123427

CHARISMATIC SPIRITUAL GIFTS

A Phenomenological Analysis

William Joseph Sneck

UNIVERSITY
PRESS OF
AMERICA

University Press of America,Inc.™
P.O. Box 19101, Washington, D.C. 20036

Printed in the United States of America

Library of Congress Cataloging in Publication Data

Sneck, William Joseph.
   Charismatic spiritual gifts.

   Bibliography: p.
   1. Gifts, Spiritual. 2. Phenomenological
psychology. I. Title.
BT767.S58   234'.13   80-8291
ISBN 0-8191-1765-X   AACR2
ISBN 0-8191-1766-8 (pbk.)

For My Jesuit Brothers

iv

ACKNOWLEDGEMENTS

I wish to express my gratitude to several communities of friends who encouraged me through this research project. First, the Jesuit Community at Ann Arbor provided fraternal support all along the way. The Novices at Loyola House, Berkley, Michigan, made a home away from home, and the University of Detroit brethren never forgot me. The Georgetown University Community saw this long journey through to its end as did the men at the Woodstock Theological Center, Washington, D.C.

Next, I am thankful to the priests, staff and parishioners of St. Thomas Parish and St. Mary's Student Chapel, Ann Arbor who challenged me into growth as a priest and a counselor.

The coordinators, research subjects and membership of the Word of God Community, Ann Arbor, were most cooperative with this project in sharing with me their very candid comments about an area of such special personal importance to them.

My colleagues in the Clinical Area, Department of Psychology, University of Michigan, built a genuinely collegial atmosphere of learning in which education became a reality, not just an ideal. I extend warm thanks to David A. Kopplin of Baylor University, Waco, Texas, whose friendship and humor combine with insight, patience and wisdom in a mentor par excellence. I am grateful also to Wilbert J. McKeachie, George C. Rosenwald and Max A. Heirich.

Mary M. Dwyer extended her hospitality to me for three years. Kathy Fry typed the final draft of this study, and blended appreciation with skill. My family made vacations times of real spiritual recreation.

For these friends and many others, I am most grateful.

TABLE OF CONTENTS

TABLE OF CONTENTS (Cont'd.)

AIM AND SCOPE OF THIS STUDY

From time to time in the history of the
Christian Churches, there have occurred surprisingly sudden and seemingly spontaneous outpourings of renewed religious fervor (Knox, Enthusiasm
1950). Such renewal movements in the past have
been marked by an attempted return to the practices and spirit of the earliest Christian communities as described in the New Testament, most
often the Jerusalem of Acts and the Corinth of
Paul's First Letter to the Corinthians. Behaviorally, Christians in these communities of renewal
have been distinguished by their stated attempts
to live more fully and more strictly according to
biblical teachings than do their less enthusiastic
neighbors. To an outsider, perhaps the first impression conveyed by renewal participants today
would be their constant exuberance, their un-
feigned joy in living. To a psychologically-minded critic, probably their most extraordinary and
seemingly bizarre behavior would be glossolalia,
the sung or spoken pseudo-linguistic utterances
heard at public prayer meetings or in private ora-
tion, and claimed to be either extant or extinct
languages, "tongues of men and of angels" (1 Cor.
13:1). (Biblical quotations in this study are
from the Oxford Annotated Bible: Revised Standard Version, 1965.) Yet glossolalia is only one
of the "spiritual gifts" noted by Paul -- indeed,
it is next to the last one listed -- and consciously sought by "Charismatic Renewal" members
(as today's enthusiastic Christians call themselves).

Now there are varieties of gifts, but
the same Spirit; and there are varieties of
service, but the same Lord; and there are
varieties of working, but it is the same God
who inspires them all in everyone. To each
is given the manifestation of the Spirit for

the common good. To one is given through the
Spirit the utterance of wisdom, and to another the utterance of knowledge according to
the same Spirit, to another faith by the same
Spirit, to another gifts of healing by the
one Spirit, to another the working of miracles, to another prophecy, to another the
ability to distinguish between spirits, to
another various kinds of tongues, to another
the interpretation of tongues. All these are
inspired by one and the same Spirit, who ap-
portions to each one individually as he wills
(1 Cor. 12:4-11).

When asked to name the spiritual gifts, modern
charismatics refer to this classic passage as it
gives the fullest list of nine in all (wisdom,
knowledge, faith, healing, miracle working, prophecy, discernment of spirits, glossolalia, interpretation of tongues). Over all these, however,
Paul places agape, love or charity, as a "higher
gift," a "still more excellent way" (v. 31). "If
I have prophetic powers, and understand all mysteries and all knowledge, and if I have all faith
so as to remove mountains, but have not love, I am
nothing" (1 Cor. 13:2).
    Presently, a group in Ann Arbor, Michigan has
evolved into the world headquarters of the Catholic Charismatic Renewal. Many members of the
"Word of God" (hereafter WoG) Community live in
common, attempt to base their lives on a strongly
committed biblical faith, and claim to experience
all of the "spiritual gifts" referred to above.
Whether in college dormitory, rented apartment, or
aged town house, WoG members submit their lives
and often their paychecks to a "head" in an obedience relationship. Married couples with children,
together with young single adults of both sexes
share food, fellowship and finances in communal
households in an effort to reproduce the lifestyles, attitudes and patterns of first-century
Christianity.
    This present work attempts to understand the
experience of "spiritual gifts" enjoyed by

charismatics. It will employ a phenomenological methodology, seek to explain the meaning of those gifts to their recipients, and try to discover what relevant psychological variables are involved in becoming and remaining thus gifted.

One "gift" has already received enormous attention, namely, glossolalia. Among many studies are found those of Kelsey (1964), Gerlach and Hine (1968), Hine (1969), Goodman (1972), Kildahl (1972), Samarin (1972), and Sneck (1973). This study will focus on others of the gifts which are mentioned in the original Pauline summary quoted above and found in WoG, most especially prophecy and healing.

While this research will concentrate somewhat heavily on the spectacular, it must be stated at the outset in fairness to the subjects interviewed, and indeed to the spirit of the community, that these gifts are not consciously sought for their own sake, but rather are reported as quite normal results of living "in the Lord," that is, a committed Christian life. Indeed the word "normal" was the one most often used by subjects to comment on events and experiences which struck the researcher as quite extraordinary. Over and over again, subjects stated that the love and support, the good fellowship and dedication to each other is what drew them to WoG, rather than the gifts. The frequency of this statement and the consistency of the life-patterns of WoG verified by five years of participant observation supports this claim.

The Charismatic Renewal burst upon the mainline Christian Churches in the fifties and sixties and shocked both the churches and the social science community which were completely unprepared for this phenomenon. In retrospect, it is possible to trace some lines of social causality, but seemingly no one did or could have predicted the sudden surge of religious interest, and commitment, and altered lifestyles which the Renewal has become on every continent. Many of those struggling scattered prayer groups and incipient "covenant communities" look to Ann Arbor for leadership for it is here that New Covenant is published, the worldwide monthly magazine of the Renewal, and WoG with its sixteen-hundred members remains the largest renewal community. The four founding fathers of WoG arrived in Ann Arbor in September of 1967, at that time in their mid-twenties (Jahr, 1975, p. 5), and began conducting weekly prayer meetings for students in their apartment above the Campus Corners grocery store. Roberta Keane's dissertation (1975) details the dynamic growth in membership and increasing organizational complexity of this community. Its international influence is exercised both through New Covenant whose circulation is about sixty-thousand, and through the Charismatic Renewal Services' team manual, an initiation handbook which has sold more than seventy thousand copies and has been translated into Korean, Chinese, French, Dutch, Spanish, Italian and Sotho, a Bantu language spoken in South Africa (Casey, 1975, pp. 4-5).

WoG, a movement which originally spoke mostly to students, now counts less than fifty percent of its membership from the University of Michigan or Eastern Michigan University, Ypsilanti. The non-student majority are towns-people, mostly single-family units. Another remarkable feature about WoG (not usually repeated elsewhere in the Renewal) is its ecumenical membership: while most of the "coordinators," the top leadership, count themselves Roman Catholics, about fifty-five percent of the community is Catholic with Protestants totalling almost forty-five percent and the remainder (some Jews and Non-denominationals) calling themselves simply "Christian." WoG insists that it is not a church, however, but a community, and members regularly attend more than fifty local churches. Weekly public prayer meetings, the focal communal and outreach activity of the group, had successively outgrown the original small apartment, the university's Newman Center auditorium, a Catholic parish's still larger social hall, a high school gymnasium, and until recently occurred at three separate locations each Thursday night throughout the year. (As of this writing, public gatherings are no longer held.)

This phenomenon has attracted the attention

of sociologists (Harrison, 1972; Keane, 1975; Heirich, 1975; Fichter, 1975), but to my knowledge no one from the psychological community has attempted in-depth research of the Charismatic Renewal. Through a phenomenological approach, this study attempts to understand the meaning-system, the structures of experience underlying the behaviors of prophecy and healing in subjects drawn from WoG. Hopefully, it will provide a contribution to the growing field of psychology of religion, and perhaps increase our overall knowledge about how the human body and psyche interact to cause emotional and spiritual well-being.

Psychologists routinely import from the natural sciences the goals of understanding, predicting and controlling a phenomenon. Phenomenological psychology, however, accepts wholeheartedly and stresses the first of these goals, understanding, while putting less emphasis on prediction, and totally rejecting the third, control. This project seeks to provide, in the tradition of William James, a description of the spiritual gifts as experienced by members of the Charismatic Renewal, and to draw psychological implications from this description. It seeks to elucidate the significance of these gifts within the living context of the subjects interviewed, of the WoG community, and of our larger culture. We shall try to demonstrate that the phenomenological method, as applied to an analysis of the spiritual gifts, provides a better tool than traditional psychological approaches to the interpretation of religious experience.

CHAPTER I

THE PEOPLE AND THEIR EXPERIENCE

Claims to intimacy with the Divine and interaction with the supernatural are as old as human-
kind and as pervasive as people seeking a transcendental experience. Except for "advanced" sec-
ularized civilizations like our own, such communication was often taken for granted and built into
the institutions and fabric of social life. WoG
represents a curious amalgam of the modern with
the intensely religious, for here are persons living in the post-industrial era who nevertheless
maintain personal relationship with God while accepting the democratic and scientific paradigms of
American culture. Before meeting them "in person"
as it were, through their experiences, we can
learn much about their set and setting by reviewing the investigations of intense religious experiences and the characteristics of those who un-
dergo them. In other words, we are asking the
questions, "What kinds of people are these charismatics?" and "What do we already know about
para-normal experiences?"

Good places to begin are four overviews.
Beyond the Classics? Essays in the Scientific
Study of Religion (Glock and Hammond, 1973) provides critical summaries of the main insights and
research generated by the theoretical traditions
of seven major modern social scientists and religious thinkers; Marx, Weber, Durkheim, Malinowski,
Freud, William James and H. Richard Niebuhr. These
theoreticians and others made contributions, now
considered classic, to our understanding of the
phenomena of religion such that the period dating
from the middle of the nineteenth century into the
first three decades of the twentieth can be considered to be a kind of "golden age" for the social scientific study of religion (p. ix). The
book seeks to ascertain whether social science has
gotten beyond the formulations and perspectives of
these founding geniuses. or is still governed by

their approaches, and concludes the latter (pp. 409-418). The cumulative record shows that we have not gone very far "beyond the classics." (It will be argued in the following chapter that precisely what is needed to make such progress, to get out of and beyond the framework established by our respected and revered predecessors is to begin the investigation with a new approach, the phenomenological.) "Instead of surpassing their founders, then, social scientists of religion focus and refocus on the classics" (p. 410). Thus the theoretical and research parameters of the field have been quite thoroughly laid out.

A second useful review of the literature is provided by James E. Dittes (1968) who summarizes both empirical and theoretical research with his emphasis on the latter. He explains that the chief reason for the primitive state of the field lies in the realm of theory and in the theoretical relevance of data: critical psychological questions and the categories of data by which they can be answered have not yet been worked out (p. 603). Such disagreement and uncertainty over strategy and approach generate four questions for Dittes: (1) Just how unique is religion? That is, are unique psychological variables involved in religion? (ibid.) A spectrum of answers emerges on the uniqueness question. (2) Next, a definitional problem presents itself: is religion a single quantifiable variable? Most studies seem to assume so, but Dittes rather thinks of religion as an "area of research" (p. 606). (3) Is religion best viewed as explicit and differentiated or subjective and diffuse? (pp. 619 ff.) Answering this question allows Dittes to review the rich research traditions represented by Allen and Spilka's (1967) typology of committed vs. consensual religion, and Allport's (1950, 1966) paradigm of intrinsic vs. extrinsic religion. (4) What is the relationship between religion and social attitudes? (pp. 627-646.) In the decade before Dittes wrote (1958-1968), two problems dominated the psychology of religion: the relationship between personality characteristics and religion, and the correlation between conservative social

2

attitudes and pro-religious attitudes. Remarking on this latter relationship first, Dittes notes that it is curvilinear, that is, as people's frequency of church attendance increases so do conservative attitudes, except that the most intensely religious reverse the trend. Very regular attenders think more liberally than less frequent attenders, and sometimes more even than non-attenders (pp. 630-631). Dittes interprets this trend as follows: "Committed religion provides (or presupposes) enhanced personal security, self-esteem and compensation, or otherwise tends to reduce the psychological motivation prompting prejudice" (p. 632).

Dittes expresses annoyance that researchers' discussion of attitudes like social conformism and intolerance of ambiguity glides so carelessly into discussions of personality factors and structures. Much research is guided by hypotheses of weak or constricted ego-structure, or severe super-ego (pp. 633-634). He mourns that the bulk of the studies in religion and personality are merely correlational in nature (p. 636). "Religion" is measured by institutional affiliation or adherence to conservative doctrines, and then correlated with awareness of personal inadequacies; with objective evidence of an inadequacy like low intelligence; with strong responsiveness to suggestions of other persons or of external influences; with an array of desperate and generally unadaptive defensive maneuvers, e.g., Jame's sick souls and divided selves (ibid.).

When one reviews these studies, one is tempted to hypothesize an anti-religious bias almost amounting to a prejudice in many researchers who seem content with linking religion and psychopathology, and seemingly ignore the curvilinear aspect of many of the correlations. They forget that the more intensely committed religious subjects often score "better" on various measures than do the non-religious, or extrinsically religious, or consensually religious.

A third useful background study, done by Michael Argyle (1958) and revised by Argyle and Benjamin Beit-Hallahmi (1975), reviews major

3

findings for both America and England. Their
search is exhaustive, their perspective, social
psychological, and their effort, an attempt to
test various theories of origin, maintenance and
consequence of religious behavior against the vast
array of empirical studies undertaken.

These authors note the amazingly rapid rise
in Pentecostal sect membership in the U.S.A., from
a thousand in 1906 to one and a half million in
1956, and this during a time of a trend toward
secularization, and the general decline of religion in both the U.S.A. and in Britain (Argyle and
Beit-Hallahmi, 1975, pp. viii and 25). To explain
this phenomenon of accelerated growth, it has become almost a sociological and social psychological commonplace to attribute the increase to variables like deprivation, low socio-economic class,
minority group membership, poor education (Boisen,
1955; Yinger, 1957). Lipset (1964) concludes that
religion, especially in the form of salvationist
sects, has served in the U.S.A. as an alternative
to political radicalism. Elinson (1965) views
sectarian activity as incompatible with, and exclusive of radical politics, and as an alternative
expression of lower class frustrations. Wilson
(1966) reported that sects in modern society tend
either to support or ignore as irrelevant the political arrangements of the wider society. (Established churches, on the other hand, function as
legitimating agents of political authority, and as
instruments of social control.) Neo-Pentecostal
groups of the 1970's show the familiar sectarian
tendency either to be conservative or else indif-
ferent to politics (Argyle and Beit-Hallahmi, 1975
p. 111). Lower class persons are less likely to
be church members, but if participating are most
likely to have fundamentalist religious beliefs
(Demerath, 1965), a characteristic of Neo-
Pentecostals and Charismatics as well. The emotional fervor of sectarians was noted quite early
too:

> Members of the working class show a dis-
> position to believe their religion more

ardently and to accumulate more emotionally
charged values around their beliefs. Religion
appears to operate more prominently as an
active agency of support and encouragement...
(Lynd and Lynd, 1929, p. 329).

Argyle and Beit-Hallahmi summarize these and
other findings in this way; church members with
higher status become involved in a "religion of
doing," while persons of lower status get involved
in a "religion of feeling" (p. 163). Middle class
persons score higher on measures of institutional
participation like church attendance and church
membership. Lower class people score higher on
measures of traditional beliefs and reported religious experiences. They are also more likely to
become sect members with a subsequent intense psychological and social involvement (p. 164). Another motive for the socially underprivileged to
join sects is that they achieve an increase of
status; not only are they accepted as social
equals, but they feel themselves as part of a
spiritual elite (Stark, 1967). The close relationship between social and church affiliation in
America is perhaps most colorfully expressed by
Winter:

The Church is now a reflection of the
economic ladder. Ascent on this ladder is
validated by escalation to congregations of
higher social and economic rank. For every
rung on the ladder there is an appropriate
congregation, with ushers of slightly more
refined dress, and somewhat more cultivated
ladies' affairs (Winter, 1962, p. 77).

We have stressed the connection between economic deprivation and religious sectarian involvement because here precisely is one of the sur-
prises provided by the Charismatic Movement: its
members are, for the most part, not deprived, not
marginal, but middle class rather than from the

5

lower end of the socio-economic continuum. The next section of this review will elaborate on this situation, found locally in WoG as well as nationally in other prayer groups studied. At this point, we shall be satisfied to note the anomaly and move onto a discussion of what Argyle and Beit-Hallahmi can tell us in response to the second of our two questions; namely, what do we know about para-normal religious experiences?

Again a bias among psychologists is evident. Quite frequently, religious experiences are felt to be abnormal rather than merely para-normal. While religious imagery, behavior, ideas and beliefs frequently are employed as the vehicle for psychopathology, no demonstrated connection exists between being religious and being psychologically ill. It is rather a question of adaptive/maldaptive religion, or growth-producing/stunting behavior. This conclusion from both philosophical reflection and behavioral science research is especially important to state at the outset of a discussion on admittedly deviant behavior like tongue-speaking, prophecy or the other charismatic gifts.

Argyle and Beit-Hallahmi note (pp. 138-139) that intense religious experiences such as glossolalia, conversion and mystical experience have often been regarded either as symptoms or effects of mental disorders. Psychopathological explanation of religious experiences, which links such manifestations to specific psychiatric disturbances, is hard to support when these experiences become common in a certain sect or sub-culture. This hypothesis concerning pathology seems even weaker since sect members are often well adjusted in all other respects, and the overall effect of sect membership is in the direction of greater adjustment to society at large.

We can begin with snake-handling, a behavior not practiced in WoG, but illustrative of the implicit antecedent prejudice linking such activity with an assumption of psychopathology. Gerrard and Gerrard (1966) mention sending MMPI profiles gathered from a snake-handling church and a conventional church in West Virginia to some expert diagnosticians at the University of Minnesota with the request that they sort out the profiles of the snake-handlers. The experts guessed that the most pathological profiles in the unmarked batch would probably be those of the snake-handlers. Actually the reverse was the case; members of the snake-handling church appear to be otherwise as normal as members of a more conventional church, and even to score slightly better than average on the MMPI. It would appear that in rural Appalachia, being a member of a snake-handling cult gives one an average to slightly superior chance at adapting to the stresses of life there! Nathan L. Gerrard (1968) suggests why. He divides his subjects into older and younger church-goers, as well as into the snake-handlers (non-mobile working class) and conventional church members (upwardly mobile working class). A first difference among older persons emerges in the way the elderly deal with illness and old age. While the older members of the conventional church dwell morbidly on their physical disabilities, the aged serpent-handlers seemed able cheerfully to ignore their ailments. Rather than being pessimistic hypochondriacs like the conventional church people, they were deeply intent on placing their fate in God's benevolent hands and acted in the light of this conviction. A second difference in the social and economic prospects for the younger people would naturally lead to the hypothesis that serpent-handling youth should be depressive because, unlike the young in the conventional church with brighter personal and financial futures, the former group can look forward realistically only to poverty. What prevents many of them from becoming delinquent or demoralized is their wholehearted participation in religious practices that provides a socially acceptable outlet for their energies, and strengthens their self-esteem by giving them the opportunity to gain "holiness." Furthermore, a hedonistic hypothesis could explain their bright affect; their mode of religious expression provides them with emotional gratification.

We do not mean to suggest that the MMPI is the only or most satisfying measure of emotional maturity, adjustment, or ability to cope with the wider cultural changes afflicting American society. While this measure of mental health registers favorably for snake-handlers in their own context, it does not predict how they might succeed apart from their fellow cult members. The role played by such cults can only be satisfactorily appreciated in a less relativistic framework than that provided by MMPI scores, for example, by means of a sociological or anthropological analysis, or a phenomenological study like this project. The example was introduced primarily to illustrate the trend among diagnosticians to equate the para-normal with the abnormal.

Turning next to glossolalia, we have Hine's (1969) study showing that American Pentecostal glossolalists appear to be well integrated and productive members of society. Despite their performance on all sorts of personality and behavioral indices, Hine finds that the opinion still persists that the gift of tongues is received only by non-verbal individuals of low mental ability in whom the capacity for rational thought is underdeveloped (Cutten, 1927), by schizophrenics or hysterics. As the vast number of WoG members are glossolalists, it is important to lay this particular ghost to rest lest he be confused with the "Holy Ghost." Alexander Alland (1961) judges the older psychological explanations of glossolalia as manifestations of schizophrenia or hysteria to be no longer acceptable in view of current socio-cultural data. Tongue-speakers of the Black Pentecostal Church Alland researched were well-adjusted to their social environment and behaved normally except for their glossolalia. Alland argues that this weakens the interpretation of the experience as indicative of schizophrenia since schizophrenics cannot limit their pathology to one segment of their behavior. Furthermore, he rejects hysteria as an adequate explanation of the trance states associated with glossolalia among his subjects. The trances are learned behavior and not _ipso_ _facto_ a result of personality disorder.

Hine (1969) exhaustively reviews four studies

attacking the "weak-ego" theory of explanation for glossolalia, but the most comprehensive work done on this question must be Kildahl's (1972). The fruit of ten years of concentrated study, Kildahl's conclusions are based on two field trips from coast to coast with observations and recordings of tongues in various geographical and sociological settings. A detailed questionnaire was distributed to glossolalists by which they could indicate their own feelings about what led them to the practice. Psychological interviews were undertaken with the subjects who ranged in age from twenty to eighty years, represented every socioeconomic class, and were affiliated with mainline Protestant Churches. On any broad criterion of emotional well-being, the tongue-speakers and non-tongue-speakers were about the same. Hence, glossolalists are neither more nor less mentally healthy than others. Can tongue-speakers be thought to represent a special personality type? This study provides an unequivocal "No" to this question. The principle difference emerging on the personality tests between tongue-speakers and non-glossolalists was that the former developed deeply trusting, submissive, dependent relationships to the authority figures who had introduced them to glossolalia.

These results confirm the work of the ego-psychologists, Gill and Brenman (1959, pp. 60-100) who have suggested that trance -- light to deep trance frequently accompanies glossolalia -- is a form of hypnosis, and hypnosis itself is a form of regression in the service of the ego in which a transference-dependency relationship is set up between the hypnotist and his subject. What appears to happen both in hypnosis proper and in trance is that the subject appears to enter into a transference relationship with the hypnotist/charismatic religious leader in which he trades self-control for a dependency relationship.

> . . . Once the trance is learned, however,
> its repetition is assured. Hypnosis becomes
> auto-hypnosis and after the first experience

> it becomes less difficult for members to en-
> ter into the trance state. We suggest that
> certain internal cues (internal sensory
> states) become hooked into a system of devel-
> oped external cues (associated with appro-
> priate time for trance) which trigger the
> behavior pattern (Alland, 1961, p. 213).

We may conclude that psychopathology can play a role in the dynamics of those involved in reli-gious experiences. In a group setting, however, these actions take on an alternative meaning, and can be functionally regarded as acts of commit-ment to the group "bridge-burning" (Hine, 1969) acts which set the individual apart from the larg-er society to some degree, and commit him to changes in attitudinal and behavioral patterns. Sects and groups which encourage intense religious experiences often contribute to the overall ad-justment of their members to their environment by providing a supportive social network and re-socializing them (Argyle and Beit-Hallahmi, 1975, pp. 140-141).

Yet a fourth useful source of references to studies of contemporary religious behavior is Merton P. Strommen's encyclopedic handbook (1971). While Argyle and Beit-Hallahmi's perspective is social psychological, Stommen's is developmental. Of the twenty-two well-researched topical essays, the two most useful are Walters and Bradley's "Motivation and Religious Behavior" (Strommen, 1971, pp. 599-654) and Walter H. Clark's "Intense Religious Experience" (op. cit., pp. 521-550).

Walters and Bradley ask what motivates people to belong to a sect, cult or underground religious movement. (The studies and data which they re-viewed reflect the pre-Charismatic Renewal pre-sumptions of social scientists.) They quote with approval W. Stark's comment (1967, Vol. II, p. 158) that the motivation of the individual who has joined a sect is typically an "overcompensa-tion of an inferiority complex" by which he goes from the bottom rung of the social-status ladder to the highest rung of religious status.

"The movement is primarily a religious solution to problems of illness, poverty and status deprivation. These problems are conceived of in individualistic terms and solved in personalistic faith" (op. cit., p. 40). These generalizations simply do not apply to members of neo-Pentecostal cults and sects in the middle and upper-middle class mainline Protestant and Catholic Churches. More recent material (reviewed below) must be consulted to find a better explanation than this.

Walters and Bradley come closer to the truth when they suggest that the religious motivation of people in all walks of life needs to be sustained by some kind of "nurturing community" (Strommen, 1971, p. 625). They refer to the study of Poblete and O'Dea (1960) who show that the lower-class Puerto Rican in New York has a need for personal intimacy which is satisfied in the sect but not in the Roman Catholic Church to which he belongs nominally. The process of becoming a sectarian is revealed in the stereotype of the testimony-style, despite the spontaneity of the witnessing. (A similar combination of stereotypical behavior with spontaneity is discoverable in WoG too. Typically, members at prayer meetings are invited to stand up and "share what the Lord has done in their lives.") The joyous testifying reveals an underlying tri-partite conceptualization: sinfulness -- conversion -- regeneration (Poblete and O'Dea, 1960, pp. 25-32). One's past sinful ways and lifestyles are contrasted with the conversion experience which includes identification with a new group and its values. Regeneration is the state in which, as regular members of the new highly solidified and supportive religious group, they are sustained in the new values which they now share with fellow converts.

Such a process is reminiscent of Durkheim's concept of anomie, a state of social disorganization in which established societal and cultural norms and forms break down. Two aspects of anomie are loss of solidarity and loss of consensus. After anomie, men may seek escape in pleasure-seeking, alcohol, drugs, a search for new meaning and the "quest for community" (Nisbet, 1953).

11

From such quests, movements develop which offer new values and new solidarities. For the Puerto Rican subjects studied, anomie was caused by the migration to New York, an alien and sometimes hostile environment and culture. Perhaps the rise of the Charismatic Renewal can be traced in part to some form of anomie resulting from the turbulence and chaos of the 1960's and the Vietnam era. This notion will be supported later.

Moving now to Walter H. Clark's survey of intense experience (Strommen, 1971), we can first repeat his definition of religious experience as an "immediate perception of the cosmic or transcendental accompanied by affect, the whole usually leading to changes in values and behavior related to the experience" (p. 522). He presents three types of nonrational religious experiences (N.B., not irrational): mysticism, conversion and esoteric. Although the first of these types, mysticism, is not the focus of this study (nor claimed by many members of WoG), Clark's mention of Stace's Mysticism and Philosophy (1960) deserves comment: while seemingly faulting him for his method, "not rigorously social-scientific" (Strommen, p. 523), Clark can't help but evaluate Stace's book as providing a very clear discussion of mysticism. Stace used a form of phenomenological methodology by extracting a "universal core of mysticism" from writings of important faiths both ancient and modern (Stace, 1960, pp. 41-133). Among its characteristics are included a sense of unity felt either deeply within the self or through the external world; a loss of awareness of time and space; a sense that one has been in immediate touch with objective and ultimate reality, etc. Stace's phenomenologically derived experience-structure has been used in turn by social scientists in more usual ways as, for example, in the often-quoted study by Pahnke (1966) concerning drug-induced-mystical experiences. Zaehner's work (1967) provides another example of a phenomenology of mysticism, but uses secular as well as religious mystical writings for analysis. For historical completeness, it is important to mention Evelyn Underhill's classic (1912) as providing an early and important stimulus to the study of this elusive phenomenon.

Concerning conversion, Clark speculates that "probably more has been written on this subject by social scientists and others, with discussions of a controversial nature, than on any other religious subject in modern times" (Strommen, p. 531). Conversion may be gradual or sudden, and can be thought of as a break with a person's past ideas, attitudes, values or behavior, accompanied by intense feeling. Whereas mystical experience is more apt to be solitary, conversion tends to be influenced by the social context. Half of the earliest volume entitled Psychology of Religion (Starbuck, 1899) concerned a study of conversion, and the earliest published article in the field (Leuba, 1896a) dealt with the same topic as well. Of course, William James's Varieties of Religious Experience (1902, Lectures 8-9) provides a wealth of case material.

Coe (1900) asks what the personality characteristics of sudden converts might be and finds his subjects to be both more suggestible and more emotional than his control group. This finding has been both supported and challenged in subsequent research and seems to depend (as in much of social science research!) not upon the rigor of methods employed, but rather upon individual differences among subjects recruited for study. Thus Kildahl (1965) found twenty sudden converts in a theological school both slightly less intelligent and somewhat more hysterical than twenty matched gradual awakeners. Roberts (1965) tested forty-three theological students along several dimensions and found that those who had been suddenly converted in the direction of their parents' faith had higher MMPI scores for neuroticism. Yet in a study of three hundred forty-seven theological students, Stanley (1964) contradicts Roberts with the discovery of a slight negative correlation between sudden conversion and neuroticism.

Clark feels that the "most suggestive and imaginative book on the subject since William James" (Strommen, p. 533) was written by the English psychiatrist William Sargant (1961).

13

In Battle for the Mind, Sargant makes comparisons
between the sudden temperamental changes in
Pavlov's dogs when subjected to fright, and the
treatment of war neuroses and brainwashing. He
shows parallels between these situations and the
techniques of John Wesley and other evangelists
in the arousal if fear, the production of exhaustion, and the raising of the level of suggestibility. While seeming to ignore the individual mystical consciousness in religious experience,
Sargant stresses the manipulative aspects of conversion and the obvious need for integrity in the
charismatic leader. He thus provides important
clues to the mechanisms of social and evangelistic
pressures in conversion.

Two studies have already concentrated upon
the conversion dynamics and subsequent processes
in WoG. Keane (1975) took her cue from Weber's
concept of the routinization of charisma. Having
been allowed by the Community's coordinators to
study the archives and interview the earliest
members, she wrote an interesting and thorough
history of the early days, and then showed how the
community has been gradually evolving and growing
more structured. Her study is lively and sympathetic, and perhaps can be faulted only in that
she seems to accept uncritically the statements
and writings of her informants.

Harrison (1972) studied the organization of
commitment in WoG. His data was gathered in 1969
from 279 questionnaire writers compared with a
probability sample of 158 non-Pentecostal Catholic
students from the University's Newman Center. (In
those days, WoG was predominantly a student movement.) Harrison showed that personal relationships with members lend credibility and attrac-
tiveness to the movement when people share its
perspective. The movement is especially attractive to people who have strong prior commitments
to personal religious devotionalism and who are
loyal to the (Catholic) Church, but seek new forms
of worship and community. ("Catholic" is here
stressed because the highly ecumenical character
of WoG had not yet developed.) Persons with
stronger occupational, educational, and familial

14

obligations were less likely to react positively to the movement and become part of it. (This statement is no longer true since at present, large numbers of community members are non-students who have developed occupational identities, completed educations, and family commitments.) Baptism is the Spirit and speaking in tongues deepen commitment by confirming the participant's sense of divine guidance and alienating him from non-participants. Continued socialization occurs through an encapsulation process involving concentration of friendship and social activities within the community, and a reorganization of leisure around the movement. Except for the parenthetical remark noted above, a replication of Harrison's study would produce essentially the same results today.

W. H. Clark's third category of religious experiences, those he calls "esoteric", are the central concern of this paper so we shall review his remarks. He mentions faith healing, glossolalia and possession. (Other experiences, notably prophecy, and other sources not mentioned by Clark will be treated more fully further on.) Clark first cites Weatherhead. Leslie D. Weatherhead (1955) writes from an integrated viewpoint on healing as provided and proclaimed by psychology and religion. His approach is historical in that he first surveys texts recording healings experienced in the early Christian Church, then moves forward in a leisurely fashion to modern times and a treatment of contemporary approaches to healing. He writes a Christian's critique of all the major schools of psychotherapy and nicely respects the contrasting claims of science and religion. No mere theoretician, Weatherhead held healing services in his London Church and worked always in a team with a medical doctor and a psychiatrist. One of Weatherhead's main points is that those claiming healing by faith inevitably speak of their spiritual experience, and often value it more highly than the physical aspect of the healing process.

Jerome Frank (1973), in a book reminiscent of Sargant's (1961), compares faith healing to

15

psychotherapy and notes similarities to conversion and brainwashing. This work will be more extensively reviewed below when we concentrate on the procedures used by healers, but we can mention a few of the common elements which allow us to group such strange bed-fellows as psychotherapy and brainwashing. Frank finds an initial intense, disorganizing, excitatory state which paves the way for a new reorganization of attitudes, followed by new information concerning oneself, or more radically, a new way of conceptualizing what one already knows about oneself. What Thomas Kuhn (1967) calls a "paradigm" for the scientific community is roughly equivalent to an individual's or society's "assumptive world," in Frank's terminology, and it is this assumptive world which gets altered by faith-healing, conversion, brainwashing etc. This process finally results in behavioral change.

Clark interrupts his literature search to record a case he himself had studied.

I myself have investigated the case of a yound woman with a month's bleeding, probably cancerous, cured by a faith healer within hours. She looks on the event as a spiritual experience and reports a distinct improvement in her disposition since the healing. This occurred over ten years ago and she is still in good health (p. 535).

Clark agrees that, to the rigorously skeptical scientific mind, faith cures, being episodic in nature, are explained away as being nothing more than the effect either of chance or suggestion in which the faith or experiential element is at best simply a facilitating or consequential factor. Yet the rigorous experiments of Bernard Grad (1965, 1966), a biochemist on the faculty of McGill University Medical School give Clark pause to wonder about a "more elusive but yet substantial dimension with which the researcher in religious experience will have to cope" (Clark, loc.

cit.). Grad found statistically detectable growth in plants as the result of the application of water in bottles held in the hands of a faith healer; also the hastening of the healing of measured wounds inflicted on mice in cages held in the hands of the same healer. In both cases laboratory personnel served as controls under carefully regulated double-blind conditions.

Clark does not deal with the mystery but moves on to consider glossolalia. This experience has already been referred to above, and here we shall merely add references to a few studies not previously mentioned since Clark covers essentially the same ground as have we. In 1963, the controversial bishop of the Episcopal Diocese of California, James A. Pike, issued a pastoral letter forbidding services of tongue-speaking in diocesan churches. In a scholarly rebuttal, A. W. Sadler (1964), urged authorities to keep in mind that the phenomenon does not necessarily involve "the neurotic mind, but perhaps also . . . the creative, the positive aspect of the unconscious, the source of our artistic creativity" (p. 90).

Positive effects on personality have been noted above in the case of the snake-handlers, and another book illustrating this result, an anthropological case study by Mintz (1960), tells of a Puerto Rican cane worker. The subject was reared as a conventional Roman Catholic, but converted to a Pentecostal Church with dancing, glossolalia and ecstasy, and experienced favorable effects on his life. Through hard work, Pentecostals improve their economic status and are in demand as good workers. In this latter respect Pentecostals are like other fundamentalist sects, but they stress more the effortlessness of their behavior, and the inner attitudes of love, joy, peace, kindness and self-control. Behavioral changes plus increased worldly goods are viewed as validations of the baptism of the Holy Spirit.

Clark's conclusion (p. 537) is that "Pentecostalism is an expression of modern Western reaction against extreme rationalism and theological emphasis in religion in favor of feeling, the non-rational, and the ecstatic."

17

Clark's final topic in possession, the belief that persons in unusual states of mind have their bodies "possessed" by spirits either malignant or benevolent. Indeed, the whole Charismatic Renewal Movement is explained theologically by insiders as evidential proof that the "Holy" Spirit is pouring Himself out in a new way upon His people, and that the phenomena under investigation here occur as direct results of placing oneself under the benign influence and sway of the Spirit of God. Thus charismatics speak of "yielding to" tongues, that is, letting the Holy Spirit pray through oneself, take over one's tongue to worship and praise God. They are either ignorant of, or discount and ignore the strong conditioning of the social environment, the work of the crowd spirit in addition to that of the Holy Spirit.

"Possession," however, is often spoken of in the context of "demonic possession," that is, influence by evil spirits from which one needs "deliverance." The belief in evil spirits constitutes part of the inheritance from primitive religions. In the Hebrew Scriptures, Saul is described as troubled by an invading, intrusive evil spirit against which David and his lyre-playing were employed as exorcists (1 Sam. 16: 14-23). Jesus is frequently portrayed as locked in combat with demons and exercising complete power over them (e.g., Matt. 8:28-34; Mk. 1: 21-28). The Roman Catholic Church rarely but occasionally employs the rite of exorcism when all other techniques known to medicine and psychiatry fail to cure certain ailments, a fact given notoriety by the publication of William Peter Blatty's novel, The Exorcist (1971) and Malachi Martin's Hostage to the Devil (1976). Aldous Huxley's The Devils of Loudon (1952) tells of a whole convent of nuns possessed of demons. The concept today is taken seriously both by pre-industrial societies and members of conservative churches. Behaviorally, subjects are either unconscious, in a state of trance, ecstasy, or other unusual state of consciousness. Ravenscroft (1965) likens these states to hypnosis and follows the usual psychodynamic explanation: the individual is in some

18

sort of dissociated state which allows his unconscious to take over.

More recently anthropologists and sociologists have made larger use of participant observation in studying possession and thus have become
more sensitive to the potential values of these
states. Eliade (1960, p. 77) notes that men sometimes become shamans, priests or medicine men
through the effects of possession. Often they
have been ill previously, but despite possession
or perhaps by means of it, they have become well,
then have become shamans just because they succeeded in getting well. Possession, then, may
offer an opportunity to express deep-seated needs
and urges in order to produce more effective personality integration and perhaps even creativity.
The R. M. Bucke Memorial Society, located in
McGill University Medical School, devoted its 1966
meeting to the study of trance and possession
states (Prince, 1968). Religious scholars and
social scientists agreed that the subject is worth
study both for the light that it provides for
Western concepts of therapy and for religious behavior.

Thus far we have been surveying four comprehensive sources of materials on religious behavior
in seeking answers to the questions, "What kinds
of people are charismatics?" and "What do we already know about para-normal experiences?" We
have seen that it is difficult to answer the first
question since the demographic characteristics and
psychological categories describing traditional
Pentecostals seem not to fit the charismatics.
The scattered studies responding to the second
question converge in a surprising conclusion:
whereas many social scientists presumed that para-
normal experiences were manifestations of a weak
ego, such experiences rather are often undergone
as part of an overall process of personality re-
structuring and maturation, and of coping with
societal stress (Eliade, 1960; Mintz, 1960; Alland
1961; Sadler, 1964; Prince, 1968; Hine, 1969;
Kildahl, 1972).

Apropos of the normality-abnormality issue,
Scroggs and Douglas (1976) ask whether religious

behavior is pathological, regressive, a sign of emotional instability, or a constructive, healthy pattern of behavior leading to true maturity. They answer that this is a question of statistical normality depending on cultural context, or a value question implying the writer's own commitment "regardless of the smoke screen of scientism he puts up to rationalize it" (p. 207). Jahoda (1959) has indicated that the dominant conception of mental health held by American psychologists is that of the self-sufficient individualist who stands on his own two feet and is not a burden to others. From this perspective, conversion to a theistic faith would likely appear as a turning from independence to immature dependence.

The approach until now has been to review large collections of literature and note material relevant to our interest. The next two sections will concentrate on each of the two questions posed.

Charismatics

We have been wondering just what kinds of people these charismatics might be, and here shall review two recent studies focussing explicitly on them: Benedict Mawn's (1975) doctoral dissertation, Testing the Spirits: an Empirical Search for the Socio-Cultural Situational Roots of the Catholic Pentecostal Religious Experience, and Joseph Fichter's The Catholic Cult of the Paraclete (1975). We shall concentrate on the theoretical contributions of the first study, and the descriptive features emerging from the second.

Mawn argues that deprivation theory has frequently been used to explain sociologically the appearance of new religious movements, but that even an extended and elaborated theory of deprivation like Charles Y. Glock's (1973) fails to interpret the rise of Neo-Pentecostalism. Mawn evolves a new explanatory category, "transcendency deprivation" (Mawn, p. 14), that is, the absence of a personal, existential, experience-based relationship to the Realissimum, to fill out Glock's

20

typology. Glock (1973) had presented the then-current status of deprivation theory as having maintained that new religious movements begin by being sect-like in character. They arise by breaking off from church-type bodies, are rooted in economic deprivation, and then gradually transform themselves into churches. Glock extended the concept of deprivation to a five-fold typology: (1) economic deprivation which leads to the formation of a sect (about the total extent of traditional deprivation theory); (2) social deprivation which causes the evolution of a church; (3) organismic deprivation, that is, physically or mentally stigmatizing or disabling traits which culminate in healing movements; (4) ethical value conflicts between the ideals and practices of society and those of individuals or groups which result in a reform movement; (5) psychic deprivation, the lack of satisfactory meaning systems by which individuals are able to interpret and organize their lives, which gives rise to cult. Felt deprivation is a necessary condition for the rise of a new religious group; the sufficient conditions are that the deprivation be shared, that no alternative institutional arrangements exist, and that leadership emerges with innovative ideas. Glock believes, finally, that religious movements compensate for deprivation while secular movements function to overcome it.

Mawn first hypothesized that the Catholic Pentecostal Movement represents an adaptive resolution of a transcendency deprivation. The bulk of his dissertation reflects a careful correlational analysis of questionnaire date showing that his four hundred fifty-five subjects do not experience in any serious (that is, statistically significant) way the five forms of deprivation postulated by Glock, but do experience transcendency deprivation. (His returns derive from a quota sample sent to strategic American Catholic centers of the Charismatic Renewal -- not including Ann Arbor.) In other words, Neo-Pentecostals do not suffer economic, social, organismic or psychic deprivation, nor severe value conflicts; rather they do feel a need for a closer

21

relationship to the Realissimum, or God, which
they can experience and feel, not just think
about. An important factor emerging from the data
is that of the strong institutional Catholicism
prevalent in the early background of most of the
subjects (Mawn, p. 91). Catholic Pentecostalism
represents a personalistic, existential, experience-based, ecumenically-adapted abreaction to the
collective, sacramentally-based spiritual experience of a prevailing standardized Catholicism.
Therefore, the social situational root of Catholic
Pentecostalism was found in the social fact of
ecumenism; the cultural root, in a felt and shared
transcendency deprivation (p. 284).

Other hypotheses tested and supported were
the following: The Neo-Pentecostal Movement, the
adaptive resolution of the deprivation, functions
to induce new religious experiences of a personal,
"contuitive" nature (p. 269). Further, the resolution induces new religious attitudes supplemen-
ting internalized institutional attitudes. The
religious movement modifies the Lebenswelt, the
humanly constructed world of meaning in which
persons live. That is, there occur modal changes
in the areas of objectifying, internalizing, and
legitimizing religious beliefs. Finally, by re-
defining the situation, the religious movement
tends to change attitudes toward environing religious and secular institutions.

Two brief examples may serve to illustrate
these hypotheses. The charismatic's Lebenswelt
is altered in that he tends to hold to a synchro-
nic concept of time rather than a diachronic concept. This means that he experiences God acting
now in his personal history, and often in a miraculous, intervening way, rather than merely in the
foundational events of the Judaeo-Christian religion. Too, the chief source of the charismatic's
internalized beliefs tends to be his own personal
experience and the shared experiences of fellow
charismatics rather than the Catholic institutional, magisterial, hierarchical source (Mawn,
p. v).

Mawn's theoretical system involves a tension
between Durkheim's structural-functional approach

22

and Weber's logical-meaningful approach. In Durkheim, the objective facticity of the societal is emphasized as being over against the individual, whereas Weber envisions social reality as subjectively founded, as ongoingly constituted by human signification. Mawn credits Peter Berger (1967) with the developed synthesis here employed. According to Berger, the externalizing or outpouring of man's physical and mental activity results in an objectivation by which the products of his physical and mental activity confront his as a reality, a facticity external to and other than himself. When this man-made external reality is internalized so as to be transformed again into the structures of the subjective consciousness, the individual experiencing this internalization is said to be a product of his society. A third step concludes the process, legitimization, a function performed by religion (Mawn, p. 109).

We have seen Mawn's main reason for adding another category to Glock's deprivation theory: none of the five types of deprivation described his subjects, while transcendency deprivation did. Another reason is that each of Glock's five forms of deprivation evolves into a definite sort of religious body, but the Charismatic Movement incorporates features of church, sect, denomination and even of cult (Mawn, p. ix). Immediately below, we shall present Fichter's argument that the term, "cult," best fits the movement.

Two other theoreticians whom Mawn finds congenial are Gerlach and Hine (1968) who noted five factors crucial to the growth and spread of a modern religious movement: (1) an acephalous, reticulate organizational structure; (2) face to face recruitment along lines of pre-existing significant social relationships; (3) commitment generated through an act or experience; (4) change-oriented ideology; and (5) real or perceived opposition.

On the other hand, Mawn sets himself in opposition to Thomas Luckmann (1967), a colleague of Peter Berger, whose thesis proposes that the common denominator of post-industrial man's mode of belief appears to be a "neutralization" of

23

official systems of belief and the emergent "privatization" of widely varying views as to the meaning of life. Western biblical religions appear to be the only ones based on cognitive belief while the non-Western religions such as Zen Buddhism are concerned with experiencing the sacred rather than with internalizing objective propositional assertions. Mawn feels (pp. 256-257) that the Charismatic Movement constitutes a serious problem for proponents of Luckmann's "invisible religion" school since it represents an antithesis to the "privatization" of religion.

While our main interest in Mawn has been to gain an appreciation and understanding of his theoretical stance, we should not pass over some of his empirical findings. Besides the important negative result that none of Glock's five types of deprivation describes the Neo-Pentecostal, he shows that transcendency deprivation afflicts a wide variety of people, and provides his own five-fold typology of the sort of persons encountered in various Catholic Charismatics groups sampled: (1) the spiritually adept who have long cultivated a life of spirituality as a matter of central concern; (2) neophytes who manifest a deepening interest in spirituality; (3) searchers in quest of a convincing religious belief system; (4) the anawim, the troubled, maladjusted, hurting individuals; (5) the dilettantes who seek to use the group as a means of gaining recognition or reputation (p. 260).

To comment now on Mawn's thesis: the ordinary descriptions regarding social class do not apply to the WoG membership. Yet the usually offered explanation for lower socio-economic class participation in sectarian movements may have an indirect application to WoG even though the members do not belong to the lower classes. Lower or lower-middle class persons have been demonstrated to gravitate to sects out of financial, social, and other deprivations and frustrations. Mawn shows a transcendency deprivation in his middle and upper-middle class subjects, but it is also possible to suggest another hypothesis: middle class persons have entered the Neo-Pentecostal and

Charismatic Renewal Movements like WoG out of
shared feelings of helplessness, frustration, and
even anger generated not by financial, social deprivations, etc., but by psychological, sociological and macro-political limitations. The dramatic
popularity of these movements rose in the sixties,
a period of great societal turmoil in the United
States when the most basic American institutions
were subjected to intense criticism, and the Vietnam War destroyed national consensus. Renewal
movements, generating intense feelings of community fellowship, especially with the Divine, re-
stored a sense of power and control to people
being propelled into a vortex of societal disorganization and personal confusion.

Mawn had been anxious to provide an answer to
the sociologists' question about just why the
Charismatic Renewal got started. Fichter (1975,
p. 140) elegantly expresses the social scientists'
surprise:

> As a sociologist of religion, I must
> confess that these four characteristics of
> the charismatic renewal were not anticipated
> by the social scientists whose business it is
> to study collective religious trends. The
> experts did not foresee that a new and vigor-
> ous spiritual cult would: (a) be inaugurated
> by lay Catholics; (b) attract adherents from
> the more advantaged middle class; (c) stimu-
> late a preference for the emotional rather
> than the intellectual experience of the
> faith; and (d) emerge in the midst of this
> scientistic, rational, American culture. If
> the Catholic hierarchy has been cautious
> about this singular development, the social
> scientists have been surprised by it.

In restrospect, it is not startling that
social scientists failed to predict the rise of
Neo-Pentecostalism because, as Mawn's work shows,
the theoretical tools had not been sufficiently
developed to accomplish the prediction. With the

addition of his concept of "transcendency deprivation," however, a similar religious revival should
be more easily predictable in the future.

Now we can proceed to Fichter's findings
about distinguishing features of American Catholic
charismatics. His book reports the results of a
questionnaire mailed to three laymen and three
laywomen in 155 charismatic prayer groups all over
the United States, at least fifty percent of whose
members were Catholics. His respondents totalled
744, a rate of eighty percent. (While Ann Arbor
and South Bend, the influential communities which
control publication of the Movement's magazine,
New Covenant, were included in Fichter's original
sample, they had to be replaced because they sent
no response.)

Fichter follows Howard Becker's (1932, pp.
627-628) revision of Ernst Troeltsch's classic
typology (1960, p. 993) of religious groups.
Troeltsch had found that the religious structures
and functions of Christianity could be sociologically categorized in three main types: the
church, the sect and mysticism. Becker inserts
"denomination" between church and sect, and sub-
stitutes "cult" for mysticism. Since all large-
scale religious bodies (generally fitting the description of church) contain within themselves
smaller groupings with characteristics that are
cultic, sectlike, and denominational, the
Charismatic Renewal is most appropriately named,
in sociological terms, a religious cult that is
both structurally and functionally contained within the Roman Catholic Church (Fichter, 1975, p.
20). In Troeltsch's words, this means that there
exists an

> . . . insistence upon a direct inward and
> present religious experience. It takes for
> granted the objective forms of religious life
> in worship, ritual, myth, and dogma; and it
> is either a reaction against these objective
> practices, which it tries to draw back into
> the living process, or it is the supplemen-
> ting of traditional forms of worship by means

26

of a personal and living stimulus (Troeltsch, 1960, p. 730).

Today's Catholics who call themselves charismatics center their devotion on the Paraclete, the Holy Spirit, the third person of the Trinity. Because Catholic Pentecostalism demonstrates personal cultic renewal within the organized Church, it cannot be called a "sect" as were the classical Pentecostal communities at the turn of the century. Those groups withdrew from or were forced out of the parent denomination: sectarians feel dissatisfaction with the routinized traditions of the established churches and a readiness to follow their own special ways to religious salvation (Fichter, pp. 21-23). Catholic New-Pentecostals, by contrast, proclaimed steadfast loyalty to the institutional Church; 78 percent affirmed that Pope Paul VI was the infallible Vicar of Christ; 75 percent felt that the Charismatic Movement could not continue in existence without the presence and aid of priests; 55 percent would obey their bishop if he were to prohibit charismatic prayer meetings in his diocese. The Paraclete Cult, then, is an internal religious cult of renewal rather than an external sectarian movement of reform (p. 32).

The Renewal manifests itself especially in the areas of prayer styles and the formation of community. Regarding prayer forms, charismatics have taken over the paraliturgical practices of Protestant Pentecostalism (p. 41). Within the hierarchical, stylized, liturgical, sacramental system of American Catholicism, emotional expressions of religious fervor had long been tamed, controlled and conventionalized. Yet activities found in Holy Roller revivalist tents are now being witnessed in Catholic churches: outbursts of spiritual enthusiasm, spontaneous prayer and prophecy, speaking in tongues, handclapping, and the joyful singing of hymns. A warm feeling of fellowship with God and other human beings seems more important than intellectual understanding of the worship service (pp. 137-138). Catholic

Neo-Pentecostals, personalized Christians, are distinguishable from conventional, institutional Catholics by these practices of prayer and by their claim to unusual and extraordinary gifts of the Spirit (p. 23). It is taught that these gifts are available to all Christians, but it is through participation in the renewal that the gifts are actualized. Personal renewal, then, is primary, and through this experience Church renewal ought to occur, and then gradually the reform of the total socio-cultural system (p. 25).

Reform and renewal of the church and of society are to be accomplished by the formation of community. This goal is expressed in their slogan; "to build a new society within the shell of the old" (p. 33). "Sharing" is the basis of this new community; first, the joyful sharing in the conversion experience to Neo-Pentecostalism; then the sharing in prayer meetings and giving testimony to what God has done for the individual; finally, in the more developed and structured communities like those at Ann Arbor and Notre Dame the sharing of living space and life patterns by members not of the same family in a "household," often with common finances. Whereas Catholic group behavior at Mass is relatively aloof and formalistic, members of the Paraclete Cult act out of a sense of intimate primary relationship; they show marked affection for one another, embracing and kissing, using first names, and showing concern for and fellowship with each other. So while the cult has its root in local communities, as a movement it extends as a social network over the whole country (p. 34), with a national "Service Committee" and "Advisory Committee" composed of persons, mostly men, who had been recognized as national leaders in the movement (p. 35). It is through the formation of community, rather than through organized, collective, social action that the world is to be changed. Although Pentecostals are not satisfied with the world, their lived conviction is that reform starts with oneself, in one's heart, and somehow spreads to other hearts until all of society is converted (p. 81). While the great majority of lay Catholic charismatics approve "liberal" programs like medicare, open housing, racially integrated schools and higher minimum wages, there is little personal participation or involvement in programs or organizations working toward such goals: the great majority of Catholic Neo-Pentecostals are hardly social activists (p. 77). The major thrust of the movement continues to be the personal sanctification of its adherents (p. 83). Less than twenty percent of all respondents have been or are involved in voter registration campaigns, peace demonstrations, grape or lettuce boycotts, the inter-racial movement, or the National Conference of Christians and Jews (p. 90). One reason for reluctance on the part of charismatics to organize their prayer groups to remedy one or more social problems derives from the fear that disagreement about political and social goals might tear the group apart. The need for internal harmony and peaceful unity seems to have become a fundamental need for the local prayer community (pp. 92-94). If groups as a whole do not tend to concentrate on alleviating social ills, neither do most individuals because there exists the feeling that secular society is corrupt, that social structures are incorrigible, and that the only solution is the formation of separate Christian communities (p. 95). In fairness to the movement, however, it must be added that there exists a high level of personal concern and care for others manifested in the "corporal works of mercy" like working with addicts, preparing meals for shut-ins, visiting the sick and elderly, and providing money, food and clothing to needy families. Instead of merely making a contribution through a formal channel provided by the parish, charismatic prayer group members are drawn to work personally, rather than through a monied organization, for the poor (pp. 96-97).

Now we consider in more detail the relationships among community members since these are to be the means toward societal renewal. In class composition, Catholic Pentecostalism is a middle class phenomenon, a feature distinguishing it from the earlier Protestant Pentecostal sects whose membership came from the lower economic classes.

There has, however, been a downward shift in class status: as the movement develops, it seems to attract more people from the working class whereas many of the original centers of activity were University campuses, specifically Duquensne, Notre Dame, Michigan State and the University of Michigan. Forty-seven percent of old-timers (in the movement three years or more) are in the upper occupational strata as compared with thirty-six percent of the newcomers (joined within the last year). A higher proportion of blue-collar workers are found among newer members (35%) than among the veterans (20%), but members with middle class occupations and educational attainments still hold the majority (pp. 72-74).

Initial contact is usually with an enthusiastic member who invites friends to attend prayer meetings. The hypothesis was supported that friendships are fostered and multiplied by membership in the Charismatic Movement: the longer a person has been in the renewal, the more likely he will be to report that he has three close Catholic friends who attend meetings with him. The most dedicated charismatics are simultaneously those most enthusiastic in encouraging friends to attend prayer meetings. The rapid multiplication of American prayer groups seems to be due to this personal evangelization (pp. 101-103). Fichter points to the enthusiastic witness to the beneficent influence that charismatic experience has on intra-familial relationships as well as noting the strains caused when only one spouse or only one generation in a family embraces Neo-Pentecostalism (pp. 106-107).

Socio-political liberalism of viewpoint was referred to above, but does not extend to the role and status of women. Even though females outnumber males by two to one in the movement, and women play a principal role in forty-five percent of the groups surveyed, they are taught by the male theoreticians of the movement to be submissive to male authority whether at home in the family or in the prayer communities. This subordination is accepted by the women themselves as the Scripturally-revealed will of God. Where women are leaders,

they want men ultimately to assume "headship," and
serve as heads themselves only by default. In the
light of such teaching, it is consistent to find
that only twenty-nine percent of respondents agree
that the Catholic Church should support the
Women's Liberation Movement, and only one-third of
them favor the ordination of women as priests
(p. 108). Nor are they in favor of the Equal
Rights Amendment (p. 85). Submissiveness and subordination do not imply passivity but rather an
invitation to men to assume the functions of
leadership. Women actively express themselves at
prayer meetings in witness, prophecy, spontaneous
scriptural quotation, and in traditionally feminine services like befriending newcomers, providing refreshments, baby-sitting and praying with
individuals (pp. 108-109).

Summarizing Fichter's findings on the personal relationships among charismatics, we note
that they desire close personal friendships among
the membership and admit as little structure and
organization as possible though intra- and inter-
community organization is developing perforce.
They are guided by the belief that they must neither hamper nor attempt to structure the spontaneous behavioral styles of persons who are completely open to the influence of the Holy Spirit
(p. 118). Liberal in political and social attitudes (though not in practice), liberal in religious behavior (prayerful spontaneity and almost
uninhibited spiritual enthusiasm), Catholic Neo-
Pentecostals nevertheless demonstrate a trend toward conservative concepts and practices in human
relationships. Such traditionalism is noted especially in their thinking on the status of women,
and their turning away from social action concerns
(p. 141).

It will be useful, finally, to review some of
the data provided by Fichter in his penultimate
chapter entitled "Prophets, Miracles, and Demons"
since this bears directly on our present investigation.

In the Judaeo-Christian tradition, the pro-
phet/prophetess provides a channel of communication from God to human beings. A person who

prophesies is believed to be delivering a message from God. Prophetic communications are regularly heard at charismatic prayer meetings, and are proclaimed more often by women than by men, with apparent spontaneity, but with a recognizable patterning in thematic statement (p. 121). In the spirit of freedom characteristic of charismatic prayer meetings, anyone present may prophesy, but after awhile, certain persons come to be recognized as specially gifted with the charism of prophecy. Leaders of the movement have analyzed the prophetic role (see the review of Yocum's work in the following section) in an effort to distinguish between true and false prophecies, and to separate these from "non-prophecy," the personal thought of an individual delivered in prophetic form (p. 122). Very few, however, of Fichter's respondents claimed to have been given the gift of prophecy (p. 124). While the common understanding of "prophet" includes the notion of foretelling the future, few specific predictions are given in prophets' exhortations. Hence while the occurrence or non-occurrence of an event foretold provides a test of prophecy, usually it is left to the judgment of the leaders of a community to consult upon and pronounce about the validity of a given prophetic utterance (pp. 124-126).

Concerning the miracle of healing, Catholic tradition has for centuries interpreted the cures of people unaided by medical procedures (whose improvement today would be called "spontaneous remission" by physicians) as instances of divine intervention. Fatima, Portugal and Lourdes, France are known healing shrines, and thousands of pilgrims of all faiths and those without any faith visit these centers annually. The faith that God heals here and now without the necessity of travel to faraway places has been widely rekindled among members of the Neo-Pentecostal Movement. Fichter asked the leaders of his prayer groups surveyed, "Have you been personally present at a prayer meeting at which the gift of healing was granted by the Lord?" Fifty-seven of these groups (37%) reported the healing of physical illnesses and thirty-nine groups (25%) told of various spiritual and psychological healings (pp. 127-128). Physical ills remedied include the following: allergies, headaches, sore throats and back pains; more serious ailments like arthritic conditions, heart trouble, deafness and blindness; dramatic cures like massive brain injury. Sixteen groups reported the healing of cancer cases. Most frequently mentioned is the lengthening of legs (pp. 129-130). Some of Fichter's respondents volunteered to produce evidence in the form of x-rays and confirmation from physicians and surgeons. The fact remains, however, that in thirty-eight percent of groups surveyed there had been no instance of physical healing, and no significant difference between the blessed and unblessed groups was discoverable in Fichter's analysis (pp. 130-131).

We now consider the deliverance ministry. Several types of healing are experienced by Movement participants. Initially, there is the conversion itself, an intensification of repentance for sin. Then there is the curing of physical illnesses noted above. Thirdly, there is the so-called "healing of memories," a cleansing of subconscious feelings of anxiety, fear and worthlessness that prevent enjoyment of life. Finally, there exists the ministry of deliverance for those who suffer from demonic oppression. While Catholics believe in the existence and operation of preter-human powers in the world, concern about their presence and influence can be traced partly to the influence of Pentecostal Protestants. Currently within the renewal there exists an ambivalence about the prevalence of evil spirits and the use of deliverance ministry. While Fichter included no question about exorcism in his survey, several respondents volunteered information about "demon-chasing" anyway. Nevertheless Fichter is convinced from his studies and interviews that a serious ministry of deliverance does exist within the Catholic Neo-Pentecostal Movement in America (pp. 132-135).

These remarks conclude our survey of pertinent literature concerning the demographic and personality characteristics of Neo-Pentecostals.

33

In the following section, we shall turn to materials concerning two main subjects of study in this paper, prophecy and faith-healing, as we reflect on the question, "What do we already know about para-normal experience?"

Para-Normal Experiences: Prophecy

Relatively little has been written by social scientists concerning the phenomenon of prophecy. The most extended treatments are found in Max Weber's essay in his <u>Sociology of Religion</u> (1963) and his fuller study <u>in Ancient Judaism</u> (1952). Accordingly, we shall supplement Weber by noting the comments of a scriptural theologian, Bruce Vawter (1968), a psychoanalyst, Sheldon Cohen (1962), and a practicing prophet in WoG, Bruce Yocum, who graciously showed me the pre-publication manuscript of his handbook on the subject (1976).

Max Weber's essay, "The Prophet," (1963, pp. 46-56) is an attempt to sort out the role and function of such a religious figure from others (mystic, priest, magician, ordinary layman) by a study in contrasts. Weber defines a prophet as a purely individual bearer of charism who, by virtue of his mission, proclaims a religious doctrine or divine commandment. Vawter's "Introduction to Prophetic Literature" provides a slightly more specific definition because his concern centers on Hebrew prophecy whereas Weber surveys a wider cultural sampling. Vawter says,

> By prophecy we understand not specifically or even principally forecasting of the future -- a fairly late conception of what is essential to prophecy -- but rather the mediation and interpretation of the divine mind and will (Vawter, 1968, p. 224).

Weber stresses that the personal call is the decisive element distinguishing the prophet from the priest. The priest claims authority because of

34

his service in a sacred tradition, whereas the prophet's claim is based on personal revelation and charisma. It is no accident that few prophets emerged from the priestly class. By contrast, the priest dispenses salvation in virtue of his office legitimated by a hierarchy directing the corporate enterprise of salvation.

The prophet is like the magician in exerting his power simply by virtue of his personal gifts but here the similarity ends. Unlike the magician, the prophet appeals to definite revelations, and the heart of his mission is teaching or precept, not magic. Yet it was only under very unusual circumstances that a prophet established his authority without charismatic authentication, which in practice meant magic.

Prophets often practiced divination as well as magical healing and counseling, but here the distinguishing factor is economic, i.e., his prophetic activity is unremunerated. This mark of gratuitous service is a further distinction from the priest, for the prophet propagates ideas for their own sake and not for fees.

Weber notes the historical simultaneity of the outbreak of prophecy throughout the Near East and Greece in the eighth and seventh centuries B.C. with the growth of world empires in Asia, the intensification of international commerce, the formation of cities and the transformation of the polis which resulted from the development of a citizen army. Concurrent with Israelite prophecy at the time of Elijah, Greece was invaded by the Thracian cult of Dionysos; Persian and Hindu prophetic movements were gaining strength; Chinese ethics in the pre-Confucian period was developing. In Greece, mystery doctrines, salvation religions like Orphism and emotional prophecy based on speaking with tongues competed with the evolving theological rationalism and cosmogonic philosophical speculation represented by Hesiod and the pre-Socratics. (Similar political and societal forces of upheaval today parallel the modern outbreak of emotional religion. While Weber confidently implies that the economic upheaval caused the outbreak of salvationist sects, modern social science admits the crudeness of its instruments in tracing such a connection precisely and firmly.)

After this glimpse at the larger picture, Weber continues his task of distinction-drawing. The prophet is not a Greek aisymnete or legislator (like Solon, or similarly, Moses) who codifies or reconstitutes a body of law systematically. Nevertheless, the Jewish prophets were passionately concerned with social reform, oppression of the poor, and other injustices violating the Mosaic code. Yet they endeavored primarily to explain God's wrath in the theatre of Yahweh's activity, foreign politics, and not mainly to alleviate social ills or instigate collective action. More correctly, I think, Vawter sees the prophets as proclaiming fearlessly the moral will of Yahweh. Calling the prophet the "conscience of Israel," he argues that his proclamation sets classical prophecy apart from that of Israel's neighbors (Vawter, 1968, p. 227). The Israelite prophets not only spoke from within the institutions of their time, but also judged them (p. 229).

Weber next contrasts the prophet with the Greek tyrant. Both seize power, but the latter through human agency, the former as a consequence of divine revelation and essentially for religious purposes.

What of the similarity between prophet and teacher of ethics? What primarily differentiates the Greek paidagogos, the Roman magister, the Israelite rabbi, and the Hindu guru from the prophet is their lack of vital emotional preaching. The style of the prophet is closer to that of the popular orator (demagogue) or political publicist than to that of the teacher. Yet Weber repeats as the hallmark of prophecy over against politics the proclamation of a religious truth of salvation through personal revelation. Nor are they merely religious reformers like the Hindus, Shankara and Ramanuja, or Luther, Zwingli, Calvin and Wesley because none of these latter claim to be offering a substantively new revelation, or to be speaking in the name of a special divine injunction. Joseph Smith, the founder of Mormonism, Mohammed, and

36

George Fox would, however, be classified as prophets.

Having tried to distinguish the role of prophet from that of similar religious and social functionaries, Weber divides his genus into two species, the ethical prophet and the exemplary prophet. Zoroaster and Mohammed exemplify the ethical prophet, an instrument for the proclamation of a god and his will, whether concrete command or abstract norm. Because he preaches as one who has received a commission from a god, he demands obedience as an ethical duty. Buddha represents the exemplary prophet, a man who by personal example demonstrates to others the way of personal salvation. The exemplary prophet's preaching lays claim neither to a divine mission nor to an ethical duty of obedience, but appeals instead to the self-interest of salvation-seekers. (Modern Neo-Pentecostal prophets fall for the most part within the camp of the ethical prophets.) Exemplary prophecy is typical of India while ethical prophecy thrives in the Near East and in cultures derivative from it. Ethical prophecy needs a personal, transcendental, ethical god, resembling an all-powerful earthly king with his rational bureaucratic regime. An element found in both species, finally, is the meaning-system, a unified view of the world derived from a consciously integrated attitude toward life. For the prophet, the life of man and of the world, social and cosmic events, have a certain systematic and coherent meaning. To be salvific, human conduct must be oriented around this meaning. The whole system is organized, however, with a stress on practical direction and consequences for living, rather than on logical or metaphysical consistency.

Weber's book, Ancient Judaism (1952), provides a more historical, less essentialist approach to the phenomenon of prophecy. The origins of Jewish prophecy go back at least to the time of the Judges, the days of the tribal confederacy. Between the individual heroes, ecstatic berserks like Samson, and the acute collective ecstasy of the war-dance stands a body of professional warriors; the Nazirites, "separated ones," were ecstatic warriors who left their hair unshorn, and abstained from alcohol and sexual intercourse. Seemingly related in function to the Nazirites were the Nebiim (singular, Nabi), prophets who provided incitement to crusade, promise of victory, and ecstatic victory magic. Samuel and Saul represented the tradition of vagrant delirious Dionysian bands of professional ecstatics, while in the Elisha tradition, resident schools of Nebiim were stimulated by music into ecstasy. Their military function as crusaders was eliminated by the introduction of the chariot and the knight class, and consequently their second function, that of ecstatic prophecy, becomes primary (Weber, 1952, pp. 95-102).

Distinct from the Nabi was the Roeh, "seer," like Nathan the court prophet of David, who had visions in solitude or did dream interpretations; unlike the Nabi, he did not employ orgiastic frenzy or mass ecstasy. Court prophets, known in all Oriental courts and in Egypt, promised good fortune. Prophets of doom lived apart in solitude for the reasons that doom-prophecy could neither be taught nor exploited for profit. Furthernore, such prophets were often outlawed by the authorities (pp. 103-109).

Many of the "classical prophets," those whose teaching has been preserved in the Hebrew scriptures, were political demagogues, objectively speaking. Subjectively, they were no political partisans, but were religious seekers, oriented to fulfilling Yahweh's commands as their religious experience led them to interpret such demands (p. 275). From a very diverse social origin, these bearers of personal charisma refused to recognize the charism of office as a qualification to teach if the priestly teacher were personally unworthy. Among the prophets there existed an attitude of cultural hostility to the genteel living and worldly wisdom of the court and cult (pp. 284-285).

It must not be thought that only the earliest prophets were ecstatic for indeed most of the pre-Exilic Nebiim were such. Their ecstasy was accompanied or preceded by a variety of unusual states and acts which were viewed as holy, God-touched, and originally, at least, as legitimations of charisma.

> When the spirit overcame them, the prophets experienced facial contortions, their breath failed them, and occasionally they fell to the ground unconscious, for a time deprived of vision and speech, writhing in cramps (Is. 21). After one of his visions, for seven days long Ezekiel (Ez. 3:15) was paralyzed. The prophets engaged in strange activities thought to be significant as omens . . . Jeremiah publicly smashed a jug, buried a belt and dug the putrid belt up again; he went around with a yoke around his neck; other prophets went around with iron horns, or like Isaiah for a long time, naked. Still others, like Zachariah, inflicted wounds upon themselves; still others were inspired to consume filth, like Ezekiel. They screamed their prophecies aloud to the world, partly in distinguishable words, partly in imprecations, threats, and benedictions with saliva running from their mouths . . . They described visual and auditory hallucinations and abnormal sensations of taste and feeling of diverse sorts (Weber, 1952, pp. 286-287).

Weber provides several more paragraphs of similarly vivid descriptive material recorded in the prophetic writings, but more useful for our purposes is the classification of symptomatology outlined by a psychoanalyst, Sheldon Cohen (1962). Cohen's theoretical paper works out of the writings of Nietzsche, Goldstein and Rank, and seeks to answer the question, "Why does there arise a single individual, a radical non-conformist, who is willing to risk his social adjustment and his life for a social superego reformation?" Cohen uses the lives of the prophets for illustrative case material, and finds in them six sorts of psychopathological cognitive processes:

(1)   Strong personal anxiety and guilt (Is. 6:4-5; Jer. 1:4-8).   Sometimes the prophets converted anxiety into physiological symptoms: Jeremiah somaticizes in the autonomic system, "the bowels" (Jer. 4:19) while Ezekiel tends to convert anxiety into hysterical failure of muscular control (Ezek. 1:28).

(2)   Hallucinations.   Insofar as the prophet claims to hear an unseen Being or to see visions which others do not share, the technical language of psychology would define such experiences as hallucinations.   Examples are found in Is. 6:1-3; Zech. 5:9; 6:1; Ezek. 1:1-18.

(3)   Delusions.   The prophets are preoccupied with events as intentionally caused, and show no tolerance for the possibility that external events may occur by chance.   They exhibit inverted Oedipal attachment to the "father" (God), passive feminine identification with God as a mother, and preoccupation with "cutting off" (castration) and with birth and womb fantasy.

(4)   Thinking in primitive modes.   They manifest over-concern with oral themes of devouring and being devoured.

(5)   Anal associations.   They engage in obsessive thinking and compulsive undoing behavior.

(6)   Distorted sense of space and time.   The prophet experiences destruction of his self, his society and the natural world in the immediate present.   The flow of time ceases; space extends cosmologically.   In Isaiah expecially, we discover "mood swings" in which the prophet oscillates between consciousness of total world destruction, mourning and melancholia, and a perfect world order at every level of existence and complete joy.   Both extremes could be considered to be irrealistic or cycloid thinking (Cohen, 1962, pp. 102-110).

Weber explains these unusual states, from his sociological perspective, as legitimating the charismatic claims of the prophets. Cohen's hypothesis, the elaboration of which would take us too far afield, proposes that prophetic thought processes involve the transition from heteronomous conscience to the formation of an autonomous creative conscience, and that in the transition to creative conscience formation, the phase of rebellion, mental illness has its psychogenesis. Cohen sees the termination of the process in the prophets as ultimately leading to a high state of self-actualization (p. 115).

Returning again to Weber's analysis, we note that a remark he makes contrasting the classical Hebrew prophets with the Christian prophets of the apostolic age is apposite today too; for the Old Testament seers, the prophetic spirit came in solitude, not in a communal gathering. The original prophets did not think of themselves as members of a supporting spiritual community (Weber, 1952, p. 292), as did/do the Christian prophets. For the latter, the Holy Spirit comes upon the faithful assembly or upon one or several of its members. This was the form of experience which the Christian community evaluated as typical.

This reference to the interrelationship between the prophet and his community can serve to introduce another topic: how was prophecy verified as "true?" As we shall see immediately below in Yocum's directives, Christian prophets were and are formed and judged in dialogue with the community. For the ancient Hebrews, as time went on it became apparent that one could not know the true prophet through ecstasy alone since ecstatic prophets contradicted each other. With this realization, the significance of ecstasy declined. For the prophet himself, the hearing of Yahweh's voice is the self-legitimation, not the nature of his holy states. His call was experienced as a free gift of grace and proclaimed as such rather than as the fruits of asceticism, contemplation, moral attainments, penances or other merits. Prophecy is always a sudden unmotivated occurrence.

The community is helped to know which prophet

41

had heard the voice of Yahweh by passages such as Jer. 23:22-29. Taking his stand on the Torah, the self-evident presupposition of prophecy, the true prophet morally exhorts the people and sanctions their sins through threats of doom. (This is not the simplistic statement that prophets of doom were true prophets, and prophets of good fortune, false, but rather that in the face of the people's sinfulness, proclaimers of good times were to be judged as liars. As a matter of record, however, the kingly and cultic prophets were mostly the proclaimers of good fortune, and were also the false prophets.) In contrast to the prophets of Greece and India who brought salvation through rituals and asceticism, the Hebrew prophets declared that salvation comes by observance of a universally binding workaday ethic. True prophets enforced this ethic and proclaimed harsh judgment upon individuals and institutions of their people which violated Yahweh's norms (pp. 293-295). Another sign, then, of the lying prophet was his failure personally to be converted (p. 299). Initially, political misfortune was secondary to an expected cosmic catastrophe, but the significance of the former gradually mounted in the prophecy of doom. The people were under contract to remain faithful only to Yahweh as their God and abide by His commandments; otherwise they would face His punishment especially in the political arena (pp. 301-302).

A final point of Weber's concerns the character of Yahweh as seen by the prophets because this understanding will perdure and color later prophecy. The prophets fluctuate between describing Yahweh as super-humanly holy and pure, and then again as the ancient warrior God with a changeable heart. Through the prophets a theodicy of misfortune was developed according to which Yahweh ascended to the rank of the one God deciding the source of the world while retaining the old features of the frightful God of catastrophe. Influenced by Persian dualism, the universally diffused folk-belief in demons only gradually penetrated the religiosity of the intellectuals of post-Exilic Jewry. According to the earlier

42

monism, there had been no need for demons since God determined the details of the world. A difference between Hebrew prophecy and Oriental mysticism is relevant here: according to the former, Yahweh is understandable by everybody; He is not an esoteric deity. A mystical possession of other-worldly godliness was rejected in favor of active service to the supernatural, but in principle understandable, God. Likewise, speculation concerning the why of the world was rejected in favor of plain devotion to the positive godly commandments (pp. 310-315).

We make a shift now to study a modern handbook of prophecy (Yocum, 1976), developed out of the experience of Neo-Pentecostal prophets. As the content will demonstrate, this move from ancient Judaism to modern religious expression is not so startling, but will demonstrate many points of similarity and continuity. The author, Bruce Yocum, a single male in his twenties, headed the prophecy team in WoG besides being one of the top men, or "overall coordinators." As was noted previously, the Christian prophets have always been tied into their communities much more tightly than the classical Jewish prophets, a fact that Yocum's position within WoG clearly illustrates.

Straighforwardly and unabashedly, Yocum details his perspective in his Introduction: his manual on how to be a prophet is derived from his personal experience. He distinguishes between knowing about God, and knowing God directly and personally, an experience claimed by all prophets (pp. 7-13).

His first chapter takes up where Weber left off with an outline-account of prophecy in the New Testament and in Church History (pp. 19-24). Luke's Acts of the Apostles provides important material: Agabus foretells a famine (11:27-28); prophets commission Paul and Barnabas (13:1-4); Judas and Silas exhort and encourage the community at Antioch after the first Council of Jerusalem (15:30-32); prophets warn of dangers in Jerusalem for Paul (21:10-11).

There are reference to prophets in the Didache, the earliest non-biblical Christian

43

writing, in Justin's <u>Dialogue with Trypho</u>, in
Irenaeus of Lyons (late second-century A.D.) and
in Melito of Sardis. There is scant mention of
prophetic activity since the third century.
Sporadic appearances are found mostly in religious
renewal movements which display a wide variety of
charismatic activities. Thus during the ascetic
movement in Egypt and Asia Minor from the fourth
through the sixth centuries prophecy appeared once
again and John of Lycopolis was an important prophet. The Cistercian (twelfth century) and
Franciscan and Dominican (thirteenth century)
Movements claimed prophets, as did the Hesychast
Movement in the Eastern Orthodox Church and the
American Second Great Awakening. Yocum concludes
his historical survey with the note that prophecy
flourishes in an atmosphere of "expectant faith."

A philosopher by training, Yocum next tries
to provide distinguishing notes (pp. 29-45) concerning "What is a Prophet?" He names four mis-
conceptions: first, a prophet is an ecstatic.
Referring to Paul (I Cor. 14:32-33), he states
that the spirits of prophets are under prophets'
control, and that genuine Christian prophecy is
not necessarily ecstatic. (This seems to be an
attempt to legislate, or at least to define, experience. It is my personal observation that
Pentecostal and Neo-Pentecostal prophets alike experience mild to deep trance. Later in his book,
(pp. 73-74) Yocum himself describes his first experience of prophecy after which he passed out.)
The second misconception is that a prophet is a
great moral leader. He might be, but this does
not make him a prophet. Thirdly, a prophet is a
visionary. Rather, prophets proclaim what was
revealed by God, not their own vision. Fourth,
a prophet predicts the future, as Jean Dixon does.
Prediction, however, is only a part of the gift.

The best description is that the prophet is a
spokesman for God; just as Aaron spoke for Moses
to the people (Exod. 4:15-17) and to Pharaoh
(Exod. 7:1), so Moses speaks for God. The prophet
has both a message and the authority to proclaim
the message publicly.

A prophet serves four characteristic

functions: to initiate an action of God as Agabus did the famine, and as some Beirut Christians, inspired in the Fall of 1975, emigrated to the U.S. (Prophecy also directed these same Christians back to Beirut in the Spring of 1976 when the situation was even more dangerous! The assumption of mantles by men and veils by women at WoG prayer meetings is ascribed to prophecy although Ralph Martin, one of the leaders, saw this practice in Grenoble, France before one of the WoG prophets declared that God wanted the members of WoG to dress similarly.) The second function consists in awakening God's people to hear His Word. Correlative to this is the third function, that of proclaiming God's Word publicly. Finally, prophets are to unleash the power of the Holy Spirit. Is. 55:10-11 contains the purpose of prophecy: encouragement, conviction, admonition, correction, inspiration, and guidance, both general and specific for the community and the individual.

In the chapter on "The Prophet's Role," (pp. 54-56) Yocum provides some clues for identifying the gift of prophecy. The elders of the community not the prophet himself, "discern" the true prophet. A true prophet will lead a solid and stable life, both from the merely human and the Christian viewpoints. The manifestation of the gift will be powerful, consistent and complex, an ongoing and consistent exercise of four or five years. It will be "powerful" in that its exercise will be effective: both life-changing and life-producing in service to the community. The prophet will be able to "stir up" the gift as Elisha did in II Kgs. 3:9-20.

This interest in "discerning" the true prophet continues in Yocum's next chapter, "The Government of Prophecy in the Christian Community." Because his perspective, like that of most renewal-minded Christians, focuses on the early Christian community as a kind of paradigm for behavior today, Yocum emphasizes the position of the elders in those days (pp. 63-69). He argues that prophets, rather than prophecies, are subject to discernment because most prophecies do not need any significant direct response as they

serve to encourage or exhort. Only rarely does a
community depend upon a single inspired utterance
to determine major directions. Help in discerning
prophecies derives from the life of the prophet
and the effects of an utterance on a community.

Before proceding to the second half of
Yocum's manual, "Growing in Prophetic Gifts," I
want to report an exchange I had with the author
concerning this matter of "governing" prophecy.
A most striking feature of Old Testament prophecy
lies in its consistent fist-shaking at the religious and secular establishments. I asked Yocum
what would happen were a prophet to disagree with
community leadership nowadays. I cited the example of the priest Amaziah telling Amos to go
away and stop prophesying (Am. 7:10-17). Following Yocum's principles, it would seem that Amos
should have ceased and desisted (pp. 68-69).
Yocum's reply shows that he puts community leadership above prophecy:

> . . . Being both a coordinator in the
> Community and exercising prophecy myself, I
> find the question a very interesting one. As
> nearly as I can tell, however, the final
> judgment in terms of what happens within the
> community has to be with the heads of the
> community, although they also are the ones
> who end up bearing judgment for what happens.
> (Personal Communication, April 20, 1976.)

He does not say what happens to the prophet,
but the stage is set for a classic confrontation
between inspiration and ideology. Such a conflict
has indeed already occurred and is a matter of
public record. In August, 1973, David Wilkerson,
author of The Cross and the Switchblade (1970),
claimed that the clearest vision he had ever received from God predicted an era of intense perse-
cution for all Spirit-filled Christians. He prophesied that the warm reception Catholic charismatics are receiving in the Catholic Church will
not continue, and that both Catholic and

46

Protestant charismatics will be forced out of their churches and form a supernatural church of true believers. This "prophecy of doom" flies in the face of the Neo-Pentecostals' vision of remaining within the Catholic Church and clouds the ecumenical hopes of the mainline Christian Churches. Ralph Martin, one of the coordinators in WoG, wrote in New Covenant that Wilkerson was guilty of sensationalism, a spirit of self-justification, and an independent unwillingness to submit his vision to the scrutiny of others. Martin believed that Wilkerson was not hearing the Lord, and that he was demonstrating traditional Pentecostal prejudice, even hostility, to the established churches. Prayer groups all over the country discussed this prophecy and discerned that it was to be repudiated because it was a one-man prophecy and not subject to the scrutiny of the proper charismatic authorities (Fichter, 1975, pp. 125-126).

Returning to the second part of Yocum's treatise we come to the practical helps for prophets. Yocum describes three sorts of prophetic inspiration in which the prophet may be told within himself the actual words of the message, or just a sense of the message without any words. Thirdly, and most commonly for beginners, it happens that only the first word or two of a prophecy is provided by the Lord (pp. 75-78). Sometimes at a prayer meeting some other person will say the words a prophet has heard interiorly. Yocum records a humorous incident in which someone was given only the words, "The owl in the night," was afraid to begin, overcame his trepidation, and delivered a beautiful message (p. 79). Receiving the authority to prophesy may be a tranquil and restful experience, or turbulent, powerful and exciting, but always basically peaceful. There is an urgency to speak plus the conviction that the message and the urgency come from the Holy Spirit. This "anointing," as it is called, often involves physical sensations: a tingling sensation on the back or lips just before speaking, tightness in the chest, or the "elevator" feeling in the pit of the stomach. These sensations accompany the action of the Spirit (pp. 80-81).

Yocum lists ten usual forms of prophecy (pp. 89-102):

(1) Oracles, plain blunt speech in the first person as if the Lord Himself were speaking.

(2) Exhortation/encouragement, perhaps the most common form in which there is greater freedom for expression than in first person prophecies, greater length and more detail.

(3) Inspired prayers like those found in Zachary's (Luke 1:68-79) and Simeon's (Luke 2:29-32) canticles.

(4) Prophecy in song. Sometimes a prophet hears words and a melody. Or he might know the words and be given an urge to sing, or only the melody. The prophet does not compose, but receives his sacred song. (Several prophets in WoG have developed this gift and produced songs of extraordinary beauty which have been recorded and are now sung nationally at prayer meetings after being disseminated in WoG records and song-books.)

(5) Revelation of a personal secret. Yocum reports a personal experience of a counseling session in which he suddenly saw a vision of a small girl and her mother. Puzzled about what it might mean, he nevertheless brought it up cautiously with the woman. The vision served to bring back a forgotten, painful memory which the woman was able to work through. Sensibly, Yocum adds two notes of importance: a counselor may be wrong in thinking he got a revelation. Secondly, it may not be the time or place to share the revelation.

(6) Personal prophecy for some individuals.

(7) Visions. Here the seer should give a matter-of-fact description of what he has seen and heard.

(8) Prophetic actions.

(9) Interpretation of a prophecy given in
tongues.

(10) Prophecy for oneself in one's private
personal prayer. (Again, it must be repeated that
this book has been written in the light of experiences already had by the author or persons known
to him.)

In this section of the book, Yocum again
takes up the question of discernment of prophecy
(pp. 105-109). An important prerequisite is a
climate of faith, a desire really to know God's
Will and to do it. "False prophets" today are
those who perform extraordinary works not necessarily influenced by the Spirit of God. Without
commenting on how he discerned this judgment, he
gives as examples of false prophecy the work of
Edgar Cayce and of mind control. Three categories
of "bad prophecy" are "impure prophecy" in which
one's own thoughts are mixed in and God's Word is
altered or distorted; weak prophecy; sloppy prophecy. A healthy Christian community is the ultimate judge of prophecy, not infallible but reliable. Mutual love is needed as well as a desire
for correction on the part of the prophets.
Several guidelines are provided for determining what is from the Lord (pp. 110-119).

(1) If the life of the prophet or the content of his message goes against Scripture or a
body of teaching central to the Christian life,
the prophet and his message are to be rejected.

(2) The prophet is encouraged to test what
spirit is behind an utterance. His own spirit
will respond and will know that he hears the voice
of the Lord. The concept of "resonance" in physics is provided as an illuminating analogy of this
experience.

(3) Judge the spiritual tone and effect of
the prophecy: it should give one pause if a prophecy is frightening, harsh, condemning, or critical. (It is hard to see how quite a number of Old

49

Testament prophecies would survive this critique!)

(4) Do those people in the community with the gift of discernment recognize the spirit behind the prophecy?

(5) Does it come to pass if it's a prediction?

(6) Does it bear fruit in the life of the community?

In his last chapter entitled "Growing in Prophetic Service," Yocum advises that attitudes contrary to servanthood are selfishness, for example, seeking a position through one's gifts, and vainglory (p. 124). One should stir up one's desire to prophesy but a servant's attitude is most basic (p. 126). Group meetings of community prophets are encouraged (p. 127), and submissiveness to headship is once again recommended (p. 131).

As one contrasts these treatments of prophecy by Weber and Yocum, two elements are especially striking. First, there is a definite continuity of religious experience between the seers of Ancient Israel and modern America. Both groups claim an inner experience which allows, or rather urges them to proclaim truth in God's name. And, they are believed! It must not be forgotten for a moment that Neo-Pentecostals are, for the most part, members of the educated, affluent middle and upper-middle classes, and that the movement, at least in its Catholic phase, flourishes in the supposed center of criticism, skepticism and rationality, the modern University.

Secondly, the degree of control exerted over modern prophets seems at variance with what is known of classical prophets until one reflects upon the phenomenon of court and cultic prophecy which was similarly tamed. One can sympathize with a community's administrators and their efforts to keep watch over any crackpot deciding to speak his mind in God's name. Throughout Christian history men and women have set forth new "revealed" doctrines and wrought havoc among the

faithful. Every two or three years, the daily
papers carry stories that yet another prophet has
set a date for the world or for a certain city to
be destroyed. (The inner dynamics of one such
group have been studied and interestingly reported
by Leon Festinger et al. in When Prophecy Fails
(1956) although their research methodology raised
moral scruples concerning their manner of infil-
trating the subjects' gatherings.) Hence, the
leaders' vigilance. On the other hand, one must
conclude that a prophet with an unpopular vision
must possess extraordinary courage if he/she has
not social support and must fall back only on the
inner light. The social ostracism and even per-
secution which awaited a Jeremiah and a Joan of
Arc do not seem impossible to reproduce given the
normally conservative and traditional policies
which administrators of religious communities
embrace.

Para-Normal Experiences: Faith Healing

When we turn to faith-healing, we are on
ground that has been worked over more thoroughly,
though again not exhaustively. We shall survey
three sorts of sources: scholarly writing; manuals on healing much like Yocum's handbook on prophecy; testimonials for and against the reality of
the experience.
Anthropologists visiting preindustiral societies have penned many monographs on the wide-
spread appearance of faith healing and folk cures.
An often quoted collection of this material is
Ari Kiev, Magic, Faith, and Healing: Studies in
Primitive Psychiatry Today (1964).
Concentrating, however, on psychologists'
writings concerning this topic, we notice a trend
to understand faith healing and psychotherapies as
points on a continuum embracing these and other
methods of influencing people through employment
of suggestibility. Kenneth M. Calestro's
"Psychotherapy, Faith Healing, and Suggestion"
(1972) is the best article on the subject, and
Jerome Frank's Persuation and Healing (1973), the

51

best book. We shall summarize both.

Calestro surveyed the experimental literature dealing with suggestibility and attitude change, and examined the various personality and situational variables associated with suggestibility. Describing the various practices of shamans and religious healers, he notes the contribution of therapeutic suggestibility to their efficacy. Without intending to demean psychotherapy, he still argues that it is the bastard progeny of a long tradition of neo-religious and magical practices that have arisen in every unit of human culture (Calestro, 1972, p. 83). Suggestibility, trust and hope appear to be major factors in the outcome of any variety of therapeutic encounters, and the importance of these elements remains constant despite changes in theory and technique. Two research traditions are compared: the placebo action in psychotherapy is seen as a special case of "secondary suggestibility" (Eysenck, 1947), defined as a change in an individual's cognitive or perceptual behavior (or both) due to subjective interpersonal influences. The other tradition starts with the materials on attitude change by Hovland, Janis and Kelley (1953).

From the factor analytic studies of Eysenck and his followers, it appears that suggestibility or susceptibility to interpersonal influence is not accurately described as a continuum between hypnotic suggestibility and waking suggestibility. Rather, at least two orthogonal factors can be discerned to describe the behaviors. The first factor, most clearly evidenced in hypnotic behavior, represents an ideomotor response to an outside agent's repeated suggestion that a response would occur. The second factor describes cognitive and perceptual responses that are influenced by a suggestive agent's attempts to exploit an individual's mental set, expectations, or need for conformity. Thus, an individual scoring high on some measure of "secondary suggestibility" is one who would be expected to rely heavily on others in formulating his values and beliefs, and to invest little value in his own objective experiences. The phenomenon described by the Yale communication group called "persuasibility" seems to be essentially the same as the "secondary suggestibility" studied by the personality dynamics experimenters. External subjective forces, rather than objective stimulus factors, elicit responses in both cases (Calestro, pp. 84-85).

After reviewing various personality and situational correlates of suggestibility (pp. 86-87), Calestro examines such variables in the natural setting of primitive psychiatry and faith healing as examples of the exploitation of situational factors facilitating suggestibility in a therapeutic context.

Studies in the incidence of deviant behavior and mental illness indicate that psychopathology is not qualitatively different cross-culturally. The symptoms, issuing from mental disorders found throughout the world, are shaped by local beliefs, norms, and general patterns of living. What does differ, at least superficially, is the particular therapeutic model employed to deal with pathology, and the Weltanschauung or assumptive system behind the model. Medicine men and shamans, like their Western counterparts, look for various symptom patterns and make prescriptions on the basis of these. Primitive peoples believe that illnesses result from a finite number of supernatural phenomena, including the loss of soul, intrusion into the body of an alien force (possession), breaking of taboos, and sorcery. Treatment almost always begins with some type of demonstration of the abilities of the shaman designed to impress upon the client the shaman's ability to control natural and supernatural forces. Various rites separate the healing from the "profane" world and identify it as an element of "sacred space and time." The nature of the treatment is related to the assumed causes of afflictions. Thus when loss of soul or violation of taboo is suspected, rituals like confession and expiation involving guilt-reducing activity are called for. Ritual exorcism for spirit possession involves techniques such as purification via starvation, bleeding and fumigation, assault on the possessing spirit, or transference of the spirit to another host. Exorcism "works" because in the assumptive world of client and witch doctor, spirits can possess individuals; the expert is assumed to have the competence necessary for the expulsion of the alien spirits; the client is eager to be rid of his affliction. When sorcery is the cause of problems, counter-magic is employed (pp. 88-91).

Calestro presents many more interesting details about the selection and training of shamans, but concludes as follows:

A variety of primitive, magico-religious techniques appears to be effective in treating certain types of psychopathology; the effectiveness of treatment is a function of its consistency with the assumptive world of the people. The effectiveness of technique is enhanced by therapeutic suggestibility, maximized by such factors as; an atmosphere of heightened emotionality; an assumption that the therapeutic situation is distinct from other mundane activities; shared beliefs in the causes of diseases and the nature of appropriate action; the status of the healer in the community gained by his recognized relationship with natural and supernatural forces (pp. 92-93).

Calestro next surveys Judaeo-Christian faith healing. Among the Egyptians, beliefs in natural and supernatural causation coexisted in harmony. The patient's susceptibility would have been enhanced by the physician's status second only to Pharaoh's. Among the Hebrews, the practice of medicine was reserved for the Levites because sickness was interpreted as a punishment for sins and the cure was assumed to be religious rather than medical. As with the Egyptians, divine intervention was not seen as inconsistent with an understanding of natural phenomena because of the theocentric assumptive system. The Christian healing rites were like many others in that they involved emotional release, physical mortification and guilt reduction. The curing agent, a monk or priest, was perceived as an individual with special powers. That Christian healing was successful can be inferred from its survival and the infiltration of similar techniques into secular medicine. The power of Christian healing fluctuates with the influence of the Church. During periods of revitalization when faith was strong, the popularity and efficacy of religious healing appears to have been proportionately high. Calestro summarizes: the model of healing is consistent with the Judaeo-Christian assumptive world; disease and pain are generally seen as the result of some supernatural intention, and the correction of these conditions is assumed to be a religious matter. The efficacy of faith healing is founded upon a participation in the system of beliefs and values. Faith healing is most effective when performed by an individual held in high regard and recognized as having certain extraordinary powers and capabilities over various forces (pp. 93-96).

We need not follow Calestro further as he studies the role of suggestibility in modern psychotherapies. We note only that given the combination of an assumptive system admitting supernatural forces, charismatic qualities in a therapist, patient need and expectation, therapeutic suggestibility is enhanced and operates on a client's cognitions and perceptions in such a way as to mobilize indigenous curative abilities in him, thus facilitating and accelerating the process of remission.

Jerome Frank's Persuasion and Healing (1973) makes essentially the same points but includes more materials on comparative outcome studies from various forms of modern psychotherapy, placebo action, as well as on Communist brainwashing techniques and healings at Lourdes. His seemingly bizarre grouping of such different forms of "treatment" is certainly justified by his discovery of the common element of suggestibility in all of them. We list here, first, his summary comments concerning all forms of treatments involving persuasion, and then his remarks specifically concerning non-medical modes of healing.

The common characteristic of persons who employ the forms of treatment surveyed is demoralization (Frank, 1973, p. 313). Four shared features of the various change processes seem to emerge:

(1)   A particular type of relationship between the help-giver and the patient, sometimes in
the context of a group, is initiated. The essential ingredient of this relationship is that the
patient has confidence in the therapist's competence and in his desire to be of help. Faith in
the therapist's ability is enhanced by the latter's socially sanctioned role.

(2)   The locale of the therapy is designated
by society as a place of healing, and the setting
itself thus arouses the patient's expectation of
help. If the setting is the sufferer's home, this
is transformed into sacred space by purification
rituals.

(3)   All therapies are based on an assumptive
system/rationale/myth which includes an explanation of illness, health, deviancy and normality.
Within the assumptive system setting forth a philosophy of life, the rationale of each school of
therapy explains the cause of the disturbance for
each sufferer, specifies goals, and prescribes
procedures for treatment. The provocative word
"myth" has been employed to stress that even
though the rationales of many Western therapies do
not invoke supernatural forces, they resemble the
myths of primitive healers in that they cannot be
shaken by therapeutic failures.

(4)   The fourth ingredient, the procedure/
task prescribed by the myth, is the means by which
the sufferer is brought to see the error of his
ways and modify them, thereby gaining relief. The
central point is that the therapeutic efficacy of
rationales and techniques may lie not in their
specific contents, which differ, but in their
functions which are the same (pp. 325-329).

The therapeutic relationship, setting, rationale and task together influence patients in
five interrelated ways to produce attitude change
and therapeutic benefit:

56

(1)   They provide clients with new opportunities for learning at both cognitive and experiential levels.

(2)   All therapies enhance the patient's hope
of relief.

(3)   They provide success experiences which
enhance the sufferer's sense of mastery, interpersonal competence, or capability. All successful therapies change the patient's image of himself as a person overwhelmed by symptoms to that
of one who can master them.

(4)   Therapies help overcome a demoralizing
sense of alienation from one's fellows. Through
interacting with the therapist and group within
the framework of the same assumptive system, one
discovers that problems are not unique and that
others can understand and care.

(5)   Finally, all forms of therapy, when successful, arouse the patient emotionally. Yet the
role of emotional arousal in causing change is not
perfectly clear (p. 329).

Methods of primitive healing involve an interplay between a patient, healer, reference
group and the world of the supernatural. The persuader is the point of interaction between those
and is seen as possessing power over the welfare
of the sufferer. The persuader puts out great effort to bring about changes in the sufferer's
bodily state or attitudes. Such systematic activity characteristically involves means of emotional
arousal, often to the point of exhaustion, in a
ritual often highly repetitive. The whole procedure can be very unpleasant, but as it occurs
in a context of hope and potential support from
the persuader and the group, tends to bring the
desired relief (pp. 95-96). Healing cults, by
making unashamed efforts to mobilize the uncriti-
cal faith of their adherents, succeed in helping
many persons whom more conventional therapies do
not reach. The cult-leader glories in his claimed

57

healing powers, exerts them without self-doubt, and his services are supported by a group of believers in his powers. These healing approaches employ emotion rather than intellect, subjective certainty instead of objective analysis. For persons who can abandon skepticism, such cults mobilize strong psychological forces for the production and maintenance of therapeutic change (p. 324).

Pattison et al. (1973) tested and interviewed forty-three fundamentalist Neo-Pentecostal church members in Seattle, Washington who had experienced a total of seventy-one faith cures. They sought answers to four questions:

(1)   Are alternate symptoms formed?

(2)   Do significant changes in lifestyle occur?

(3)   Do those claiming faith healing exhibit a typical personality?

(4)   Why do people participate in these rituals?

Interviewed subjects were asked to talk about their life patterns and medical history prior to and subsequent to healing, and their perceived function of the healing experience. The subjects were skilled blue-collar and white-collar workers whose social life and religious life were co-extensive. The interval between the healing and the interview was two weeks to fifty-one years with the mean being fifteen years. An important indicator of the subjects' suggestibility lay in the discovery that their perception of the healing was related to participation in a healing ritual, not to a change in symptomatology. That is, symptoms often lasted after a claimed healing! Half of the seventy-one cures were instantaneous and half were gradual. Most of the subjects had consulted physicians both before and after their cures since doctors are "useful and necessary and given to us by God" (Pattison et al., 1973,

p. 400). No symptom alternation occurred nor was there a change in lifestyle. The one major change was in attitude: subjects testified to a deeper certainty of belief in God and their religious convictions markedly increased.

Concerning the personality status of the participants in the study, their self report indicated them to be high energy people who rarely experienced anxiety, worry, restlessness, depression or anger. "God can take care of everything," said one (p. 401). Yet the interviewers' impressions contradicted these personal viewpoints. Subjects would deny or minimize anxiety, worry, etc. and seemed to want to see themselves in a good light. On the personality indices administered, both male and female subjects fell within normal ranges on the Cornell Medical Index; psychiatric items on this test also were within normal limits.

On the MMPI no statistical difference between males and females was registered, nor was there significant deviation among subjects, and so a composite profile was drawn. An L scale of sixty indicated a tendency to report oneself in a highly socially acceptable manner. The difference between K and F was 13.7, showing defensiveness against psychological weakness and a distortion of self-image in the "good" direction. The clinical scales showed no gross pathology though an Hy of sixty-three tells of reliance upon repression and a denial of emotional difficulties, exactly the qualities noted in the interviews. Anxiety and repression scales were within normal limits but R was high, a confirmation that repression and denial are major coping devices. Of the thirty-nine possible items to check for social desirability, this group averaged 32.5. Subjects like these with high K and Hy and low F and Sc are described clinically as affiliative, constrictedly over-conventional persons who deny difficulty and have a Pollyanna perception of all events. Even in the face of catastrophic failure they resolutely maintain that "things are going fine." Feelings of defeat seem to be intolerable to such persons.

Finally, as to why persons seek faith cures, it must be remembered that science asks, "Does faith healing cure the illness?" while an applicant asks, "Am I living in the right way?" In societies undergoing rapid cultural change from a pre-scientific to a scientific Western form of society both types of healers are employed by the populace for different reasons. When a patient perceives an illness to be due to an impersonal, natural cause like a germ or an accident, he will seek treatment from a medical doctor. But if the illness is understood as being due to conditions culturally defined as personal sin, evil intent, or violation of taboo, a faith healer of the whole person is sought out. Persons in conservative religious groups maintain religious beliefs about the supernatural cause of events and hence feel no inconsistency in seeking out a faith cure. The primary function of such a belief system, then, is not to reduce symptoms, but to reinforce an assumptive worldview consonant with the subject's subculture. There is a continuum ranging from magical belief systems like witchcraft in which evil is controlled up to Christian Science in which evil is denied. The psychodynamics are similar in all systems, but the systems vary in their degree of abstraction. Within such an assumptive world, magical belief systems are not abnormal, but part of a coping system that provides ego-integration for individuals and social integration for the subculture. Healing reflects a control over one's self and one's world while the system provides a mechanism for externalization and an explanation when anxiety and misfortune occur (Pattison et al, 1973, pp. 401-409).

The studies reviewed thus far have all been written from within the assumptive system of Western science. What happens if one adopts a viewpoint that is midway between that of science and those of pre-industrial societies? Lawrence LeShan (1974) attempts to do that by working toward a general theory of the para-normal. His book compares three types of consciousness and the realities of which each is aware: the medium experience clairvoyant reality; the mystic,

60

transpsychic reality; the physicist, sensory
reality. Western scientism gives primacy to the
last of these, but LeShan attempts to study each
carefully, and claims to have performed healings
in "secular clairvoyant reality." By not giving
primacy to sensory reality, but nevertheless by
insisting on careful explication and understanding
of the alternative realities, LeShan avoids the
error of scientism and its prejudice against the
para-normal. His careful collection of the experiences and writings of mystics and mediums produces a persuasive case for the legitimacy of the
para-normal and against Western reductionistic
materialism. It is hard to accept his evidence
and reject his viewpoint!

We turn now to the second type of literature
on faith healing, various manuals concerning its
practice and written within a Christian assumptive system. (Other publications, like those of
Edgar Cayce, for example, or the prodigious number
of volumes on psychic healing and the occult,
could be quoted but the group studied is Christian
and it seemed good to survey literature available
to the subjects interviewed.)

An old-time favorite is Agnes Sanford's The
Healing Light (1947). Basically a personal statement of her experiences with spiritual healing, it
provides a simple and clearly outlined method for
use with oneself and others: choose the same time
and place everyday; make yourself comfortable and
relax. Remind yourself of the reality of a life
outside yourself -- this phraseology is adapted
for use with non-theists who nevertheless can be
brought to a feeling for something more than the
material world. Ask that life to come in and increase life in your body. Make a picture in your
mind of your body as well. See it perfect and
shining with God's light. Give thanks that this
is being accomplished, and say "Amen," so be it,
like a command (Sanford, 1943, pp. 36-37).

The Gift of Healing (1965) by Ambrose A.
Worrall is the autobiography of Worrall and his
wife, Olga, and details their earliest beginnings
in dealing with a spiritual reality, their doubts
about using their strange talents for precognition

and healing, and their current dedication of all
their spare time to a free ministry based in
Baltimore but with beneficiaries world-wide. The
work is fascinating both because of its wealth of
case material, and its specificity in suggestions
about procedures which latter we reproduce here.
There are five basic principles to healing as understood and practiced by the Worralls:

(1) Spiritual healing is not in opposition
to medicine.

(2) The spiritual therapist has no power of
his own. The gift is not a gift of power itself,
but of the ability to be used by the Power, to
direct, to channel the Power to others.

(3) We can and must learn the art of allowing this Power to work through us. The art involves learning to make contact with a force, to
be receptive to the forces around us, to the impression that comes, to the inspiration, to the
knowing.

(4) The healer must care.

(5) The individual who seeks healing must
have a right attitude. The person who is openly
hostile makes it extremely difficult for the
spiritual therapist to cure. The patient must allow healing to work. (Worrall explicitly refuses
to pry into the individual's personal business or
religious affiliation. Nor does he tell the
patient that he must believe in him or in his
theories.)

Ten steps are then listed describing the actual healing interchange --

(1) The patient is educated regarding habits
and posture.

(2) He is further instructed regarding the
healer's basic theories about an available healing
force, the need for receptivity, the affinity

between healer and patient.

(3) The "tuning in" technique: this means that the healer waits until the patient and he are on the same "wave length," until the healer becomes attuned to the client's wave length so that the healing force can flow.

(4) Massage.

(5) Laying on of hands.

(6) Passes of the hands with light contacts.

(7) Treatment of the patient by prayer and affirmation, but without contact. Subjectively on the healer's part, there may be merely a complete personal affirmation of truth, followed by an allowance of his thoughts or being to drift free in the field of consciousness itself. The healer is aware subconsciously all this time that the Power is at work.

(8) Treatment without the patient having any awareness that he is being treated.

(9) Explanation of what treatment he is using and why.

(10) Employment of the definition of Faith as "the lack of resistance to that which you hope to receive" (Worrall, 1965, pp. 194-197).

As Worrall's secular profession is engineering, he comfortably employs electrical metaphors to describe the transmission of healing energy:

> . . . the energy by which the healing is to be accomplished flows in the form of a current through what we could call the healer's equivalent of a primary circuit. A change in frequency seems to occur in the healer's body, perhaps by induction in a neural secondary circuit, then the current flows

through this circuit from the healer to the patient. There is, in effect, an inner transformer that adjusts the current to the frequency that can be received by the patient . . . I believe the healing currents utilize the nervous system and that placing the hands on specific nerve centers produces the fastest results (p. 166).

In direct physical contact a tingling sensation is often experienced by both the healer and the patient. Worrall says that in his case the "current" appears to flow from his solar plexus. Unlike the heat experienced in the laying on of hands, the current from the solar plexus appears to be cool. He speculates that low frequency current is involved in healing with physical contact and high frequency in healing at a distance. He experiences in both cases the sensation that something similar in consistency to heavy air is leaving him (p. 167).

Worrall argues, however, that spiritual healing is a natural phenomenon, occurring in accordance with natural laws. He acknowledges that this power is demonstrated through people of many religions and through some who have no religious affiliations. His own personal belief is that the healing power has its origin and source of supply in the Supreme spiritual power that governs and controls all things (p. 164). Except for this last statement of private belief, his experience and explanatory scheme parallels that of LeShan.

A most thorough treatment, especially of physical healing, from the Christian Neo-Pentecostal perspective is Francis MacNutt's Healing (1974). A disciple of Agnes Sanford who has been active in the healing ministry in the United States, Peru, Bolivia and Chile, MacNutt estimates that about half of those prayed for are physically healed or notably improved, and about three-fourths are healed of emotional or spiritual problems (p. 14). He stresses the increasing frequency and ordinariness of the healing phenomenon within the Christian community; on a typical

Pentecostal retreat when he asks for a show of
hands of those who have seen the sick healed
through prayer, half the hands go up (p. 10). Indeed, he must spend his first hundred pages attempting to convince a skeptical educated
Christian audience that healings do occur and can
be legitimately prayed for because of the theological tradition of the value of suffering and
the Cross, and because of the Elmer Gantry and
Marjoe-type faith healers exposed as charlatans.
MacNutt sees the revival of the healing ministry
as a return to a more authentic living of Christ's
teaching and the earliest Christians' practice
about illness than had been the case since
Augustine taught that miracles were only for the
beginnings of the Church, and since the "sacrament
of the sick" had been transformed into "last
rites," a preparation for death instead of health.
He shows constant and prudent concern that guilt
not be generated in those prayed over by over-
zealous healers who might be tempted to shift the
blame for no cure to the lack of faith in the patient. "My faith is in God -- not in my faith"
(p. 120). He makes the interesting and important
distinction between the faith in healing that all
Christians have and the special gift of faith in
the healer. The latter is associated with the
"gift of knowledge" to pray with the confidence
and certainty that a certain intention will be
granted, e.g. that the one prayed for will indeed
be healed. The prayer of such people is more like
a command than a petition: "Be healed." People
with this gift of knowledge are also given to
understand for whom they are <u>not</u> to pray for
special healing. God in some way or other has revealed his will to heal/not heal at this time; the
ministry of a person with such a gift is not only
praying to God but addressing the sick person as
God's spokesman. Many of the problems in the
healing ministry are caused by persons imitating
the styles of others who have gifts they themselves do not have: guilt-induction can be caused
by such an approach (pp. 125-130). He also cites
examples of healings occurring when no one, neither healer nor healee (neologism for "person

65

healed"), had faith beforehand and a cure still occurred: in such cases, God simply wants to manifest his goodness (pp. 131-133).

The remaining two hundred pages of this comprehensive handbook contain a compilation of testimonies, examples, and practical guidance for the minister of healing. Though there is too much to summarize in detail, we can nevertheless note the following high points. A spirit of caution and concern that sick people's guilt not be aroused nor expectations manipulated perdures throughout. For example, he warns against expanding any one method or experience into a universal method; the practice of "claiming your victory" (i.e., declaring that one has been healed once prayers have been offered, even though symptoms remain) should be undertaken only if the sick person himself feels that this is what God wants, and has been truly inspired to accept his healing as an already accomplished fact (pp. 137-140). An advocate of the team approach to healing (physicians, psychiatrists, healers and clergymen working together), he is sensitive to the differences between what therapy and prayer can effect:

> I recently talked to a mother and father who spent $70,000. on psychiatric help for their daughter. This professional help kept her alive and gave her a vocabulary to describe her problem but did not cure her. She has since been healed by prayer (p. 181). . .

> . . . The most I was ever able to do as a counselor was to help the person bring to the foreground of consciousness the things that were buried in the past, so that he could consciously cope with them in the present. Now I am discovering that the Lord can heal these wounds -- sometimes immediately -- and can bring the counseling process to its completion in a deep healing (p. 187).

MacNutt lists four kinds of healing and

suggests practical helps with each: repentance for sins, inner healing, physical healing, and deliverance from evil spirits. For example, the visualization suggested by Sanford in doing healing is again recommended by MacNutt when attempting physical healing. "For instance, if we are praying for the healing of a bone we can ask the Father (or Jesus) to take away every infection, to stimulate the growth of the cells needed to restore the bone and to fill in any breaks" (p. 202). Yet while suggesting that the healer visualize as clearly as possible what he is asking God to heal, he follows his own rule about not making any procedure a universal method by recommending the alternate approach of simply relaxing, emptying the mind of all thought and effort, and letting the love of God flow through him. He further specifies that such imaginative prayer should be positive, emphasizing not the present state of sickness but hope for the body as one would like to see it -- whole. Praying while imagining the patient sick in bed is often unsuccessful (p. 203).

Quite frequently, practicing healers blame lack of faith in the healee as the reason for no cure so it is refreshing to read MacNutt's chapter entitled "Eleven Reasons People Are Not Healed" (pp. 248-261). In it he provides causes like "Refusal to see medicine as a way God heals," "Not using the natural means of preserving health," and "Now is not the time" in addition to more "spiritual" reasons like sin in a person's life and a false value attached to suffering. In sum, MacNutt blends common sense, counseling expertise, and the "higher wisdom" taught him by his prayers for healing to write a book at once psychologically and theologically sound.

Finally, we list some volumes giving testimony for and against the reality of healing. Most famous is Kathryn Kuhlman's I Believe in Miracles (1969), a collection of case studies concerning persons healed at Ms. Kuhlman's popular services. Most comprehensive is Will Oursler's The Healing Power of Faith (1957), a journalist's well researched succinct study of many different American and European communities of healing, individual healers, and healing shrines. Oursler makes the same distinction in terminology which MacNutt and others had used between "healing" and "miracle." Healings, both psychological and physical, are frequently claimed but "miracle" has been usefully defined by physicians at Lourdes to specify only the cure of an organic disease which must continue for at least a year without regression, and must be inexplicable by any other means except divine intercession (Oursler, 1957, p. 52).

This concept will be useful to recall as we survey the final volume in this search, William A. Nolen's Healing: A Doctor in Search of a Miracle (1974). A surgeon, Nolen confesses that he had always been skeptical of healers, but that his faith in Western medicine was shaken in 1971 when it was reported that New York Times editor, James Reston, had been cured by acupuncture in China (Nolen, 1974, p. 8). This event set him on a course of researching the claims of various healers, specifically Kathryn Kuhlman, Norbu Chen of Houston who was sponsored by astronaut Edgar Mitchell, and the Philippine psychic surgeons. His conclusion: no healing of organic disease, one with structural physiological alterations, was discovered. (Physicians at Lourdes, however, do have such healings on record.) Healings which did occur were "self-limited" cases in which the cure is basically accomplished by the body itself. Suggestion can and does influence the outcome of "functional ailments" caused by the malfunction of an organ or system under the control of the autonomic nervous system (p. 244). Healers, whether by their machinations, their rituals, or their sheer charisma, possibly stimulate patients to heal more rapidly than they otherwise might, just as a charismatic doctor might accomplish more through rapport than through impersonality and brusqueness. This is the usual statement of the suggestibility hypothesis though Nolen adds that the "charismatic stimulation of the healing process probably occurs through the autonomic nervous system" (p. 243). People go to healers because the medical profession had let them down with

nothing curative to offer. Healers offer more
warmth and compassion than physicians do. Healers do help: they relieve symptoms and cure some
functional diseases (p. 270).

This quick accounting fails to do justice to
the wealth of novelistic detail Nolen provides as
he recounts his travels, feelings, puzzlement
(especially with the Philippine surgeons until he
figures out their technique), and intelligent
disagreement with the claims of any and all healers. It has been necessary to include Nolen because of his sincere efforts to find even one organic cure, and because he represents clearly and
interestingly the skepticism of the medical profession about the validity of faith cures.

The Researcher's Personal Statement

This survey has attempted to move from the
general to the particular in researching two questions: who are the Neo-Pentecostals, and how describe their para-normal experiences? In addition
to the particular conclusions reached by each
scholar consulted, we have seen a more general
philosophical issue surface from time to time, the
problem of choice of assumptive-system or world
view. It is clear how the framework of science
will cause a writer to attribute to suggestibility
what a framework of Christianity will cause a believer to interpret as a gift from "the Lord." Of
the scholars reviewed, LeShan and Worrall seem to
have the most pliant overall framework. I wish to
conclude this section with a personal statement of
my own Weltanschauung regarding miracles, prophecy
and healing. (This is a different question from
the methodology of this study which is dealt with
in the following chapter.)

Most formative in my reflection on this question has been the Scottish Presbyterian theologian, John Macquarrie. In the section entitled
"Miracles" in his Principles of Christian Theology
(1966, pp. 225-232), Macquarrie nicely articulates
the stance of a theist like myself who am attempting to live and profess Christianity in a

demythologized, postindustrial, scientific society. Minimally, a miracle is an event that excites wonder, but in a religious context, it is believed that God is in the event in some special way, that He authorizes it, that He intends to achieve some special end by it. Such an act of God may be a vehicle for revelation, grace, judgment, or all three. While I believe God to be active in the whole world-process, some happenings count for more than others (e.g., the Exodus, the Resurrection, my own faith-cures.) So I avoid the flat generalization of nineteenth century idealist theologians who say that everything is miracle and thus make the concept devoid of content. But I also reject the traditionalist view that miracle is distinctive because it breaks into the order of nature; that in a miracle the laws of nature are suspended and a super-natural agency takes over. Such a conception of miracle is irreconcilable with our modern understanding of both science and history: I accept the scientific "act of faith" that incomplete accounts of world events will be filled out by further research into factors just as immanent and this-worldly as those already known. I accept the two principles of historical method of analogy and correlation enunciated by Troeltsch. According to the first, historical events are only those happenings analogous to events occurring in our own experience; according to the principle of correlation, all events belong within the context of an immanent process. Thus, miraculous healings reported in the Bible can be classified as historical because similar events occur today although the natural laws governing such experiences are still unclear. Yet a believer can still experience wonder and know God's presence and activity within such happenings without representing the event as a supernatural intervention. Such an interventionist view of the Deity would gradually see His powers shrinking as knowledge of man and nature got extended, and would represent Him also as playing favorites.

The true meaning of miracle, then, does not lie in some extraordinary publicly observable event, but in God's presence and self-manifestation in the event. The mythological way of thinking tries to express this distinctiveness by making the event itself something magical or supernatural, thus shifting the focus from the essence of miracle (the Divine self-communication) to the happening. Miracle has the character of ambiguity: from one point of view, the event is seen as perfectly ordinary; from the viewpoint of faith, it is an event that opens up Being and becomes a carrier for Being's revelation, grace, judgment, or address.

When asked about God by Napoleon, the mathematician Laplace is supposed to have said, "I have no need of that hypothesis." Similarly, the Exodus event (Ex. 14:21) of the escape from Egypt by the Hebrews can be viewed as a stroke of good fortune, a chance happening, or the foundational event of a People in its relationship to a covenanting God. (The extra details in the subsequent verse about waters standing like a wall to either side are a mythological addition stressing the magical in the event and distracting from the faith experience). From the assumptive system of scientism, the perspective of faith is a subjective addition to the raw publicly observable data: a crowd of ex-slaves walks over a shallow watercourse, and a pursuing army gets its chariot wheels mired in the mud and rising tide. Yet to this motley crowd, now become a community, and to its physical and spiritual offspring, Holy Being has communicated His concern, interest, care and compassion. A network of subsequent experiences, communal and individual, support and extend this relationship. Through a day-by-day living of the Law which reveals the will of Holy Being, and through special events seen by the community as miraculous, the understanding of Being's self-manifestation deepens, and the vision of His presence becomes an even more complete and real way of knowing than scientific data though the latter are respected too. This philosophical view of miracle applies, therefore, to the healing experiences of Neo-Pentecostals.

It is necessary, finally, to reconcile Weber's (1952) and Cohen's (1962) psychological evaluative account of ancient Hebrew prophecy with my own abstention from pathological characterization. In their view, the immanence of God manifests itself in that which appears pathological within a this-worldly assumptive framework. Because my own "myth" develops from the thought of Macquarrie, LeShan and Worrall, I prefer to conceptualize prophetic experiences as "para-normal" rather than "abnormal." Nor is the distinction merely semantic: having taught "Abnormal" Psychology for several years, I realize how linked a culture's definition of pathology becomes with its assumptive system. For example, when Cohen (1962, pp. 103-104) calls the prophetic visions and auditions "hallucinations" and "delusions," he is casting his vote with those who are blind and deaf to the prophet's insight; he is being judgmental rather than merely descriptive, and importing his assumptive framework into the analysis. It seems far better to take a Jamesian approach, to judge the experiences "by their fruits, not by their roots" in determining whether a particular prophet's claims are a schizophrenic's ravings, hence abnormal, or a visionary's interaction with the para-normal.

This project, then, tries to understand the para-normal experiences of prophecy and healing from a this-worldly phenomenological perspective, but the author remains open to the validity of the claims of the subjects that they have experienced and heard Being revealing itself in the events to be recounted.

CHAPTER II

METHODOLOGY

An explicitly phenomenological approach is
employed in this research. What is that? My concrete exemplar was William Jame's Varieties of
Religious Experience (1902), a study which moves
effortlessly from data to generalization, from experience to observation, from life to insight.
Among the various methods available to a psychological researcher today, I believe that the phenomenological is best suited to handle the material of this study. The task here, then, is to ex-
plicate this inductive style of investigation.
Other well-known examples of social science research written from the phenomenological perspective are Goffman's Asylums (1961), a study of total institutions, The Presentation of Self in
Everyday Life, (1959), and Becker et al., Boys in
White (1962), an inside view of hospital life.
This chapter will contain four sections:
(1) a brief historical review of our psychological
predecessors who developed and employed the phenomenological method; (2) a generalized description of the method; (3) objections to its use and
an attempt to answer these queries; (4) a more
specific account of the method as employed in this
study.

The Development of Phenomenological Psychology

The historian of philosophical phenomenologies, Herbert Spiegelberg, traces the influence
of this method in psychology and psychiatry
(1972). Equally useful is the summary of Amedeo
Giorgi (1970), himself a psychologist, whose
thinking structures the following excursus. Giorgi
shows the fruitfulness of the phenomenological
method by outlining the approach of those psychologists who viewed the discipline as a human

science.

The two words, "human" and "science" capture his insight, psychology has been excessively narrowed by its past strivings to ape the style of the natural sciences instead of developing itself as a characteristically human science, a goal of a vocal minority of psychologists from the beginning. Furthermore, such development would still guarantee psychology's identity as a science, not an art, not a return to a covert tutelage to philosophy or theology, nor a mere extension of the therapeutic attitude. In his own words,

> . . . what I mean to communicate by the term "human science" is that psychology has the responsibility to investigate the full range of behavior and experience of man as a person in such a way that the aims of science are fulfilled, but that these aims should not be implemented primarily in terms of the criteria of the natural sciences. (Giorgi, 1970, p. xii, italics his.)

Giorgi follows the thinking of psychologists about the word, "science," from its birth in Wundt's laboratory in 1879 up to the present day, and details how the majority of psychologists, in straining to shake the field free from domination by philosophy, plunged headlong and unthinkingly into the camp of the natural scientists. As a result, psychology has been shackled by a method which prevents it from being true to its subject matter, the full human person in all his behavior, especially his interiority and more properly human functioning.

> To be sure, natural scientific psychology does yield legitimate data about aspects of man, but there is serious question whether or not the aspects that are amenable to the natural scientific conception reveal the humanness of man in an adequate way (p. 2).

74

Mainstream psychology conceived as a natural science is characterized as being empirical, positivistic, reductionistic, quantitative, genetic, deterministic, predictive, and founded on the idea of independent observers (pp. 61-62). This approach which succeeds so well in physics and chemistry had been taken over uncritically by psychology in the late nineteenth and early twentieth centuries. Now, a century after psychology's founding, it is appropriate to reflect thoughtfully on this methodological presupposition, and if it is found wanting, to articulate an alternate paradigm. Is this approach of the natural sciences problematic? Giorgi lists six criticisms by psychologists, past and present, detailing the limitations of the approach:

(1)   Psychology lacks real unity.

(2)   Psychology lacks direction.

(3)   Psychology has not been investigating meaningful phenomena in a meaningful way.

(4)   It lacks holistic methods.

(5)   Traditional psychology does not do justice to the human person.

(6)   Psychology's relevance to the life-world (Lebenswelt) is deficient (pp. 79-87).

The import of these criticisms is that psychology has demonstrated stronger commitment to natural scientific methodology than to its subject matter, the human person in his totality and fulness. Criteria derived from natural science have limited the phenomena allowed to be investigated, and conditioned the kinds of questions psychologists are permitted to ask about the phenomena. The criteria culminate in the measurement question, such that "How do you measure . . .?" has become key, and measurement precedes existence, as

75

it were (pp. 64-65). If a phenomenon is to the
extent that it is measureable, then failure to
measure will guarantee psychological irrelevance
such that peculiarly human experiences like humor,
grief, friendship, love, courage, or freedom will
lack treatment in psychology textbooks. (Of
course, we do not mean to imply that a human science would be unconcerned about more ordinary,
prosaic behaviors like perception, etc.)

So much for critique: what are the characteristics of the "human science" which Giorgi and
other phenomenologists have striven to put in the
place of the natural scientific perspective?
Giorgi begins by demonstrating that from the start
of psychology's independence as a discipline in
its own right, voices have been urging an explicitly human approach to the field. In the late
nineteenth century, Wilhelm Dilthey (1944) demonstrated that the <u>Geisteswissenschaften</u>, human
studies, could be rigorous and systematic, but in
a way that was different from the natural sciences. Human sciences are not a mere welter of
subjective impressions, but have rigorous methods
and controls of their own. Whereas in the natural
sciences, we aim for knowledge and explanation,
prediction and control, in the human sciences we
seek understanding and interpretation. In place
of clearly formulated theories which can be tested
by experiment, we have an attempt to analyze and
describe the concrete complexities of life. Instead of explanation of particular events and processes through general laws, we develop an appre-
ciative understanding of the meaning and value of
the unique individual.

Dilthey speaks further of the distinction between a system of laws or sciences, and a system
of significant and value-permeated existences or
world-views. Because the natural sciences deal
with the non-human world, it is quite permissible
to take phenomena out of context, substitute symbols for them, and mathematically manipulate these
symbols to create algebraic laws of phenomenal behavior. Since, however, the human sciences study
a human world, the product of consciousness, these
sciences describe and interpret phenomena as

expressions of a humanly meaningful reality. The human sciences cannot remove phenomena from their historical context as it is precisely this context which gives them meaning. So the human sciences build up a structure of knowledge based on corroborative evidence which Dilthey called a world-view or Weltanschauung. Consequently, such a science can do justice to the higher functions of human thought and action.

Dilthey continues to elaborate the distinction between natural and human sciences by speaking of the former as "explanatory" science and the latter as "descriptive" science. A "descriptive" science finds its units and laws through empirical analysis, or close examination of what is actually given in experience, whereas an "explanatory" science is one which takes its units and laws from a methodological assumption which determines their general nature beforehand, as in modern physics. Natural scientific psychology, modeling itself after physics, adopts its hypotheses of unit sensations and feelings, and other hypotheses which go behind the facts of experience. Because mental life is a functional unity which cannot be reduced to or built up theoretically out of non-functional units, the real unit of mental life is not a sensation, not a feeling, not even an isolated intentional act with its content, but a total reaction of the whole self (Erlebnis) to a situation confronting it. Each such Erlebnis includes cognitive, affective and conative elements whose interrelations are called the "structure" of the mind. A "descriptive" psychology, then, rests on the fact that this structural system is not discovered by inference or hypothesis, but is given in lived experience. Here is a further contrast between these "structural" relations and causal relations: whereas causes can be inferred, structural sequences have their meaning in themselves, and in them the essence of the mind is perceived. Understanding, therefore, is a process of grasping meaning, an insight into the working of the human mind, a mental operation which can be defined in terms of other mental operations as little as can seeing or reasoning. Understanding is an inside

77

view of human nature that we all possess (Giorgi,
1970, pp. 21-26).

Franz Brentano is the next thinker presented
by Giorgi as representing and carrying forward
the human scientific tradition. Brentano's
Psychology from an Empirical Standpoint appeared
in 1874. Best known, perhaps, through his influence on Gordon W. Allport (e.g., 1950, pp. 143-
144), the Austrian Brentano concentrated his attention on the acts of the mind whereas the more
dominant and prominent Wundt and his followers
developed a content psychology. For Brentano,
intentionality was the most crucial characteristic
of the human mind: to act mentally was to intend
an object that represented one's goal. The gram-
matical part of speech most typical of mental life
is thus the active participle for at every moment
the individual is engaged in thinking, discerning,
feeling, loving, studying, etc. The important
thing is what the individual is trying to do in
relating himself to the objects of his own thinking. (The greater relevance of Brentano's act-
psychology over behaviorism or other forms of
natural scientific psychology is immediately seen
in psychology of religion where the subjective
thrust of the mind is important to understand, and
where overt behavior, as measured by such crude
measures as church attendance statistics, is far
less revealing.) Mental phenomena are distinguished and specified as occurring when an object
has intentional existence in an act of the mind.
Accordingly, psychic activity is characterized by
directedness toward an object. While the "Act"
psychologists accepted activity as the essence of
the mind and tried to analyze it, the "Content"
psychologists who stressed the objects toward
which the mind was directed won in the struggle:
the palpability of the content and the ability to
analyze it with the known methods borrowed from
the natural sciences were decisive factors in the
outcome (Giorgi, pp. 28-29).

William James can justly be claimed to belong
both to the camp of the natural and of the human
scientific psychologists. The latter would claim
him because of his style of thought, his way of

treating psychological problems, and the type of problems selected. Not only his Varieties of Religious Experience (1902) but also his Principles of Psychology (1890) explore such topics as stream of consciousness, will, experience, areas outside the province of behaviorism. It was definitely James's adoption of a descriptive attitude towards experiential phenomena that enabled him to uncover so many important aspects of them and revealed them as they were experienced (Giorgi, p. 31). In a perceptive essay, James E. Dittes (1973) shows how the human scientific psychologists, as we have been calling them, hold even more of a claim on James than do the natural scientific psychologists. To write about the relation between William James and the social science of our time may be "to identify estrangement more than continuity" (Dittes, 1973, p. 292). Rather than his ideas being discussed, advanced, tested, elaborated and extended by social scientists since his day, his concepts and method are most usually summarized in historical surveys, but do not feed into contemporary empirical research. James gets treated the way most aged parents do: his blessing is sought and invoked piously at the beginning of a new (research) venture, and then his psychologist offspring go and do as they please, or more accurately, submit unthinkingly to peer pressure from their sibling natural scientists. This study attempts to reflect James's benign parental influence by consciously evoking and abiding by his introject!

In James's own view nothing is more crucial than the context and the function of an idea. Ideas for him do not have, as they do for the contemporary scientific outlook, reference to a constant, objective reality, equally perceptible to all observers in the same way, observers whose perception is gradually clarified, gradually made more like the reality itself, as they share their individual perceptions and ideas about this reality. For James, an idea about reality and, for

79

that matter, reality itself, exists for par-
ticular persons in particular circumstances.
The ideas are _for_ the thinker, here and now
(Dittes, 1973, p. 293, italics his).

Dittes goes on to reflect that psychology is beset
with a continuing battle between those who most
value regularity, generalizability, reproducibility, and those who value even more highly individuality, depth, richness and meaning. "James
stands with the latter, endorsing, even insisting
upon individual distinctiveness and depth"
(p. 296). Dittes uses the familiar image of the
blind men feeling different parts of the elephant
to illustrate what is _not_ true for James -- rather
the opposite holds truth for him. The image implies that there exists a synthesis, a unity which
could be constructed from our multiple perceptions. It implies further that individual distinctive perceptions are somehow the product of
our own defective inadequate perceiving. Thirdly,
it suggests that our comprehended particularity
results from where we happen to be standing,
rather than, as James would argue, from the vali-
dating and validated outcome of personally focused
energy and searching. Though rejoicing that there
are other truths, one must not discount his own
personal discovery by thinking of it only as a
glimpse of truth which is potentially clearer, or
a part of a truth which is potentially more complete, to be integrated with other truths, or
added to by "further research" (Dittes, pp. 320-
321).
  What James' style and spirit especially adds
to an understanding of phenomenological method is
his active emphasis on passionate searching. He
rejects shotgun empiricism, the "fishing expedi-
tion" approach to data as when one reviews one's
computer printout for findings of high correlations and constructs one's predictions _a poste-
riori_. While taking a reverential and respectful
stance before reality that it might yield up its
secrets, the phenomenological researcher, or at
least one influenced by James' spirit, comes to

reality like a suitor with definite intentions in mind. James is not sponsoring any mindless Baconian induction whereby one goes for a walk outdoors and writes down everything one happens upon. The result would be chaos, not research much less poetry or phenomenology. One approaches reality not as a spectator, but like a greedy gold-miner seeking evidence for a rich vein of truth.

For the natural scientific psychologist, reality is evidenced by regularity, communality, reproducibility, and homogeneity, precisely for the reason that these characteristics reassure him that he has kept out of his inquiry the subjective and any individual differences which he regards as contaminating intrusions. But it is for precisely this same reason, the exclusion of the individual's subjective involvement, that James regarded these characteristics of regularity and homogeneity as barriers to reality (Dittes, p. 337). Whatever is idiosyncratic; whatever is most likely to issue from the interaction between the observed material and the observer's own history and expectations; whatever is most functional for him -- this, James would declare, holds a clue to the truth. It is not to be written off as "error variance," a subject's response set to be controlled for "contamination." Following James, this study will search for response sets, will seek evidence of interaction between the research situation and the subject's history and motives as indicators and vehicles of characteristics and behavior really of crucial import to the investigation of spiritual gifts.

Furthermore, I shall not neglect my own reactions and input, but shall count it as data by using my self-as-investigator in three ways:

(1)   As a fellow-subject, responding to a situation in parallel fashion and presumably representatively, along with other subjects. For example, I have been present when prophecies have been uttered, and have a few times been a subject of prophecy.

(2) As a controlled stimulus from which I can gauge and interpret subjects' responses.

(3) As a kind of living meter, responding to subjects' responses (Dittes, p. 339). These approaches admit, rather than ignore, that the interaction of researcher and subject is a complex sociopsychological situation, and that the complexities must be used to enhance the investigation, rather than artificially partialled out.

Our purpose here in reviewing the thought of psychology's ancestors is not merely to establish that phenomenological methodology has always had spokesmen within the field, but also to learn from these writings how to proceed ourselves. Having dialogued with William James, we pass next to Eduard Spranger, Dilthey's successor at the University of Berlin. Known mostly for his typology of Values which lies behind the Allport-Vernon-Lindzey Test (1931), Spranger is of interest here because of his concept of objectivity, a concept much broader than that of natural scientific psychology. In his Types of Men (1928), Spranger outlines his thinking. Spranger strives for understanding. Unlike explanation, understanding aims not for basic causality, but rather for a nexus of meaning relationships. Understanding is that complex theoretical act in which we grasp the inner, meaningful core in the life and actions of individuals. Subjectivity is always related to objective creations. Because the subject with his experiences and creations is interwoven with the configurations of the historical and social world he is freed from the isolation of purely subjective states and consequently related to objective realities. Spranger considers these realities objective for three reasons: (1) because they are attached to physical forms, which forms may function as direct carriers of value, such as signs, or as means of artistic expression; (2) because they have been developed from the reciprocal relations of many single subjects, and are thus collectively determined forms;

(3) because they are based on definite laws of meaning which have a supra-individual validity. Here then is an attempt to clarify the meaning of "objectivity" in terms of the actions of human subjects, rather than in relation to the criteria of natural science. Calling his approach "structural psychology," Spranger felt that he bypassed many dilemmas of traditional psychology such as the mind-body issue; the relating of psychic phenomena to a specific form of the objective world, namely, external nature, which is actually a correlate of only one human cognitive attitude; the explanation of complex mental processes in terms of their elements. Structural psychology is thus opposed to a traditional "psychology of elements" (Giorgi, pp. 32-33). Spranger's notion of objectivity will be the one adhered to in this presentation.

Ten years after Spranger's Types of Men appeared, William Stern's General Psychology (1938) was published in English. One of the earliest psychologists to denominate himself a "personalist," Stern calls psychology the science of a person having experiences, or capable of having experiences. Experience in this system is understood as a matrix which is unified by a goal-directed person. Human personality is a self-determining, purposive, meaningful totality. Far from being independent of the environment, personality and environment are "convergently" related to each other. His system is broad enough to allow for both nature-subject interactions and culture-subject dialectics. The life of the personality presents itself in a dual aspect: as expression and impression. The body is expressive and the psyche is impressive. Experience occurs not only as expression or expressive action, but as consciousness, it is simultaneously an impression upon the experiencing subject. Hence, expression and impression are two forms of the same experience, and can enter into diverse combinations in a unitary personality (Giorgi, pp. 34-35). Spranger's and Stern's theoretical formulations will prove to be expecially helpful when trying to understand the experience of spiritual

83

gifts, especially healing, which if approached with the mind-body dichotomy, can hardly be "understood" much less "explained."

Up to now, William James has been the only American voice heard representing the phenomenological tradition, but William McDougall can certainly be cited as well:

> . . . In physical sciences the student needs only to refine upon the methods of observation and reasoning which he has learned to apply in dealing with the physical world about him, regarding all events as links in a mechanical chain of cause and effect. Most students have begun, by the time they approach psychology, to regard this as the true and only way of science.... Having begun in this way myself, and having slowly and painfully extricated myself and found what seems to be a much more profitable attitude toward psychological problems, I held that the path of the student may be made smoother by setting clearly before him at the outset the alternative routes.... The two principal alternative routes are (1) that of mechanical science, which interprets all its processes as mechanical sequences of cause and effect, and (2) that of the sciences of mind, for which purposive striving is a fundamental category, which regard the process of purposive striving as radically different from mechanical sequence (McDougall, 1923, p. 36; pp. 39-40).

Modern phenomenlogical method speaks of psychological phenomena as being intentional, and intentional analyses as being the approach of the "science of mind" (or human science as we are saying here), but the meaning is clear despite different vocabularies. The following sentences could have been written fifty years later by any modern-day phenomenologist:

> The most general and fundamental facts
> about experience . . . are two. First, ex-
> perience or experiencing is always an ex-
> periencing of something . . . even when, as
> in psychologizing, that object is itself an
> experiencing or thinking. Secondly, all ex-
> periencing . . . is the experiencing or
> thinking of *some one*, some subject, some per-
> son, some *organism* (loc. cit., italics in
> original).

Later phenomenologists would speak of the reciprocal implications between man and the world, intentional relationships with the world, and body-
subject. McDougall here anticipates the developed
notions of his successors. Phenomenology cannot
be rejected as a European import replanted on our
soil, but rather as a development of much that was
more than implicit in American psychologies.

Maurice Merleau-Ponty has also influenced the
spirit and method of this research project. Both
psychologist and philosopher, his general position
is that the perceived life-world is the primary
reality, the really real, and that from this basis
we proceed to other levels of experience. (Thus
his foundation and starting point contrasts with
that of Idealism for which mental constructs are
the really real; with Materialism which teaches
the primacy of physical matter.) His thesis:

> . . . By these words, the "primacy of per-
> ception," we mean that the experience of per-
> ception is our presence at the moment when
> things, truths, values are constituted for
> us: that perception is a nascent *logos*; that
> it teaches us, outside all dogmatism, the
> true conditions of objectivity itself, that
> it summons us to the tasks of knowledge and
> action. It is not a question of reducing
> human knowledge to sensation, but of assist-
> ing at the birth of this knowledge, to make
> it as sensible as the sensible, to recover
> the consciousness of rationality

85

(Merleau-Ponty, 1964, p. 25).

James Edie, in his introduction to Merleau-Ponty's
<u>Primacy of Perception</u> (1964), summarizes the ap-
proach in this fashion. The structures of perceptual consciousness are our first route of ac-
cess of being and truth, and these structures un-
derlie and accompany all the structures of higher-
level intellectual consciousness. What distinguishes Merleau-Ponty's "phenomenological posi-
tivism" from the classical teachings with this
name is that Merleau-Ponty never claims that
higher-order experiences can ever be reduced to
perception. Neither does he define perception in
terms of a few privileged qualities or sense-data
as did traditional empiricism. The world given
in perception is the concrete, intersubjectively
constituted life-world of immediate experience.
It is a world of familiar natural and cultural
objects, of other persons, the world in which I
act. Perception itself may be defined in terms of
a sensory-motor behavior through which the world
is constituted for man as the world of human consciousness prior to any explicit or reflexive
thought about it (Edie in Merleau-Ponty, 1964,
p. xvi).
     Yet man lives not only in the real world of
perception. He also dwells in the realms of the
imaginary, of ideas, of language and of history.
Because there are various levels of experience,
phenomenology is open to all of them and recognizes in each its own irreducible specificity, its
own meaning and value structures, its own qualitatively distinctive characteristics. Therefore,
from a phenomenology of perception, it becomes important to proceed to a phenomenology of intersubjectivity, a phenomenology of truth and of rationality, a phenomenology of aesthetic, ethical
and religious experience, etc. Distinctive of
Merleau-Ponty's interpretation of phenomenology is
the conviction that in all these other levels of
realms of experience, we will rediscover the fundamental structures of perceptual consciousness,
but transformed and enriched and thus irreducible

to perception as such. Although there are "many ways for consciousness to be conscious" (Merleau-Ponty, 1964, p. 124), we never completely escape from the realm of perceptual reality. Even the seemingly independent structures of categorial thought, of rationality, are ultimately founded in perception.

Merleau-Ponty's thought will be made more clear by contrasting it with several other phenomenologists. Edmund Husserl and Merleau-Ponty are related as thesis to antithesis insofar as Husserl's lifelong efforts are spent in elaborating a phenomenology of reason, categorial thought, and science, and only then turned to perceptual consciousness as the foundational mode of experience; Merleau-Ponty proceeds the other way round by beginning with perception and, in his published works, does no more then pose the problem of a phenomenology of rationality (Edie in Merleau-Ponty, 1964, pp. xvii-xviii). Merleau-Ponty was not concerned with utilizing phenomenology as a means towards establishing a more rigorous science in the Husserlian sense, but believed in establishing phenomenology as the dominant Weltanschauung of the human sciences. Experience precedes essences: the latter disclose, and are dependent upon experience. By grappling with experience, Merleau-Ponty avoids the idealistic transcendentalism of Husserl and puts, as it were, the essences back into existence.

Furthermore, in Husserl's notions of knowledge, there are always two poles: the noesis (I-pole, or knower), and noema (object-pole). Intentionality comes down to knowledge of an object. For Merleau-Ponty, knowledge is an ontological relationship, a subject-object-body interaction. It is through our body that we experience the world. By placing the body, rather than the mind, in the center of existence, Merleau-Ponty undercuts the Mind-Body dualism of Cartesian philosophy for body and mind interpenetrate. The unity of body-mind also removes the dichotomy between objectivity and subjectivity. World is not an object-out-there, but the natural setting from which all acts emerge. Accordingly, there no longer is an

"inner" and an "outer" man. It is the subject
actively constituting the world through perception
which lends meaning to the world.

At first glance, Merleau-Ponty appears close
to Heidegger. Both clearly agree on the unitary
character of human reality as a world-directed,
active intentionality. Through the experience of
this intentionality, the world is constituted as
the human life-world. However, what radically
separates Merleau-Ponty's existential analysis
from Heidegger's is precisely his thesis of the
primacy of perception, and his acceptance of the
perceived world as the primary reality. It is the
perceived world which gives us the first and tru-
est sense of the "real." For Heidegger, on the
other hand, it is not this world but the "Being of
beings" which is the primary reality. Any analysis of human experience, perceptual or otherwise,
is only a means to pose the more fundamental question of this Being. Heidegger's "thought of
Being" escapes the methods of phenomenology al-
together and certainly has nothing whatever to do
with perceptual consciousness (Edie in Merleau-
Ponty, 1964, p. xviii).

Thirdly, Sartre conceives of consciousness as
"pure" consciousness, utterly independent of being
absolutely free, without content or structure.
Against this position, Merleau-Ponty developed his
philosophy of the "incarnate cogito" whose most
fundamental behavior is exactly the perceptual
constitution of a world of which it is nevertheless always a part and participant (ibid.). For
Merleau-Ponty, consciousness originates in "I am
able" not in "I think." Consciousness accordingly
has an action-praxis-will component. Meaning
originates in the interactive presence of organism
and situation.

Three more precursors of modern phenomenological method will be briefly mentioned before
shifting our focus from its heralds to the method
itself. Donald Snygg (1959) protested the inadequacy of the objective approach for the prediction of human behavior, and proposed in its
place a phenomenal system that takes the point of
view of the behaving organism rather than of the

researcher. R. B. MacLeod (1947) worried that the methods of physics and psycho-physiology would be simply carried over into social psychology, and wanted as reference points not some pre-established categories real for the researcher, but rather real for the subject with whom the psychologist is dealing. Finally, Gordon Allport (1947) wrote two succinct sentences which can conclude this brief historical excursus:

> Addiction to machines, rats, or infants leads us to overplay those features of human behavior that are peripheral, signal-oriented or genetic. Correspondingly it causes us to underplay those features that are central, future-oriented and symbolic (Allport, 1947, p. 190).

Allport's preference for "idiographic" over "nomothetic" methods would indicate his solid support of this line of psychological theory and research, human scientific psychology.

Much more could be quoted, and further historical elaboration supplied, but of far greater use at this point would be a synthetic distillation from many writers in this tradition of their methodology which shall now be provided.

A Generalized Description of the Method

The great historian of philosophical phenomenologies, Herbert Spiegelberg (1965, Vol. 2, pp. 655-701), after passing in review the giants of the movement, extracts seven processes he believes to be essential to the method.

(1) The first process consists in investigating particular phenomena, particular experiences of, say, force. This involves three subphases:

a) An intuitive grasp of the phenomena. To prevent a philosophical or researcher's

89

infinite regress, this first step basically involves the act of pointing to an experience.

b) The analytic examination of the phenomena. The precise subject matter at this point consists of certain linguistic expressions. The objective of the analytic examination is the discovery of descriptive expressions preferably consisting of a smaller number of terms with a simpler structure to take the place of the original expressions. This, of course, is preparatory to a study of the referents, i.e., of the phenomena meant by the expression (p. 669).

c) A description of the phenomena. This description is to be negative by excluding irrelevant data and selective, i.e., a precision about referents and qualifiers (p. 673).

2. The second process involves investigating general essences. Edmund Husserl, (1960), the main early proponent of phenomenology, spends many pages describing this process which he names "eidetic intuition," a movement from the linguistic expressions and descriptive modifiers of the first process into an apprehension of the essential constituents of the things themselves as they impinge on human consciousness.

3. Apprehending essential relationships within and among essences. One way to accomplish this task would consist in free imaginative variation by adding or subtracting components, for example, by adding/subtracting sides/angles of a triangle and seeing whether what remained were still a triangle. The goal of this third step is to arrive at generality and necessity, so-called "synthetic a-priori" knowledge or categorial intuition (Spiegelberg, 1965, Vol. 2, pp. 680-683).

4. Watching modes of appearing. Here the phenomenologist questions just how the things impinge on human consciousness. What clue does the mode of appearance provide for a deeper understanding of the essence? Might the mode of

appearance throw one off guard, or distract from the essential reality? Hence one's "watchfulness" must be simultaneously sympathetic and guarded without becoming overly involved, on the one hand, or wary on the other.

5. Watching the constitution of phenomena in consciousness. Here the focus shifts from the "things" back to human consciousness once again. One seeks to determine the typical structure of a phenomenon's constituting itself in consciousness by an analysis of the essential sequence of steps (p. 688). Spiegelberg gives two helpful examples by reviewing the processes by which one becomes oriented in a new city, and by which the personality of a new friend takes shape. Both these human experiences constitute examples of gradually growing structures of consciousness. Such structuring is normally spontaneous and passive, but may be active as after disorientation, one works to reorient one's spatial field. Phenomenological methodology seeks to explicitate, on a higher level, just how this structuring happens. There is a definite affinity here between the laws governing the way this occurs and the so-called laws of "good gestalt."

The remaining two steps of the method will be included merely for the sake of completeness. The contested step 6, the "phenomenological reduction," has never proven to be common ground for all those who have otherwise associated themselves with the Phenomenological Movement. Merleau-Ponty for example, refused to accept the phenomenological reduction. This present research project will not attempt a phenomenological reduction both because it is the author's conviction that the first five steps of the method are sufficient for discovering an essential intuition into spiritual gifts, and because greater minds than his own are confused and divided over the purpose and worth of the sixth step.

6. Suspending belief in the existence of the phenomena (Epoche). Husserl never succeeded in formulating the meaning and function of the

reduction in an unambiguous and definitive fashion. Husserl associated this reduction with mathematical "bracketing" (Einklammerung). Phenomenologists are instructed to detach the phenomena of
our everyday experience from the context of our
naive or natural living while preserving their
content as fully as possible. Without going quite
as far as the Cartesian doubt, Husserl wants a
suspension of belief in the existence/non-exis-
tence of this content. Then he can concentrate on
the essential "whatness" of the phenomena. This
perspective should then facilitate genuine intuiting, analyzing and describing of the given: thus
one can consider all data, real, unreal and doubtful, as having equal rights and proceed with the
investigation without fear or favor. Husserl himself, however, thought that the "eidetic reduction" (step 2) or idealizing abstraction provides
an adequate foundation for the essential intuition
without the added step of the phenomenological reduction (this step 6), (pp. 690-692). This exclusion, of course, does not mean that the usual
clinician's skepticism about any self-report of a
subject will be lacking; phenomenological reduction is a more properly philosophical undertaking
and need not be imported into the psychologist's
methodological tool-kit.

7. Interpreting the concealed meaning of
phenomena. Heidegger's Sein und Zeit (1962) has
the fullest demonstration of this step by a meta-
physician. Philosophical "hermeneutics" proclaims
similar goals to those of psychoanalysis; to interpret the "sense" of certain phenomena, to discover the meaning not immediately manifest in our
intuiting, analyzing and describing. Here again,
we shall attempt a discovery of latent content but
with psychological rather than philosophical intentions. Our focus thus is on man, rather than
on ontological judgments about Being Itself.
Spiegelberg concludes his summary of the phenomenological methodology (pp. 699-700) by providing several distinctive notes. This method
provides a challenge to the reductionism of
Occam's razor. On all levels, a phenomenological

approach is opposed to explanatory hypotheses because it confines itself to the direct evidence of intuitive seeing. The unity of the phenomenological procedure is found in its deliberateness, in its unusually obstinate attempt to look at the phenomena and to remain faithful to them before even thinking about them.

Objections to Phenomenological Methodology

That psychologists at large share the unease over too narrow a methodology, too mechanistic an impression of man is reflected especially in two recent Presidential addresses at the American Psychological Association meetings by Donald Campbell and Wilbert McKeachie in which the speakers strove to begin fashioning a "new image of man." Furthermore, Division Thirty-Six, Psychologists Interested in Religious Issues, in 1976 sponsored a three-hour panel on contrasting methodologies, and a two-hour discussion on past, present and future models and paradigms. So the issue is far from settled, but despite such controversy this author has made a value judgment in favor of phenomenological methodology. It is only fair, however, to present a sampling of opposing argumentation. A brief and recent statement in the literature attempting to resolve the dichotomies between "empirical" and phenomenological approaches to the Psychology of Religion is Hansford's (1975). A fuller treatment is provided by Giorgi's two articles entitled "Phenomenology and Experimental Psychology" (1965, 1966). Yet we choose to summarize the lively exchange between the behaviorists Brody and Oppenheim (1966, 1967) and their respondents and critics Henle and Baltimore (1967), and Zaner (1967).

Referring to pure phenomenological psychology as "ppp," (an abbreviation which twits the opposition) Brody and Oppenheim locate three points of tension between the methods of behaviorism and phenomenology, and then attempt a discussion of rapprochement. Brody and Oppenheim cite various authorities in the phenomenological tradition to

93

buttress their claim that the type of experience involved in the method of ppp is nonconceptualized experience. Hence, the first area of tension between behaviorism and ppp is in the domain of theory construction and evaluation (Brody and Oppenheim, 1966, pp. 296-299). Any effort to describe a nonconceptualized experience can do so only through a process of conceptualization which distorts and impoverishes the experience. Thus an experiencer who tries to convey his nonconceptualized experience without such loss of content must in fact be speechless, or at best present not a description but only an exclamation. The following are four characteristics of nonconceptualized experiences:

(1) During such an experience, the experiencer cannot distinguish himself conceptually as experiencer from that which he is experiencing, and is thus in union with the experienced.

(2) The experiencer is not capable of assigning a locus to his experience in a public spatio-temporal coordinate system, but only in a private frame of reference.

(3) Nonconceptualized experiences are ineffable. Consequently they are also propertyless since properties involving class terminology cannot be assigned to them.

(4) Nonconceptualized experiences are solipsistic.

Because these experiences have such characteristics, they do not provide the basis for the construction of any conceptual system (especially because they are ineffable), much less for the criticism of any conceptual system, but are at best propaedeutic to the development of psychological theory.

The second locus of tension between behaviorism and ppp flows from the first. Since explanation in science involves the use of some theory, and since ppp provides no basis for the construction of theory, explanation is not compatible with the method of ppp.

Thirdly, methods of testing provide the final locus of tension. For the behaviorist, any psychological theory, law, or statment must ultimately be testable with reference to intersubjectively observable aspects of phenomena. But whoever accepts this requirement becomes a methodological behaviorist, since his conceptual system rests ultimately on a behavioristic base, and ppp is used only in the context of discovery. Advocates of ppp could avoid this implication only by rejecting this insistence. What Brody and Oppenheim are saying is that any advantage inherent in nonconceptualized experiences is gotten at the price of their irrelevance per se for science (art. cit., p. 302).

Rapprochement would be theoretically possible but practically difficult in that complementary roles of constructing or testing theories might be assigned to behaviorism and ppp, but this logical possibility flies in the face of prejudices and arguments proposed by each side (pp. 302-303). Even terminological rapprochement has its difficulties: while terms like "red" could be coordinated and assigned compatible designations in behaviorism and ppp, concepts like "fear" acquire modified meanings by virtue of having entered into a network of theoretical laws and relationships which specify the concept's meaning. The modified meaning of such a term may or may not be directly experienced or coordinated with an immediately given experience.

Titling their rejoinder, "Portraits in Straw," Henle and Baltimore (1967) show that Brody and Oppenheim misconceive the nature of phenomenal experience as it is employed by the psychologist, as well as the nature of nonconceptualized experience. Additionally, methodological behaviorism is shown to rest on the use of the investigator's own experience. After repeating the four characteristics of nonconceptualized experience mentioned above, they demonstrate that the ordinary experience of human beings, the phenomenal data used by psychologists, simply does not possess these characteristics. Even the nonconceptualized experience of subjects without language, such as infants and animals, is not characterized correctly by Brody and Oppenheim.

Opposing the first characteristic, they note that with the exceptions of recovery from unconsciousness, mysticism and related experiences, the most obvious differentiation in naive adult experience is that between the phenomenal self and the phenomenal environment. Rather than being in union with the experienced, both adults and individuals without language act in a way that distinguishes between self and the environment (Henle and Baltimore, p. 326).

Refusing to agree that the experiencer cannot assign public spatio-temporal coordinates to his experience, Henle and Baltimore appeal to behavior; an adult is able to behave with reference to the world of another person as if it were at least roughly the same as one's own. Again, comparative data from infants and animals suggest that the localization of experience in public space and time does not depend on conceptualization (loc. cit.).

Thirdly, they dispute the claim that nonconceptualized experience is propertyless by referring to the vast literature on form and other discriminations in infants and animals. Experiences are endowed with properties prior to the assignment of words or class terminology to them; for example, squares and circles are differentiated in perception before the class names can be assigned to them.

Finally, they simply disagree that either conceptualized or nonconceptualized experiences are solipsistic. They conclude their rejoinder by pointing out that the behaviorist is required to make use of his own private experiences in making his observations, and to rely on the experience of his colleagues for intersubjective validation; hence he should have no objections to refer also to the experience of his subjects.

Zaner too (1967) objects that Brody and Oppenheim's view of "ppp" is not the one commonly held by practicing phenomenological psychologists, especially on the point of equating "experience" with "nonconceptualized experience." He emphasizes that the methodological decision to bracket presuppositions is in no way equivalent to doing without any concepts at all. He repeats at greater length the argument given by Henle and Baltimore that Behaviorist A, in asking Behaviorist B for confirmation of data, is relying on experience, is assuming the existence of Behaviorist B with the latter's perspectives, competencies, etc., and not that Behaviorist B is simply more data (Zaner, 1967, p. 322). The very scientific requirement of "intersubjective verifiability" hoists the behaviorist on his own petard since he must rely on his experience, not on his researches that indeed there are others there to appeal to. There is a double petitio principii here, a double begging of the question; first, as to the existence of another behaviorist rather than merely more "data;" second, as to the meaning and justification of "publicly observable." Phenomenologists, on the other hand, have taken up intersubjectivity as the main focus of their problem. The latter refuse to demand only one test (sense perceptual proof) for all situations. Sense perception is irrelevant to proof in mathematics. Just as numerical entities and relationships are not private to the mind of the individual mathematician, neither are the reflections on my own consciousness and its objects.

Brody and Oppenheim's rejoinder (1967) is no less spirited. The critique of their opponents forced them first to restate their position in the form of eight propositions with comments. At the root, however, of their disagreement with Henle and Baltimore is their position that the subject matter for psychology is not experience per se (the phenomenologists' claim), but rather inferences about experiences made from first and third-person reports (Brody and Oppenheim, 1967, p. 332). From this epistemological opposition flow the two separate approaches toward the subject matter of psychology. Their reply to Zaner is a categorical assertion that, as they understand phenomenology, it implies the exclusion of all language as its logical extreme, and with language the exclusion of all concepts and means of communicating, theory-building and testing. Further, they reject the basis for Husserl's doctrine of intentionality (art. cit., p. 333).

To comment on this exchange: we are dealing here in the metapsychological realm, in the domain of deciding just what is the subject matter of psychology. This debate shows forcefully that philosophical presuppositions are involved in adopting behaviorism, phenomenology, Freudianism or any other approach to the data of human behavior and experience. A good deal more is involved too, like previous training, socialization, prejudices and feelings, a point made by Kuhn (1967). The author's reasons for choosing phenomenology are spelled out in the previous two sections of this chapter. By summarizing this clash of viewpoints, we have hoped to illustrate the involvement of philosophies in deciding on a method for science besides merely presenting a series of carefully articulated objections. It appears clearly that, after awarding points to critics and proponents on both sides of the issue, many here reach the impasse over differing philosophical presuppositions.

The Method of This Study

Having spoken about the history of phenomenological methodology and the attempt to define psychology as a human science, we now present the specifics of this approach to the present project. Because the author feels that biases are best revealed by making them explicit, a few biographical remarks about the degree of participant observation employed are necessary. This study grew out of five years of involvement with the Word of God Community. Initially the researcher was contacted in his role of priest to celebrate Mass for some student members of the community on a weekly basis in their homes. This service commenced in the Fall of 1971. He made many friends within the group and attended his first WoG prayer meeting in

January, 1972. Feeling the need to learn more about the group, he took the usual prescribed introductory course of seven weekly meetings called "Life in the Spirit" seminar in June and July of 1972, and attended the next socialization experience, the "Community Weekend." Attracted by the idealism, friendliness, and support of the group, he took the next step of becoming a novice in the community, referred to as "going underway," in December of 1972. This brought with it three commitments: to attend at least one of the two weekly prayer meetings; to attend the "Foundations Courses," a series of information and discussion sessions about life within the community; and to discern whether one was indeed called to become a full member of the group. He did manage to attend meetings almost weekly for a year and a half. He decided in the Fall of 1974 to withdraw from the underway commitment due to disagreement with policies of the community's leaders especially about the exercise of their authority, but even more basically because he did not feel called to living the Christian life in precisely this way. Throughout his five years in Ann Arbor, however, his relationships with those in charge were friendly, and members of the community continued to request his (unpaid) services as counselor, and as priest for regular celebrations of the weekly "charismatic" Mass (until Fall, 1975), for baptisms of children, weddings and funerals. He was especially called on by people who, like himself, had grown to be skeptical of some of the community's claims and practices, but who needed reassurance from a church authority that separation from the group would not imply a rejection of Christianity.

When this study was conceived, it was first proposed to the community "heads," and permission was denied because it was felt that such studies were not really useful to those involved. Concern was also expressed that my questioning might "upset" my subjects.

Feeling that the second reason was the more important one in the minds of the leaders, the author appealed to their personal knowledge of his character and style as revealed by weekly sermons in local churches, and the known results of his interactions with community members in the various sorts of services mentioned above. They relented and granted the permission. It is to their credit that they did so even though at this time he had withdrawn from his underway status and was now merely "related," a category reserved for friends of the community who were not members. The author presented to them the list of questions given below and asked to be informed of any negative feedback from the experience of being interviewed. None came.

Subjects were recruited by putting a brief ad in the Community Bulletin, a weekly announcement sheet distributed at the Sunday gathering for community members only. The ad requested subjects "willing to share their experiences of healing and prophecy" to contact the author by phone. The ad was run only once; those subjects responding were contacted, and if others known to them came up in the interview, the latter too were contacted in turn by the author.

In the initial rough experimental design, it was proposed that twenty healers, twenty prophets, and twenty healees be interviewed. It turned out, however, that these were not pure types; all had experienced the gift of tongues, most had experienced prophecy, at least in their living units, or "households," if not at public gatherings as well, and most of the healers had been healees too. Prophets were healers/healees and vice-versa. The typology was abandoned, and subjects were encouraged to speak freely about their experience of all the spiritual gifts with the result that much was learned about other gifts like deliverance, word of knowledge, word of wisdom -- behaviors connected intimately with the two most important to the author.

An interview, recorded on tape, of an hour and a half in length became standard though some subjects needed more time, some, less. The interview was conducted most often in the author's office in the University of Michigan's logical Clinic. Because the office was shared by other

100

therapists, and because of the very tight sched-
ules of subjects, other places were used as time
made them available: the subjects' homes, the
author's home, the author's church office. All
knew that the author was a priest in good standing
with the WoG Community, was doing the project for
research purposes, and would respect the confidentiality of their remarks.

The following questions served as an outline
for the discussion, but were not slavishly adhered
to. In the style of phenomenological research,
the author was guided by the remarks of the subject, and by questions which occurred to him as
the interview proceeded. An attempt was made to
make the process an non-directive as possible.
The questions --

(1) Please tell me in your own words how you
experienced a single occasion of physical healing/
prophecy.

(2) What is the history of your experience
of spiritual gifts?

(3) Is the way you experienced these gifts
similar to what has happened to others in the Word
of God Community?

(4) Have you thought out or been taught a
theology of healing/prophecy/the gifts, i.e., how
do you understand what has happened to you?

(5) Please tell me about yourself, a short
biography.

(6) Earliest memories; earliest of father;
earliest of mother.

Phenomenology is the study of phenomena as
experienced by persons. The primary emphasis is
on the phenomenon itself exactly as it reveals itself to the experiencing subject in all its con-
creteness and particularity. Hence the first
question above seeks to get an unvarnished statement of just what happens when gifts are

experienced. The second question broadens out the perspective to include related but similar experiences. The approach of phenomenology is characterized by the attitude of openness for whatever is significant for the proper understanding of the phenomenon. A subject is led to concentrate on the experience of the phenomenon exactly as it is given to him, and tries not to prejudge it, nor to see it through any specific perspective simply because of previous knowledge about the phenomenon. Hence, the third and fourth questions aim at unraveling the effects of WoG socialization and teaching, and to bracket these from the subject's own personal experience and interpretations. The fifth and sixth questions aim at providing some data to make a brief personality assessment, to trace continuities between upbringing, personal history and the religious experience. Insofar as upbringing and personal history extend into and are preserved by the religious experience, the former are meanings which endure and constitute the latter experience.

The method of phenomenology, intuition, reflection and description is thus engaged in by the subject, but especially by the researcher as he begins to make thematic generalizations within and across subjects both during the interviews and afterwards when reviewing the tapes. These data and generalizations, analyses and descriptions of the essence of the phenomena follow in the chapter on results. An interweaving of buttressing quotations from the subjects will support the conclusions derived. The author will conduct the analysis "out loud," as it were, without benefit of computer and invite the reader to follow along, making the phenomenological process his own along the lines suggested above on pp. 89-93. This procedure ensures the maintenance of an intersubjective realm of discourse, and allows constant checking for the objectivity of the research. Human rather than mathematical "control" is thus provided.

CHAPTER III

THE GIFTS AND THE GIFTED

Concerning the gods, there are those who
deny the very existence of the Godhead; others say that it exists, but neither bestirs
nor concerns itself, nor has forethought for
anything. A third party attribute to it
existence and forethought, but only for great
and heavenly matters. A fourth party admit
things on earth as well as in heaven, but
only in general, and not with respect to each
individual. A fifth, of whom were Ulysses
and Socrates, are those that cry: "I move
not without Thy knowledge." (Epictetus, 60-
120 A.D.).

Having apparently conducted a phenomenological analysis of his own in the ancient world, the
stoic philosopher Epictetus arrived at a typology
which includes most positions on the spectrum of
belief-unbelief among persons asking questions
about the inter-relationship of deity and human-
ity. Among the first class came Leucippus,
Democritus and other "atomic scientists" of anti-
quity. Aristotle with his "Unmoved Mover" or
"Self-Thinking Thought" represents the third
group. The subjects of this research would without exception place themselves in the fifth
category.

Nine males and thirteen females were interviewed for this research. More subjects could
have been consulted, but as the dialogue continued
various themes and patterns emerged and repeated
themselves with such regularity that further con-
sulation seemed superfluous. What these persons
supplied could safely be reported as typical and
in some sense usual for the rest of WoG.

Before displaying the essential elements in
an understanding of the experience of spiritual
gifts, a personality profile of each of the

103

subjects will be sketched. Since their words will
be quoted in much of what follows, it will be
helpful first to make their acquaintance briefly.
Each will be given a pseudonym beginning with suc-
cessive letters of the alphabet. In order that
confidentiality may be maintained, biographical
information which could identify the subject will
be ommitted or slightly disguised.

ABIGAIL, a middle-aged single woman, spoke
excitedly of the various kinds of physical and
emotional healings she had experienced since becoming a member of WoG. Without being asked, she
had brought along to her interview the various
testimonies of physicians to her cures. During
our conversation, she also read to me various prophecies of hers which she had written down and
treasures. A simple, uncomplicated, "ordinary"
woman, she was able nevertheless to speak clearly
and eloquently about these happenings which had
transformed her life and her meaning-system. Our
discussion also covered the phenomena of deliverance, and of being "slain in the Spirit" wherein a
person falls to the ground in a trance-like state
during a prayer service. Abigail works as a sec-
retary in a professional's office, and it was
there where she first experienced gradual healing
of her near-sightedness even before becoming part
of WoG. Although she had had eye problems from
childhood and wore glasses, during office prayers
one day (when all were praying for the needs of
the office and the staff and not for anyone's
healing), she noticed suddenly that she could read
the print in a magazine without her glasses. For
the next eight months a continuous clearing of her
eyes took place. Her response was to thank God,
and to refrain from wearing glasses except for
driving until she retook her driver's exam, was
able to read all the lines on the screen, and had
the requirement for reading-glasses removed from
her license. A similar second unrealized healing
of photophobia followed: ordinarily bothered by
bright light, she knew that this problem had been
resolved when she absent-mindedly drove without
sun-glasses on a summer day. During the two and a
quarter years between the office prayers and our

interview, her only prayers for her own healing
concerned addictions to alcohol and nicotine, but
she was healed of these and other maladies as
well. Abigail noted a pattern in her healings.
Others would often point them out to her as when
someone in her household remarked on the cessation
of symptoms of bronchitis and emphysema because
her nocturnal loud coughing had stopped, or when
a friend jokingly called her attention to an emotional healing of violent temper-tantrums by
stating that "you used to have the disposition of
a wounded tigress." This remark and others revealed in her a healthy ability to laugh at herself good-naturedly. Her piety is shot through
with witty common sense: in describing an intense
prayer experience when she felt "lifted up from my
chair," she recalls that "I opened my eyes to make
sure I was still grounded." The import of her
various healings, prophecies and other contacts
with "the Lord" was conveyed by her ability to recall exact dates of their occurrence without the
aid of notes. Considered solely from a therapeutic point of view, Abigail's membership in WoG
has done her immense good. While many of the problems she reported could be diagnosed as psycho-
genic in origin, her ability to deal with them was
enhanced by the relationships and support provided
by the community. Rather than conveying a sense
that her healings were finished, she rather looks
forward to increased growth, a deeper Life in the
Spirit.

BETTY is a vivacious nursing student in her
early twenties. One of the most intellectually
curious young women I met in WoG, she never was
afraid to ask questions, express doubts, argue her
viewpoint. As I had anticipated she might, she
later left WoG in a dispute with her male "head"
because of the rigid controls he was placing on
her life. Nevertheless, she still maintains positive relationships with and feelings about members
of WoG. As in Abigail's case, Betty's healings
occurred first even before she became involved
with the Community. When she was a child, her
father had prayed over her and her sisters while
they were sleeping, and various healings had

occurred. Betty's conversation reveals her to exhibit a cheerful familiarity with God even though she remains appropriately deferential. Thus when praying to get over a sore throat so that she could be accepted as a member of the Easter choir, she reports herself praying, "Lord, look, I know you don't normally do this for me, but please do it anyway. You want other things first." (By this she meant her understanding that God had to make some spiritual changes in her life before dealing with other physical problems). Betty is very self-reflective, psychologically-minded, and quite critical of what she is taught her experience "should" mean. She would rather figure things out herself, and hence was a good research subject for this project. One of the middle children in a large family, she perhaps developed this style so as not to escape being noticed. Despite this intellectual approach to life, she is ready to name a miracle when she experiences one, whether it be the rapid and unexplained healing of a stomach ache or nerve spasms, or the return of a kneecap to its proper location with a "sense from the Lord" that it is "O.K. to take your bandages off now." Yet her struggle to understand what is happening does not resemble a researcher's quest so much as a person trying to penetrate the dynamics of a human relationship. "Miracles mean that God isn't dead: He isn't even unemployed," she laughed. "Miracles are normal, something an average Christian ought to expect because of God's great love. God cares for the universe, an individual, a stubbed toe."

CHUCK had begun his adult career as a high school dropout. With the help of WoG, he could report proudly that he was the first member of his family to finish high school. A University freshman at the time of the interview, he predicted confidently without boasting that he stood a very good chance of earning a Ph.D. Possessed of a clear narrative style, from among all those interviewed Chuck provided some of the most vivid descriptions of the inner feelings associated with delivery of prophecy or performing a healing. Because he had used drugs extensively before becoming a Christian, Chuck would make some clear distinctions between a drug "high" and an intense religious experience. Although his joining WoG meant the end of all drugs, he has maintained his individuality in keeping his long hair. This is a somewhat unusual achievement since the men in the Community are ordered to cut their hair and not wear flowered shirts. Upon joining WoG, most young men both "go straight" and begin to appear "straight." Chuck has done the former, hence winning acceptance, but resists the latter. He relates in a warm, honest fashion, and appears to be quite popular both among his peers, and among the toddlers with whom he works in the Community's baby-sitting service. While he speaks much of the time in an almost poetic mode, he does not manifest the intellectual curiosity shown by Betty. When I asked him how he handles unanswered prayers for healing, he brought up the Community's most difficult case, a young father, aged twenty-nine, who had died suddenly of leukemia, whom several of the most respected prophets had declared would be healed. "These are questions the Lord hasn't answered for us yet," commented Chuck with finality, but he has enough faith that somehow these and other difficulties will ultimately be understood.

DAPHNE, a twenty-three year old single graduate student, majors in language studies. "Publicly committed," and therefore a permanent member of WoG for several years prior to our discussion, she had risen almost as high as a female could in the male-dominated hierarchy of the Community. A member both of the initiation team and the Community's prophecy team, she lives in a residential household while herself being a head of a women's "Christian Living Situation" (a term for an apartment or residence whose members do not share finances in common, nor have as deep a commitment to "headship" as do household-dwellers). Thus she is entrusted by the Community to oversee the growth of those under her direction in the Living Situation, to help with socialization of newcomers through work with initiation, and to be open to inspirations from God in prophecy. Although anyone may prophesy at a Sunday gathering for

Community members (after getting immediate prior
approval from the man running the meeting), only
officially appointed members of the prophecy team
could speak on Thursdays at the public meetings
open to all. Daphne does not take herself overly
seriously, however, and her pleasant, relaxed,
open manner of communication shows that the coordinators have chosen her wisely for her services
and responsibilities. Daphne speaks her prophecies out of an intense and constant sense of God's
presence. While most of the subjects referred at
one time or another during their interview to this
sense of God's nearness, this theme dominated her
remarks. The intensity dated back at least to her
conversion experience, classically Jamesian in its
content --

> . . . I had a real belief that God existed,
> but no personal relationship with him. Six
> years ago, I was a sophomore at _____
> College. I had applied to Michigan, broken
> up with a guy. My life was not going well.
> I wondered if maybe I should consider doing
> something different in my relationship with
> God. I told God, "You've got to take charge
> of my life." In the middle of the night I
> was awakened. I felt God put His arms
> around me. There was light in the room and
> a sense of God's love. I heard, maybe audi-
> bly, "Love me as I've loved you. Trust me as
> I've trusted you. Obey me and don't be
> afraid." I became frightened. I tried to
> turn it off, but couldn't; it wasn't under my
> control. There was no touch on my arms, but
> it felt like when someone was embracing you.
> (Interviewer: And the light? . . .) God was
> behind me. I had the sense of a person sur-
> rounding me.

Her description of prophetic activity will be reviewed below. This excerpt demonstrates a rich
inner life accompanying her abilities of leadership, coordination, and the evocation of trust

superiors and subordinates.

ELAINE, publicly committed for a year and a half at the time of our interview, had experienced all three of the gifts being researched: she is an official Community prophetess, a member of the "healing team" which exercised its ministry to the sick weekly after the Thursday night public prayer meetings, and a healee. An attractive young woman of twenty-two, she like Daphne had risen far in WoG. She was head of the single women's household in which she resided and worked on the University dormitory initiation team. She was majoring in education. Her interview was especially valuable in its description of the way healing and prophecy have begun to be socialized and institutionalized through the two teams to which she belonged. Elaine was also reflective enough and articulate enough to discern the difference between a "sense from the Lord" and her own inclinations, desires and feelings. At the same time, it was quite evident from her statements that she had thoroughly internalized the Community's official stance toward the various gifts she exercised, and saw her own experience in the light of the public teaching. Despite her position and her gifts, however, Elaine manifests a profound peace, humility and security in her service and calling. She attributes the good results of her work to the Lord, of course, but phrases her belief very personally: "Soon the Lord will work more miraculously, more often. What we experience is not the result of the wisdom we've gained, but of His power. I don't feel we have to 'get better' at it." This theme of humble security in the Lord's working through her manifested itself several times in our discussion, most usually by her cautioning me that "techniques" of healing or prophecy did not exist, but rather that the Community was attempting freely to respond to the Lord's leading. (She answered my questions more comfortably when I changed my stimulus word to "patterns," rather than techniques.) Furthermore, unlike several of the women, she did not betray a sense of nervousness in her exercise of the gifts, but because she had been using the gifts for quite some time,

Elaine felt at ease in performing her various services. "I relate in a cautious way; I'm not real bold when I exercise spiritual gifts because when you're speaking for the Lord, you must be careful. As I do it, I will grow more confident."

FRANK is Elaine's partner on the healing team. A liberal arts major at the University, he heads up a dormitory household, and works on the "Evangelism Team," a group which in secular terms would be called the Community's recruiting arm among the University students. The son of parents involved in the helping professions, Frank had "come to the Lord" as a high school student and experienced the gifts before arriving at the University. His accounts of the early days of the deliverance ministry contained some hair-raising tales, and his early experiences of moving confidently and forcefully against evil spirits were reflected in his later style of conducting healing services. While being very sensitive and compassionate toward the particular sufferers with whom he prayed, Frank would agressively rebuke the presence of evil in the sickness or the spirits oppressing someone. He would encourage his healees toward active mastery, toward stepping out in faith by appealing to them to try (within reasonable limits) to use some afflicted bodily organ. Frank admitted a need he felt to be "under rather than over God's Word," by which he meant that he had to be more receptive, more submissive to God. Naturally healthy, outgoing and active himself, he behaved energetically in the healing sessions, would challenge but apparently not threaten his subjects, but would also struggle to follow the Lord's inspiration. Frank described thoroughly and in great detail the procedures of the healing team, and spoke of its significance in affecting other areas of his life, especially in becoming more open to God's direction and guidance. It could be predicted that Frank will always have to work at balancing his natural intensity and self-directedness with his desire to follow rather than lead the workings of the Spirit of God. He is involved without being hyperactive, exuberant but not naive, commanding but not overwhelming. An

110

avid sportsman and accomplished athlete, Frank is
well chosen by his heads to work in Evangelism and
to serve as a role model for "younger Christians"
in the dorms.

GERALDINE, another member of the healing team
had also served for two years on the prophecy team
at the time of our interview. Like Elaine, her
service on both teams made her an especially valuable interviewee to get an inside view of the
Community's official practices. Many of the other
subjects had prophesied occasionally, had now and
again prayed for healing and had their prayers for
health answered, even at times dramatically. Yet
these two women fulfilled the prescriptions of
Charismatic Renewal Theology that a gift must be
frequently exercised to be perfected and used by
God for His people. Geraldine has been in college
but had left before finishing and was now working
as a waitress. Despite this low-status occupation
in "the world," her spiritual gifts were recognized and appreciated. In addition to her team
responsibilities, she was non-resident head of a
women's living situation while herself residing in
a married household. While many of the subjects
clarified various issues, Geraldine spoke most
eloquently of the meaning of "faith" in the life
and expectations of the Community, of herself as
an instrument of God, and of those she served. In
appearance, intellect, and talents, Geraldine
strikes one as average. Yet she and the Community
see her as one tremendously blessed by God and
having concomitant duties. Accordingly, she is
serious without being stiff or gloomy, and a committed exponent of the official views on things.
Still, however, she could describe her own experiences, especially in their incipient stages, with
originality and freshness. Although her explanations for things were quite orthodox, at least one
of the prophecies she described seemed more predictive than most and, as it turned out, correct
in its fulfillment. Hence, she would be a vehicle
for new directions within WoG while herself remaining very much subordinated to headship and the
party-line. Unlike Betty, she is comfortable with
"Community Order," and will probably remain so as

the years pass and she continues receiving attention and support for her ministries. Before passing on, a comment will be made about Geraldine's
use of what could be labeled the "teaching tone."
When subjects are elaborating upon central tenets
of the group, they spontaneously adopt a monotonal
style of expression perhaps modeled after the
speaking patterns of the overall coordinator of
the Community when he is delivering a "teaching,"
or set of theological/ethical directives. Many of
the subjects slip into and out of the "teaching
tone;" Geraldine used it more than most. In
listening to the taped conversations, it is possible quite easily to distinguish when subjects
are presenting dogma and when they are speaking
more from their own experience by the presence/
absence of this pattern and tone of speech.

The final person interviewed from the healing
team, HILARY, brings the number of subjects up to
four of the officially commissioned practitioners.
This twenty-two year old graduate of the University had been a "head" in his dormitory while in
school, and at the time of the interview was working full-time in Community-related employment.
Like a growing percentage of the membership,
Hilary spends very little time away from Community
members and activities because even his work day
involves "brothers and sisters." Perhaps the most
frequently used word in his conversation was
"sometimes" in that he resisted my attempts to
have him generalize either from his experiences of
healing or his explanations of them. In qualify-
ing most statements with that "sometimes," he
manifested an attention to the details of various
different healing events, and a refusal to accept
premature closure. His social science background
helped him maintain a questioning (but not skeptical) attitude toward the ministry he performed.
Hilary drew the spontaneous distinction between
people who really do have the charismatic gift of
healing, and himself whom "the Lord used in this
way. It's the way the Lord wants people in general to pray with other people for healing." The
pleasingly humble manner in which this was uttered
suggests Hilary's personal detachment from his

112

role and function, and indicates his ability to reflect objectively about his service. Yet his nuanced reflections and comments do not imply any lack of enthusiasm in actually performing the healing rituals: having heard his descriptions of his work and seen him in action, I can only employ adjectives like "vigorous," "involved," "commanding," and "charismatic" (despite his demurring). Perhaps his thinking has developed so deeply on the topic because he had prayed for the healing of his own father who had subsequently died. This had occurred a year prior to our talking together, during which time he had continued exercising his ministry with other healings occurring. Another seeming obstacle to his faith which he took in stride is his own suffering from a chronic, though minor, ailment for which he has been both medicated and prayed over, seemingly to no avail. To say that his father's and his own illnesses have challenged and deepened his faith would be half the story only: they have enlarged his compassion and have forced him to think through a rationale for healing that seemed more profound than most due to its personally appropriated character.

ISIDORE, a twenty-seven year old day laborer, holds no offices in WoG and lives by himself. He claims that he experienced a series of visions (three visual, one auditory) eight years ago. The visions constituted his joyous conversion experience, and he uses all the superlatives he can muster to describe their content (Jesus' mother Mary, and each person of the Trinity) and effect upon him. Most of the prophecies he has received since then (numbering, he says, about a hundred) have contained words of encouragement to him, exhortation to patience, and guidance for getting through his life without the intensity of the time of the visions. Isidore spent more time at prayer than any other subject since he worked at odd jobs and devoted the remainder of his days to Scripture and praying. As with his prophecies, so too did most of his conversations with me over the five years I knew him reflect his central concern; how to cope with living without the intensity of feeling experienced in his visions and the happy eight

113

weeks immediately after. The ordinary pleasures
of his daily life seemed to hold no appeal for him
though he finds fulfillment in sculpture and flute
playing. Conversing with him, one thinks spontaneously of John of the Cross's "Dark Night of the
Soul." He seems somehow to have been begotten in
the wrong era, belonging instead perhaps to the
third century when he would have tried the life of
a hermit in the Egyptian Desert. Isidore lives
the life of a monk in the world: making just
enough money to survive on the barest necessities
of life, he prays at home or in the open country-
side waiting for a clearer direction from God's
revelation about how he is to spend his life.

JULIE, like Betty, has left WoG since the
interview though she had made her public commitment as a full participant, and had been an official member of the "Prophecy Squad," as she
called that team. A twenty-two year old University graduate, she worked full-time as an administrative assistant in a professional office.
From the beginning of her contact with the Community, she seemed marked out for the work of prophecy because she frequently experienced a feeling
that the Lord wanted to speak through her, even
before she knew much about the gift. Her vocation
evolved naturally since, in her dormitory, only
she and another woman experienced this gift. As
her talents became recognized and she rose to official status, she could never recall having a
leader of a prayer meeting discern that her prophecy was incorrect. This fact was not a source
of pride for Julie, just a consoling confirmation
of the rightness of her functioning. Her interview provided a charming history of her development and socialization into this gift through
early naive phases of ignorance and timidity,
through periods of greater self-confidence, to a
plateau of useful service to individuals and
groups in their attempts to discover how best to
proceed in God's service. Julie enjoyed her prophecy team meetings more than any other of the
various gatherings she had to attend. Then, however, a period of "some disorder" in her spiritual
life followed as she became confused about the way

the Community was going. During this period (the year prior to our interview) she prophesied perhaps only three or four times as she began distancing herself emotionally and ideologically from WoG. Her confusion was compounded by the fact that sometimes her prophecies supported her criticisms, while at other times she felt herself to be unjustly "rebellious" against her heads; at still other times she felt the label of rebelliousness from them to be unwarranted. Although this interview was conducted during a period of personal stress for Julie, she still provided quite useful data about the growth in the exercise of prophecy and its correlation with Community appreciation and recognition. Unlike Isidore and other subjects interviewed, she never prophesied to herself because that procedure "seemed silly." Her conversion to Catholicism had also influenced her prophetic activity as she noticed that her pronouncements became more "Catholic" in tone, and she was even rebuked after a prayer meeting once because her word had changed the direction of the meeting. (The leader did not object to this turn of events in principle; he had only wanted her to check with him first before imposing this switch.) Julie exemplifies a conflict observed in many young women in WoG between the ideals of "liberated" womanhood enunciated in their secular work-lives, and their own needs for community and acceptance by a body with a different notion of liberation; namely, through submission and subordination to headship. Many women remain within WoG; others, like Julie, ultimately leave even though their gifts had been appreciated and developed.

KAREN is a twenty-one year old senior in the University who was brought up in a non-Christian family. Her father is a professor; her mother, a woman quite active in community affairs in their home town. Through a high school date, she had become aware of the Charismatic Renewal, joined WoG while at college, and has also converted to Roman Catholicism. She was a National Merit Scholar in high school, and kept up good grades at the University despite heavy involvement in WoG.

Karen's relationships with her immediate family
seemed healthy and open: the tension and strain
surrounding her conversion to Catholicism had been
resolved. Karen claimed three extraordinary experiences of healing: a severe cut on her foot
from broken glass was quickly healed in a few
minutes after prayer; a chipped bone of her ankle
was healed in three days instead of in the three
weeks predicted by the doctor; her knee, thrown
out during a dance, was also healed through prayer
although the doctor had anticipated surgery for
it. While her self-description portrays a young
woman seeking the truth both cosmic and personal,
she also manifests much more cooperation than
Betty or Julie did, in that she has complied will-
ingly with directives of heads in the Community
that she break up a relationship with a man that
was "getting too serious." (The reason for this
rupture was explained in work-related terms; a
relationship would take time from her service in
the Community. She is already committed to attending a meeting each night of the week.) She is
both practical and idealistic: in speaking of her
future, she plans to get a teaching job upon grad-
uating, but wishes ultimately to save up enough
money to attend law school. Karen wants to support herself through her professional training
even though her parents have more than enough cash
to finance her way.

LOIS is a forty-year old woman whose lifelong
battle with cancer has been won through prayer for
physical healing. Coming from an intellectual
family, she reported that she had never believed
in miraculous healing. "I wasn't going to risk
discouragement," she reflected. Her entry into
WoG was consciously made for reasons other than
health. She was "looking for what I could feel
was the Body of Christ . . . I could find radiant
individuals, but the problem was to find a whole
body of them." In her view, WoG is "a people who
had really found out about God's love and could
communicate with each other." From these few
quotations it can be seen that Lois represents an
excellent subject who blends skepticism with piety
critical judgment with religious faith. Her first

few months in WoG brought her confidence that a permanent physical healing was possible, and that her yearly tissue scans for a possible return of cancerous cells would in the future always be negative. Medically speaking her first year in WoG was traumatic: another fibroid growth was discovered at a different site in her body. Lois's courageous spirit comes through as she sums up that difficult year with its uncertainty and temptations to depression by saying, "That was the most exciting adventure I'd ever had." (On paper this sentence appears to be naive, perhaps tinged with denial, but the context and tone of her spoken words convey the strength she gained in toughing out her ordeal.) Certainly the most broadly read of the subjects, her interests extended deep into literature, philosophy, history and religion. Perhaps partially because she was a Protestant in a predominantly Catholic community, her thinking along ecumenical lines was fostered. She spoke of "interior visions" about Church unity:

> I saw a great many towers standing in a particular country. As long as one goes along the ground floor, he is struck by the differences in the towers. But as you climb up, your view gets more and more similar to the view of people climbing their own towers. If you reach the top, you look across and shout, "Isn't the view magnificent?"

Like several other subjects she displays her sense of humor even in circumstances when she is dealing with the Almighty. At the moment of her healing, she felt hands in the two afflicted areas of her body "like the most gentle and thorough medical examination, but with no hurting." She began to cry and to think, "I don't deserve this." A voice within her mind said, "Don't be irrelevant. That 'worthiness' has nothing to do with the subject!" Narrating this incident, she spontaneously laughed aloud as did I. Lois was also sensitive to the burden placed on the sick by faith-healers who

claim that the Lord wants all persons healed here
and now: her own experience had taught her to
wait, to be silent with expectation, but not to
blame herself, much less others, for lack of sufficient faith.

MAX, a husband and father, came to the interview with an affliction that had not been healed
after prayers, but related several absorbing accounts of healings accomplished for his wife and
children. Quite a successful businessman, Max
had given up his job in a different state and
taken a drastic pay-cut to come to Ann Arbor and
join WoG where his considerable administrative and
executive abilities were given a new outlet. Employed by the Community, he exercised both financial and spiritual headship within the body. Both
he and his wife are known for their common sense
and good advice in both practical and spiritual
realms, and accordingly both enjoy much respect
and officially delegated authority in the Community. Max has a no-nonsense way of talking, and he
easily blends worldly pragmatism with an unblink-
ing faith in the supernatural and miraculous. His
own child, rather than Community ideology, introduced him to physical healings because, prior to
his joining WoG, his daughter had asked her parents to pray over her. While he had prayed, "O
Lord, let this happen if it be your will," his
child's attitude was that the healing was going to
happen, period. The problem had centered around
an ear infection, and when the physician looked
into Max's daughter's ear, he asked whether it was
the wrong ear he was examining since nothing was
wrong with it. Furthermore, the healed ear showed
not even a sign of a scar.

Similarly, Max's wife's healing caused surprise and consternation for her gynecologist: he
had discovered a lump in her breast and scheduled
surgery three days later, but after being prayed
over, Max's wife needed no operation as the lump
was completely gone. Max spontaneously contrasted
his own and his family's joyous response of faith
in a God with the cautious happiness of the physicians consulted. The doctors all seemed to him
to side-step the issue of divine intervention.

While they would happily agree that it was great that a recovery had occurred, none was willing to say that a miraculous healing had taken place. More than many subjects, Max shared the researcher's quest for understanding of the phenomena, and because illness was such a constant in his family, Max had almost routinized procedures for praying when sickness struck. Yet even though his discussion sounded so organized, business-like and logical, it was clear that all the "procedures" were carried on in the context of his personal relationship with his God. Perhaps because of the striking nature of the various healings accomplished in his family, he was invited to be a member of the healing team, but later resigned from it. Max reported that he felt "out of it," and "disarmed" in the healing prayer-room. Ultimately because he felt that it was "not my ministry," he withdrew after no significant experiences in that service although he still believes in its efficacy for his family and himself despite his own health problems at the time of our discussion.

NED had been a member of the Community since its earliest days. A young married father, he worked full-time in a local hospital while going to school part-time. Because psychology was a side interest of his, he expressed great interest in being interviewed, and provided the longest set of comments by any subject. His remarks ranged widely over his experiences in his own life and within the Community, and are valuable because of his perspective on the evolution and growth of customs and practices within WoG. His perceptive comments covered all the areas here researched, but most especially the history of his own experiences as a prophet and how his prophecies were received by the official leadership, how his personal growth was fostered and directed by the experience, how the gift appeared, developed and matured. The simultaneous seriousness and good humor with which he viewed his gift are illustrated by his reaction to the news that his first child was a boy despite the fact that prophecy had declared both the sex and the name of his expected baby. "My thought was, 'How could the doctor

119

err?'" Although Ned is a reflective man and psychologically-minded, he does not let his musings
get in the way of his experiences as they are
going on and thus destroy or interfere with them
by taking such a spectator approach. In fact, one
of his stated reasons for enjoying our interactions was the chance they provided him to step
back and integrate his history with his life in a
fuller way. He enjoyed one of the widest ranges
and repertoires of prophecy as he experienced it
in reference to his own personal life, in the reception of insight, encouragement and counseling
hints for helping those in his household, and in
direction for the Community at large. Both he and
his wife OLGA (see next interviewed subject) had
experienced the curious but beneficial blessing
of leg-lengthening, and had had their skepticism
about "the gifts" considerably reduced. Like the
other college-educated subjects in the sample, Ned
struggled in trying to integrate the scientific
world-view he lived by in his daily life, especially at work, with the extraordinary phenomena
taking place within him and around him. As he put
it, "I feel like I'm on the front line where the
metaphysical and tangible world intersect." Yet
Ned's interest was not merely theoretical or spec-
ulative because he found that his effectiveness at
work in the hospital was definitely increased when
he would pray silently for his patients' health.
As an employee, he did not conduct healing rituals
publicly, but had gathered evidence sufficient for
himself that prayer "worked."
    OLGA, Ned's wife, was interviewed indepen-
dently of and subsequently to Ned. She had worked
in an ordinary clerical position and had gone to
college up through her sophomore year when she had
her child. Content to stay at home with her baby
until her husband finished his own schooling, she
had plans of returning to school and hoped to become a lawyer. My interest in recruiting her as a
subject had been heightened because she had once
given me a written prophecy which had startled me
with its clarity and appropriateness even though I
had been in Ann Arbor less than a year, and had
met her only casually when the prophecy had been

delivered. A quiet, reserved person, Olga nevertheless acted decisively when she felt impelled to
prophesy. Yet she is appropriately self-critical
too: "I'm always afraid it's something I'm coming up with out of my head." Olga especially
feels this trepidation when she is given a "discernment" concerning the personal life of another.
While fearing that she may be rebuffed for "med-
dling," she delivers her word and has never been
so rebuked. "I feel compelled to say something
If I don't, I feel miserable, and if I do, I feel
miserable until I say it at which time I feel relaxed." Like Ned, Olga had been a participant in
the Renewal for many years, even before her coming
to Ann Arbor, and consequently she added to her
remarks the perspective of time plus the living
out of the challenge she frequently felt to square
what she was experiencing with her traditional and
vigorous Catholicism. Besides corroborating her
husband's account of her leg lengthening, she
painted a brief history of deliverance as practiced in the early days before the practices and
procedures became institutionalized, and the more
hair-raising, spooky, preternatural aspects of
deliverance were suppressed by social consensus
and control. In addition to the tensions she
feels between her shyness and the gift of prophecy
between her Catholicism and the fundamentalist
brand of Christian Theology governing the Renewal,
Olga also strives to integrate her "bent for the
mystical" with her felt duties as a wife and mother. When reaching out for deeper prayer forms,
she smilingly recalls the Lord saying to her, "Cut
this stuff. I've got other things for you just
now. You're dissipating your energies, fighting
with your child, fighting with your husband: this
is not in My plan for you." Accordingly, Olga's
piety and lifestyle are taking a very "this-
worldly" direction, and the Lord's love for her is
specifically related to her growth as a Christian
woman, she feels.
    PAULA, a nurse in her early twenties, had
just made her public and permanent commitment to
WoG two months before our interview. Living in a
residential household run by a married couple, she

personified the happy young person for whom the
Community met almost all needs, personal, social
and emotional. Working in a traditionally feminine occupation, she did not experience the strain
felt by other young professional women between
career goals and striving, and the Community's approach to submission. She was in a "relationship"
with a young man approved by both sets of superiors, his and hers, and anticipated marrying and
living in WoG for the indefinite future. A healee and prophetess, Paula breathes an infectious
enthusiasm as she recounts her conversion experience which was accompanied by a most dramatic personal healing of an hereditary degenerative bone
disease. This had occurred in high school, and
her ultimate decision to settle in WoG was preceded by several attempts to live "peacefully" in
other communities: her home town, and that connected with a group in another state. Propelled
by a desire to "be part of a people really living
their lives together for the Lord," she and her
"heads" ultimately discerned that she should journey to Ann Arbor. Previously, she had had a great
deal of experience speaking before high school and
church groups about "the Lord," and had herself
founded several prayer groups. Yet she always
felt that, despite her success in leadership positions, she would prefer more headship and is now
quite comfortable in her present situation. Endowed with natural gifts of a warm, cheerful personality and a healthy family situation, Paula
nevertheless experienced many other gifts when she
"came to the Lord" such as an ability to overcome
her basic shyness and speak before groups. (She
noted explicitly that she had not been prepared
for this challenge by participation in high school
debating.) Hence, like many other subjects, her
own definition of "spiritual gifts" is not confined to those mentioned in Scripture. Rather she
sees all of reality as gift, and is made more conscious of a gift's special nature, of course, when
habit, inclination or previous expectations would
not have led her to anticipate that she could have
behaved in a certain way, that events would have
turned out fortuitiously, etc. Obviously a

recipient of many gifts, Paula is generous in her turn for she and one other young man (not her intended spouse) cheerfully turn over their paychecks monthly to the head of their household, and thus provide most of the financial support for the several adults and children living there "in common." In this way she enables the others to serve pastoral roles in the larger WoG Community or to attend to the human needs of her fellow household members.

QUENTIN, a college senior in an honors program, majored in psychology and planned to become a physician. His special interest was in the area of epidemiology. As a boy, he had almost died from allergic reactions to certain foods. He suffered for seven years from these allergies. From time to time, he would experiment in the hopes that he had outgrown them, but would develop a "sore throat, cold, runny nose if I'd even eat a hot dog!" Two years prior to our interview, Quentin had been completely healed of all his allergies in a single evening's healing prayer session. Possessed of what might be described as a reverently curious nature, he had tried to explain first to himself and then to me the various experiences, feelings and events which surrounded his healing. After a girl had prophesied to him at an earlier prayer service that "The Lord will heal you soon," he had taken a student's approach to the problem: "I read lots of books on healing, went out, ate beef and got sick!" Later, however, he experienced a "sense from the Lord," (a phrase used over and over again by many subjects) that he should be prayed over in the healing prayer room. He recalls that the whole happening wasn't a very emotional experience: "Having studied psychology, I thought a person could work themselves into a state to change their body chemistry. I don't think there was any emotional involvement at all." As inner conviction grew, he knew interiorly that he had been healed and so the very next day he started eating the previously dangerous foods, but had not recurrence of any difficulty. He relates his story calmy, matter-of-factly, humorously, not adding details he can't recall, "I didn't

123

attribute the healing to the person praying for
me; I can't even remember who was praying for me."
While he uses his education to carry him a certain
distance in understanding the phenomenon, only his
religious faith can provide the clue that explains
what turned out. He sees the healing in the context of his loving and trusting relationship with
the Lord. While not an official member of a healing team, he has successfully prayed for friends'
healings, and related several tales of twisted ankles and legs during athletic contests where he
and his companions prayed with fellow players who
then stopped writhing in pain, hopped up and finished their games. His accounts of the experiences of prophecy and glossolalia parallel others'
but are briefly and sharply expressed, clearly
analyzed, and related with a certain amount of wit
and verve which make his interview, the briefest,
stand out above many others.

ROBERTA, my oldest subject, is a deeply reflective woman whose healing was only partial and
temporary, but whose wise and rambling musing on
many subjects besides healing revealed a personality seasoned and mellowed by her years. She had
joined the Community and become publicly committed
quite early in its history when it was still predominantly a college-students' religious movement -- this despite her protest expressed several
times that she finds young people's thinking and
lifestyles difficult to adjust to. Roberta
nevertheless communicates a certain quiet vitality
and freshness of viewpoint, and makes people feel
comfortable in her presence. Like Quentin, she
experimented after the healing prayer for her eyes
by not wearing her glasses; unlike his situation,
the initially satisfying results seemed to disap-
pear after a traumatic visit with relatives, and
she reluctantly resumed wearing her glasses. In
retrospect, Roberta's case seems to be one of a
hope unfulfilled, but a hope so strong that for a
time, it seemed to be realized. Yet her own discussion of the incident and its outcome reveals no
bitterness, nor naive denial, but rather a peaceful integration of the disappointment and its
aftermath into a life lived in joy despite

124

frequent tragedies. Spontaneously contrasting her own imperfect healing with the full recoveries of others, she remarked quite simply that "there is no 'why?' with the Lord." Her contemplative appreciation of nature, life and people showed itself through her frequent use of the adjective, "beautiful," to describe someone or something. A peaceful serenity seemed to fill the room as Roberta talked about her past, her hopes fulfilled or dashed, her present happiness in WoG. Still, she was able to be calmly critical of the Commmunity's outpouring of efforts on new members, and its failure to manifest more continuing concern and support in the way she felt she needed it. All in all, however, Roberta expresses contentment with her situation and the pattern her life has assumed since her entry into the Community.

SHEILA is a young mother of several children, a housewife, and an official member of the prophecy team. She provided valuable information about the institutionalization of the gifts while she could also describe clearly her own beginnings with the gift and her use of it in many varied contexts. Like others who had first come to the Renewal in their college years, she had been initially quite skeptical about any and all of the gifts, but as experience yielded to experience, she felt her doubts melting. Sheila still had difficulties with physical healings, however, despite her great fluency in prophecy, but because she had been healed herself of a pregnancy-related problem, and had taken part in several healing prayer sessions, she was becoming more comfortable with this gift too. Thus her interview also stands as an illustration of a person deeply practiced in one gift while somewhat hesitant concerning another, and shows different stages of "maturity in the gifts" within the consciousness of a single individual. Sheila is one of the most vocal of the prophets at public gatherings of the Community, and seems in many of her utterances to reinforce the line of teaching adopted by the coordinators. It is difficult to judge from our interview just how conscious Sheila has become of her role of legitimating the leaders' direction,

125

but what is evident is her own sensitive use of the gift in various life situations aside from the formal meetings of WoG. In no way a "yes-person," she lives life energetically and enthusiastically while feeling comfortable with the subordination she experiences vis-a-vis her husband and the (male) head of the prophecy team. Yet she is aware of the attention which exercise of the gift draws and she complains that she feels "more trouble than when somebody compliments me as a mother." Thus she signals her acceptance of the Community's warning against spiritual pride in this or in any gift. Sheila provided information on a topic rarely mentioned, the giving of a prophecy through dreams. Sheila, finally, is a woman for whom the gifts of prophecy and deliverance provided personal help in dealing with many past family problems and hurts: the gifts can benefit the giver as well as the larger community for whom they are primarily intended.

THOMAS, a minority group member, is in his early forties, a husband and father, and works as a supervisor in a health care facility. His interview contained the greatest number of mentioned incidents of healings, prophecies, etc. He speaks in a slow, deliberate fashion and punctuates his vignettes with dashes of gentle self-deprecatory humor. Though a naturally shy man, he seems to gather courage when asked to speak about his experiences before groups, and in one-to-one conversations has mastered the technique of sharing his experiences of the spiritual without forcing them on his hearer. Thomas grew up in poverty, but now lives in a modest middle class neighborhood. His own illnesses were among the most severe to be reported cured. His occupation allows him many opportunities to "witness" to the gifts from the Lord in his own life, and to pray with the sick for their own healing. For Thomas, rapid healing of his own ailments and of the patients brought to his hospital has become a way of life, that is, he spontaneously and frequently prays for and receives the healings he requests. Accordingly, he does not dwell for long on any one incident but passes rapidly over many in grateful review as he narrates his tale. He declares that much of his life is spent in conversation with the Lord: about his problems at work, his patients, his family. Thomas chuckles and notes that his favorite saying is "Take over, Lord: I can't handle it." This should not be interpreted as a flight from responsibility, but rather as a living out of his sense that God is working powerfully through him, rather than that he himself is accomplishing the healings he and his associates so desperately need. Not only does he converse with the Lord, but also about the Lord: "Years ago I played baseball and talked baseball. Now I talk about the Lord." His familiarity with the Divinity is further nuanced by his description of early healings of his own which he would use as occasions to "test" the Lord's love for him. Thus Thomas is a man who has integrated the experience and practice of the gifts into his whole lifestyle. Because he is so involved in health care, and because illness had been so much a part of his own and his family's past, he very naturally lives by the Community's teaching and understanding of healing. Whereas other subjects' cures were dramatic if infrequent, or confined to a special setting like the healing prayer room, the drama of Thomas's situation lies in the frequent occurrence of extraordinary phenomena.

URSULA, a fortyish single female, a minority group person like Thomas, was chosen by me for an interview because I had heard from Chuck that she was experienced in leg-lengthening. She readily and independently corroborated the procedures already provided by Chuck, and told me that she herself had been similarly treated and healed. In addition, she described her personal ministry of "healing of memories" to which she had been assigned by one of the coordinators. This service involved a supportive relationship of prayer and informal individual counseling with several young people in the Community who had had relatively serious emotional problems. (It must be added at once that her service was not a substitute for professional therapy, but was freely provided because the more usual intervention techniques

127

seemed not to be doing much good.) A kind, warm, motherly sort of woman, Ursula seemed admirably suited for this mode of assistance. She enjoyed her role, and from my acquaintance with two of those with whom she worked, seemed to be accomplishing much good despite her own self-confessed hesitancies about her lack of formal training as a counselor. Relying on prayer and intuition, she was both a good listener and sensed when to ask appropriate questions, make suggestions, and consult others when she was stuck. Ursula also worked with the Community's younger children, and had the confidence both of the parents and the youngsters themselves. Like Roberta, she wished that more attention was paid to the needs of the older people in the Community, but patiently accepted the realities of living in a group composed predominantly of much younger people than herself. Perhaps because she herself had experienced serious physical infirmities, she was drawn to pray for others' illnesses and psychological disturbances. Despite inner reluctance, she also employed the prayer for deliverance with those in psychological distress and found it to be effective especially in combating suicidal tendencies. "An atmosphere of love is curative," she commented as she discussed the healing movement of the Lord through herself and through the whole body of the Community. Because she correctly sensed that many in the Community feared those with psychological problems, she would sometimes take a walk with her "clients" so that "people could see us together" and not be afraid to associate with those in such need. To round out our discussion, Ursula also spoke concerning her experience with prophecy, but because she had been given a message which caused worry for the recipients, she hoped that she would not have this happen too often again.

The final subject, VICTOR, a twenty-five year old single male, was also someone I recruited because he had been with the Community since its beginnings, had an excellent memory for details, and knew about the history of the group's practice of deliverance. Victor's sense of humor made him popular and liked by all, and because he has a talent for organization and close attention to detail, he frequently supervised large community projects though he had not become appointed to the hierarchy of coordinators. Like many young people in Ann Arbor, he had graduated from college and decided to work a few years before pursuing his education in political science. Involvement with WoG delayed his entry into graduate studies, but Victor throws himself wholeheartedly into community and church affairs. He serves as an excellent right-hand man for the many assignments which he is asked to complete. While feeling critical concerning certain trends within the Community, he nevertheless manages to live happily and peacefully with developments and takes the long view towards problems of which his sensitivity makes him aware before others notice. He is informally consulted as an "older brother" by persons new to WoG because his innate common sense is quickly recognized, and because he is not an official who must pronounce the party line. He gave the fullest exposition which anyone supplied concerning the evolution of the various phases and stages of deliverance, and his remarks completed the picture puzzle whose pieces had been occasionally hinted at by other subjects. His cautious acceptance of this practice is revealed in this statement: "I thought it was a good thing, but wasn't sure the approach was best. People get too hung up on blaming evil spirits instead of working things out in other ways." This characteristically balanced approach permeated all his answers to my requests for information, both about his experiences with deliverance and with prophecy.

This concludes the personal description of each research subject. Further details of their personalities will become evident in what follows as each is allowed to speak for him/herself in describing each gift.

What follows is a description of each gift as experienced by the subjects interviewed. The phenomenological method described in the previous chapter will be employed. Lest the reader get lost in the welter of data, a brief overview will be provided first in the form of twelve propositions which might be said to characterize the meaning-system, the world-view, the Weltanschauung, the myth of the subjects and of WoG. Though none were so systematic in their comments, it is possible to list this series of propositions enumerating their main tenets of belief regarding the spiritual gifts.

(1) God exists and is personal and active in His world, not remote and unconcerned.

(2) Through Scriptural revelation especially, but also through the continuing revelation called prophecy, He calls a people to Himself to worship Him and serve each other.

(3) God wants to initiate a personal relationship with this people and with each individual person.

(4) Living in a community is a necessary condition for this relationship; a community provides the locus of the relationship and of the reception and practice of various signs of God's favor, the spiritual gifts.

(5) Praise is a most important human response to this relationship, and is often proclaimed "in tongues," ancient, extinct or foreign languages not studied or learned by the one offering praise.

(6) God speaks to the heart and mind of each person. Sometimes this "speech" takes the form of actual words heard interiorly. This interior prompting to utter prophecy, to heal (or not to heal!), to behave in some definable fashion is called the "Lord's leading," or a "sense from the Lord."

(7) Through the exercise of the gift of "discernment," one learns by practice to

distinguish between one's own thoughts and desires, the "Lord's leading," and promptings of "the Evil One," or the devil/Satan/demons. (The demonic realm is just as real for charismatics as is the divine.)

(8)   The Lord's will is that men be whole and sound, physically and psychologically.   Trust in Him has physiological and emotional correlates: healing the hurts of body and spirit should occur regularly and normally in a Christian community.

(9)   Often the "Lord's leading" takes the concrete form of a "Word of Wisdom," some concrete, practical and sound advice for a person or the community when a decision must be made.

(10)   A "Word of Knowledge" is another concretization of the "Lord's leading" wherein a counselor suddenly intuits a definite fact about his counselee's past life, often embarrassing and even forgotten by the latter, and employs his knowledge to further the process of inner healing.

(11)   "Expectant faith" is the best attitude for all to cultivate in anticipation of the Lord's dealing with His people to promote their personal growth, increase their numbers, and generally make the planet into a loving unity of brothers and sisters.

(12)   The history of cultures is best interpreted apocalyptically and eschatologically, that is, people, nations and political systems not dedicated to the Lord are moving toward their own destruction, but the Second Coming of Jesus Christ will quite soon initiate a universal Kingdom of justice, love and peace.

Now the subjects will speak for themselves as

131

they describe the experience of each gift.

Prophecy

Chuck describes his first encounter with prophecy, i.e., interpreted as meaning the use by God of human persons to communicate His thoughts and wishes --

> I felt the Holy Spirit in a physical sense. I had this awareness even when my eyes were closed . . . There were no boundaries: I sensed that I could reach out around myself to infinity. I knew it was the Lord. I felt words coming, but the words weren't mine. I felt elated. Now I understood why the apostles appeared to be drunk. I had no idea whether I was talking or not. I felt like I was floating.

The content of prophecies could be divided several ways: encouraging ("My People, I love you") and exhortatory ("Repent. Change X in your life."); intended for the whole Community or for just a single individual; pragmatically concrete or poetically haunting. With eyes closed, the prophet speaks or sings in naturally flowing cadences, and in the first person as though in the name of the Deity. Often crucial phrases are repeated. Contrary to the popular understanding of the term, relatively few prophecies concern the future.

Abigail, self-described as cranky and crotchety, was told in prophecy, "The lion must be tamed slowly. I will diminish your snarl." She attributes her greater success in controlling her temper and her tongue to this and other similarly supportive prophecies.

Here is an example of a prophecy spoken to the entire Community:

Remember the darkness that I have called
you from and rejoice. Remember the bondage
from which I have freed you, and rejoice.
Remember how you were alone and spread far
apart, and see how it is that I have brought
you together and made you into a people, and
rejoice. It is I who have brought you to
birth, and it is I, myself, who have called
each one of you by name. Yes, it is I, myself, who have promised to be your God and
have made you into a people, and know that
you have only begun to see what I would do
among you.

Prophecies which do deal with the future often refer to coming political, economic and social
cataclysms and warn the people to prepare especially through loyalty and obedience to their
leaders. Prophecy has, to some extent, been
brought under the control of the Community's leadership in that there is a "prophecy group" to
which experienced prophets belong and who alone
are entrusted with the task of prophecy at the
large community gatherings -- though all are encouraged to "yield to" the gift in smaller group
settings, e.g., the households.
Sheila, a member of the prophecy group, provided the following definition of prophecy:

"Prophetic" for me is less, really less
a prediction of the future -- I haven't had
any experience with that -- as it is just
really speaking the word of God's love, God's
wisdom, God's plan for the body, for my life
as an individual, for our life as a family.
It's operative in our family life . . . I've
been learning what it means to move more from
a general sort of sense of what God wants to
a more specific -- speaking of God's love in
general for us is always good; I think the
Lord will always speak generally of His love
for us. I guess by the word "prophetic" what
I mean is getting a sense of how God sees

things more clearly. The Lord wants to give us wisdom in different areas, whether a direction for the whole Community or a specific word of wisdom for somebody there at that meeting: God's Word, in a sharper way than just by reading Scripture, really penetrates through and speaks out.

In addition to defining prophecy, Sheila speaks concretely about her belief in and experience of the realities called (by the researcher) propositions one and three noted just above; namely, that God's existence is not debated but a reality woven into daily family life; furthermore, that humans can and do enter into relationship with God; that God provides direction, encouragement, support, "wisdom," the various other gifts, etc. This experience of a relational awareness of and interaction with the Transcendent forms the fundamental basis of the religious experience of Community members. Whereas many Americans' primary experience of religion seems to be in terms of adherence to a moral code, or holding to a body of dogmas, or loyalty to an institutionalized church, this quotation and many more will show that people in WoG freely communicate with "the Lord." Of course, participants in WoG have their moral code, their dogmas, their institutional loyalties too, but the distinguishing characteristic of participants, over against many other Church people of the same denominations but not in WoG, remains this highly developed and deliberately cultivated sense of communication and interchange with the Deity. This point will be repeated time and again by each subject and forms a sort of background music behind all the testimonies. It must be explicitly noted here at the outset because, like the lines on a football field or the rhythm in a tune, it merges into the total experience and might be overlooked without explicit attention having been provided.

Prophets are people whose sense of the awareness of God draws them on to communicate what they are convinced is a message intended for themselves

in private; for one other person; for a small
group like a household; for the entire Community
gathered at a prayer meeting. Even when the message is just for himself alone, a person will
still use the prophetic mode of behavior and speak
aloud to himself or at least write down words
which cross his mind. Elaine, for example, during
her personal prayer time, will speak out what she
feels are the Lord's words to her, and then write
them down. How does she know that the words are
from the Lord, are the right words? Elaine compared the experience to that of knowing but for-
getting someone's name: if someone says the name,
you know it's right. Sometimes the event itself
will confirm a prophecy: Elaine had prayed that
she be granted in-state residency so as to be allowed to pay lower University tuition; she received a sense from the Lord that the prayer would
be answered; it was. Nor is the prophecy always
to one's liking. Elaine was considering her career of education, felt she didn't like it, but
"in prayer the Lord said, 'Stay. This is for
you.'" Elaine and others are convinced that the
truth in a Word makes something happen, i.e., that
words themselves are sources of dynamic causality -- a typically biblical and Semitic notion.
For Elaine, the prophetic experience is like hearing a friend on the phone or reading a message in
a letter as opposed merely to knowing something
just as a fact.

Hilary provided the best response to my
query, "Why do you rely on this sense from the
Lord?" "It's all we've got," he laughed. "It's
a fallible instinct. We don't always hear Him
perfectly. Still I believe God speaks and we can
hear Him!"

Before proceeding to describe what it's like
to deliver a prophecy before others, we shall give
a few more descriptions of what happens when one
receives prophecy. Ned described the feeling-
content as being awe, but not fear, during the
"experience of the majesty of the divine God. The
other half of my feelings are of the tenderness of
the Father God." The Charismatic Renewal had filled Ned with the experience of God as a Father and

135

himself as a particular son, not just one of a
group. Prophecy is an "instrument tool, but not
audio-hallucinations. I talk, and God talks
back -- clearly discernible, not my own thought
patterns." Unlike Elaine, Ned allows personal
prophecies to go on "in my head," does not proclaim them aloud, but writes them occasionally.
Receiving a prophecy on Community order, praying
on it, he said, "Lord, I'll write; you talk." He
produced several pages.

Describing his life as "intellectually-
oriented" and calling himself an "internal-
control" kind of character, Ned had to forge a way
to deal with such paranormal happenings. In his
words --

> . . . I found I could pray and somebody would
> talk back with formulated thought. I was
> concerned about "going off the deep end." I
> made a deal: "Be consistent and don't lead
> to wrong, or I'll turn off the voice." In
> seven years it has been consistent, and never
> led to evil. "Dialogue prayer" is a better
> formula than "prophecy." I found a number of
> people had experienced it. (In 1969 and
> those early days) there were no teaching
> mechanisms in the Community yet. One morning
> when I was working on the ambulance I awoke
> and didn't want to get up. So I prayed,
> "What would Jesus do?" The answer came,
> "Get up and get to work." So I did and began
> washing the ambulance. Sure enough, we got a
> call and I hadn't washed my face or combed my
> hair!

In this vignette, we can see that what non-
Community members might call "talking to oneself,"
members of WoG interpret as prophecy, and justify
the term by insisting that (1) the source of the
ideas, revelations, messages, etc. arises outside
oneself, and (2) the thought pattern is different
from one's own. Additionally, the supposedly
chance demand for the ambulance gets interpreted

as a "confirmation" of the validity of the prophecy. The cognitive-style of WoG members is bol-
stered, however, by more dramatic experiences
which are eagerly "shared" at the public meetings
and in private conversations. They would insist
that, rather than practicing "eisegesis" or reading meaning into an experience, they rather are
performing exegesis or unfolding the genuine
depths and implications of a happening.

Returning to Ned, we meet a man whose conversion experience occurred through a prophecy
delivered by someone --

Here's how I met God: at that time, I
didn't believe in a personal God. Kenny G.
was in from New York and one day I was street
evangelizing with him. We went into St.
Mary's (the University's Catholic chapel).
Kenny knelt down and I was walking up and
down the side aisle. I said, "I want to believe in you, but I can't." I was angry that
I didn't have faith. But Kenny, who had a
high squeaky voice, said in a deep voice,
"Ned, my son, I love you. Where ever you
run, where ever you hide, I will find you;
and I will love you." Internally I said to
myself, "Yeah, That's God. That's it."
Another part of me said, "Don't do anything
rash. You're emotionally upset." Somehow I
managed to step on this second feeling about
having to be careful about "these neurotic
personality types." I was saying to myself,
"Yeah! Yeah!" and at that moment he came out
with his second prophecy which was, "Welcome
home, my son, you are in my love." You know
how dim that place is, but the lights got
brighter and brighter in exactly five stages
just like somebody was clicking a rheostat.
I closed my eyes and thought, "My God!
You're having hallucinations!" The part of
me that had just gotten stepped on said, "I
told you so." The other part of me said,
"No, no, that's really true. God is really
giving you that sign." Somehow I managed to

think, "That really was God, and you're
gonna look up, and it's gonna be there
again." So I opened my eyes and looked at
the altar, and the lights got brighter and
brighter again in five stages. It wasn't a
blinding light or the manifestation of a person, or even a locus of light, just the general lighting available. At which point I
said, "I gotta have a cigarette." From that
exact instant, I can date the real existence
of faith in God and that He cared for me despite whatever other problems I've had. That
was a dramatic way in which prophecy from
somebody else affected me and my life. The
real confirmation was my internal sense, but
there was the external sign too -- his prophecies, and the manifestation of faith on
his part. I was critical and outspoken then
too, always have been, and he spoke out his
second prophecy with no confirmation that the
first had been apt or appropriate.

Again in this statement, we meet the notion
of "confirmation," an additional clue for the prophet or the recipient of prophecy that the Word is
valid and accurate. Previously we saw Elaine's
trust in prophecy confirmed by the subsequent
event of being granted in-state residency: an
event foretold and then occurring is the strongest
confirmation. Other confirmations were the ambulance call to Ned interpreted as a proof that the
call to rise on time was indeed from the Lord, and
the delivery by Kenny G. of the second prophecy
when he had been given no hint that the first had
been accepted and internally acted on. Another
form of confirmation frequently attested to comes
in the experience of having given a prophecy to a
group, and being told by others that they too were
just on the point of delivering the same message.
An alternate mode of this form happens when a person senses he should deliver a prophecy but "sits
on it" through nervousness, shyness, fear that
it's not "from the Lord," and then someone else
gets up and shares the very same message. Because

138

so few prophecies deal with explicit events, confirmation by some alternate mode gives added strength to the faith of the hearer.

Ned's story also introduces the related area of concomitant physical manifestations during prophecy (or healing and the other gifts). Already in the first comment from Chuck in this section, we had heard allusions to physical reactions to the gifts, and like the underlying theme of a personal relationship with God, this experience of physical effects needs explicit attention at the outset here because their presence is frequent but not always mentioned by the subject. Members of the Community tell of "anointings" which are more than ordinarily strong internal promptings to utter a prophecy and are frequently accompanied by a physical, bodily change of state. Chuck called his experience (quoted above) an anointing, and was especially helpful in distinguishing such an experience of prophecy from the consciousness-expansion due to drugs because previous to his conversion, he had frequently been high on hallucinogens. Under the influence of drugs, he felt like an observer of the experience whereas in an "anointing" by the Spirit, he felt like a participant. Often in a drugged state no emotions were felt whereas in prophecy he frequently, even usually, felt love, peace and happiness. When hallucinating, "consciousness had trapped me and I couldn't get back. I flew along with it, and it dropped me, and I had to work my way back." In an "anointing," however, "you are where you started, only you feel changed for the better." A fourth difference expressed was that a drug-high caused by grass or L.S.D. was oppressive. "I couldn't stop it even though I often wanted to." Yet an "anointing" isn't oppressive. It's consciousness-expanding but like "standing on a beach and walking into the water. The water wouldn't move you unless you wanted to be moved."

Geraldine, noting that the experience of the gift of prophecy had changed for her over the time she had been on the team (two years) described her first reception of the gift as --

139

. . . a physical anointing, a direct wave
whereby I know the Lord wanted me to speak in
prophecy. Also there was more fear involved
then; I was more inhibited. My heart would
start beating real fast; I guess that was due
to nervousness. I'd feel a rushing going
through me: it wasn't quite like a pounding;
I'm not sure how to explain it, it's been so
long ago. I guess I always knew I was to
prophesy because I experienced something
physical happening at that time. It was
something like a bursting within me; a quick
sensation of something going through me.
(Was it in the area of your head, your stomach, your legs, or all over?) All over; but
it didn't happen every time. Over the last
year and a half though, prophecy has changed.
Now I don't always have an emotional or sensational experience, but rather a clear sense
of what the Lord might want to do at a meeting. Now I won't necessarily get a direct
word, but when I began I would have a direct
word about what I should say or what God intended to do at that gathering.

In this statement comes an echo of Sheila's comment
that prophecy means a more specific concretization
of God's Will for someone/the group than is contained in scriptural directives, a special manifestation here and now of the Divine purpose.
    Julie also spoke of changes over time in her
style of prophesying, changes in physical accompaniments as well. In the beginning of her prophetic career, she would feel "like when drinking
coffee on a fast day: my stomach would be nervous." The "heavy anointing feeling" was of the
Spirit surrounding one. "Did you ever watch Star
Trek with the 'beaming-up' and 'beaming-down?'
It's like beaming-up, a deep level of communication."
    A final example: Karen was told by someone
that the Lord wanted her to have the gift of prophecy. Several weeks later she gave her first
prophecy:

It's what drew me into the Community in the first place: hearing that God talks through people. I got a sense in my head or in my stomach that "That was the Lord." Or I got an idea to do something. It would turn out good and I would conclude that it was the Lord.

Thus far we have been concentrating on prophecies delivered to a single individual. These next three concluding testimonies recapitulate most of the points already illustrated. Olga keeps notes during her prayer time, and if she sensed that the Lord wanted to tell her something, she would write it down. Sometimes it would amount to a page and a half; sometimes three lines; occasionally, only a single sentence. Her personal prophecies are also quite specific: "I rarely get ambiguous prophecies. Sometimes I get a consciousness of the Lord loving me in a way specific to my growth as a Christian woman." Hence, she has been warned against dissipating her energies fighting with her child and her husband. This behavior is not in the Lord's plan for her. (Other subjects referred also to the "Lord's perfect plan" for individuals and for the Community.) Quentin, in speaking of personal prophecy, puts it this way:

God speaks to me in a pretty direct way by placing thoughts or words in my mind that come from nowhere and are <u>there</u>, are ordered. Individuals have distinctive speech patterns: When I experience God speaking it's different from my way of thinking, for example, "You're concentrating too much on your self-image." My reaction is to say, "Huh? What?" I go before the Lord and have Him expound on it. The Lord leads my mind to dwell more on the thought.

We shall conclude this discussion on personal

141

prophecy with a few quotations from the hundred or
so rendered to Isidore. They have come to him
either in prayer or through others. The first
came through a priest at a monastery who spoke in
God's name and declared, "I have glorified my name
in you and I will glorify it again." A second,
delivered personally to Isidore without any other
human intervention, drew this reaction from him:

> The sentence began with "My son . . ."
> The sound of His voice, though not actually
> "sound" filled an undefined immensity. I
> later reflected that were it audible to other
> people, they would have heard it as far away
> as the east coast of the United States. But
> it was all within, where He is. Though I'd
> studied no theology I could see how He con-
> serves me in existence by perpetually creat-
> ing me. Thus I could see His Fatherhood. I
> was surprised to hear God speaking English
> perfectly, ravishingly.

Isidore claims to have submitted all his prophesies to his "heads," or spiritual directors, and
"was discerned O.K." He adds that he has been
careful to ask that he be helped in this way only
when he has reached the end of his rope. This attitude is consistent with those many others already quoted who expect God to speak directively,
but it contrasts with the easy familiarity implicit in most speakers' expectations. The following
prophecy was given for Isidore by a University
student as seven prayed over him (Isidore):

> I will make you a bright star in the
> black velvet of the night. Everyone will see
> your great joy and they will ask themselves
> "What is this?" Then they will ask you,
> "What is this?" Then you will teach them how
> to enter into My Joy. But do not be afraid
> and do not worry about what to say at that
> time for I will give you the words to say and

many starlets will be borne from you. I will
glorify My Name in you. Be patient. I have
everything perfectly timed. Everything is
worked out. Everything is taken care of. Do
not worry about anything. Be patient. Do
not ask why, where, how, or when. Do not
worry about anything at all. Simply love the
Father and Me.

Note the spontaneous use of poetic imagery in this
message, and the fact that it is delivered in the
name of Jesus, the Son of the Father. Prophecies
are delivered in the name of the Father and of the
Son, but this researcher has never heard a prophecy attributed directly to the Holy Spirit during its proclamation although, of course, theologically all of the gifts are attributed to the
Spirit.

We pass on now to consider more fully the
characteristics of the event just recorded: the
giving of a prophecy to someone else. Many of the
characteristics of prophecy to one person are
found in this latter experience as well, but additional features must be noted and discussed.

A first and most crucial experience in the
prophet is a sense of urgency that s/he deliver
the message. Various subjects report a sense of
being driven to the proclamation, and list the unpleasant effects of silence.

Victor's case is mild: when the internal
sense came to him that he should speak out, he remembers feeling, "If I don't, I'll burst."
Victor's explanation for the sense of urgency, especially when one is just beginning to use the
gift, is that "The Lord has to get your attention
the first time. Once you're willing to respond,
you don't need to be beaten." He is fond of quoting the passage from Sirach 2:1, "My Son, when you
begin to serve the Lord, prepare yourself for an
ordeal." (Parenthetically, we might note that
Victor "received this passage" when "praying for"
one: this Protestant practice of praying for a
Word of Scripture from God and then opening the
Bible at random and letting the finger alight on

143

the first verse has been uncritically adopted by
Catholic charismatics everywhere and not merely in
WoG.) Victor went on to explain that if you don't
speak forth the prophecy there is no divine condemnation, but if you do, "the fruits of the
Spirit will be in the situation." Cautious before
speaking, Victor would wait, discern, pray for
passages, ask the people around him at the meeting
if they sensed something needed saying. Sometimes, "just the right thing would occur; you
sense a real surety that this is to be done. The
last thing you would think of is exactly the right
thing." Most of the time the sense would come
from nowhere, and along with it a "feeling of
peace and rightness." As with others who have
yielded to and practiced the gift for a while,
Victor has grown in fluency and comfort:

> Now there's not much urgency; it's more
> a peaceful, gentle persuasion. I get a sense
> that the Lord wants to say something about
> "X." I try to feel with the Lord what he
> wants to say. I demand more than the opening
> two syllables, at least a sentence or two,
> something to step out on, plus a sense of the
> whole. Generally, I'm reluctant. (Why?) I
> don't do it much publicly. I don't feel that
> it's my ministry. It's more important to
> feel it's what He wants. Speaking in the
> Lord's name is an awesome thing. We need
> Fear of the Lord.

These remarks from Victor speak of the sense of
urgency, and two others will speak about that immediately below, but it is also necessary here to
call attention to some descriptions of the "sense
from the Lord" or "Lord's leading" (Proposition
six) which Victor provides and others have noted
along the way as well. The essence of the experience seems to be a feeling of peace, rightness,
appropriateness, harmony with the flow of a meeting or situation, congruity with what the subject
feels to be God's Will for the here-and-now. We

notice also the phenomenon of subjects' being given a word or two, a sentence or more before actually speaking out. (Rarely, however, do subjects testify that they have been given a whole prophecy word for word, except when they stand up at a prayer meeting to confirm "word for word" what another prophet has just uttered! We may wonder about the effects of social conformity here and pass on.) Note, finally, the explicit reference to awe of God, fear of the Lord. The majority of the prophets interviewed spoke of this sense of God's majesty and their own sense of fright while speaking in His name. Otto's category of <u>tremendum</u> from <u>The Idea of the Holy</u> (1917) comes to mind as one listens to them. The terror was distinguishable from natural nervousness anyone would feel who is unaccustomed to public speaking.

Thomas also experienced this sense of urgency but when he didn't speak out "The Lord took away the gift when I was disobedient. A brother told me he had expected more prophecy at the meeting today. 'Let it out, man,' he had said. 'It's not for you.'" Thomas reports physical concomitants: "a feeling in my chest, sometimes in my head; a full exciting feeling." Despite this urgency, "the hardest thing for me is to start. Lots of people say they have fears about starting to prophesy, wondering whether the Word is from the Lord or from themselves. Or what if I get stuck in the middle of a sentence?" These were indeed commonly reported causes for not plunging right in: if one is to speak in God's name as the prophetic form is structured, then what if the prophecy is "impure," i.e., with an admixture of one's own thought? This fear is based on respect for the Word; the other fear rises from the fact that one is usually given a sense of the prophecy and the first few words at best, not the whole message. One fears becoming embarrassed and not finishing a message. Hence, the conflict between the urgency and the hesitancy can make prophecy-bearing an uncomfortable gift.

Ursula told the most painful story of all those associated with any of these gifts. She had been given a "strong sense" that if a young couple

pursued a certain course of action, the wife would
become seriously ill. "I couldn't tell them, but
I couldn't rest. I was praying in church, not
about them, when it was dumped out on me." Ursula
took the story to a friend of hers who "had good
discernment." They prayed together. That night
Ursula has a sense of the awesomeness of God. She
"got a passage" in Scripture with the directive,
"Don't play around with the things of God." Since
she sensed that this "really was from the Lord,"
she waited two months and then told the couple.
They were upset, of course, and the husband was
angry. "I told the Lord to take care of it, but
it affected our relationship. The husband became
distant. Once he asked, 'Are you waiting to see
what happens?'" Ursula's response was that she
only did what she thought the Lord wanted her to
do. Later when the couple had gone on to do what
they had planned, and the wife hadn't gotten sick,
Ursula still felt that the prophecy had been accurate, but only temporary. When I asked if she
had felt "unpeaceful," she responded, "No, only I
didn't want to do what the Lord wanted. I hope I
never get another one like that!" Though she had
prophesied in other contexts, this was Ursula's
only experience of a personal prophecy. When I
asked her for a criteria of genuine prophecy, she
provided five which restated the comments of many:

        First, there's an urging in the context
    of what the Lord is trying to teach. The
    prophecy is related to the work of the Lord;
    it's timely. Second, through faith and dis-
    cernment you believe it's God's Word, not
    yours. It didn't come from a plan or idea
    you had. You have a strong sense that the
    Word is from the Lord. Third, you know He's
    gonna give you the Words. You have a mental
    sense of a message. Fourth is the delivery.
    You have to put it in words that will convey
    that message. The urging of the Spirit to
    give the message is very much a part of the
    experience. Fifth is the clarity. The Lord
    gives the gift of the ability to give the

                        146

prophecy with clarity.

This is a useful list because it provides a chance
to recapitulate some of the characteristics previously discussed under personal prophecy, but obviously applying more broadly. Ursula, Thomas and
Victor have all been quoted as experiencing the
urgency or need to speak. They remind one of the
words of Ned, Chuck and Geraldine about anointings
and their physical accompaniments. We shall say
more later about the gift of discernment (Ursula's
second point), but here we can recall proposition
seven where it was noted that through discernment
one distinguishes between the Lord's Word, one's
own thought, and promptings of "the Evil One."
Quentin and Ned, however, both spoke about the
differences between one's own thoughts and the
word patterns in a prophecy. More will be sub-
joined immediately below concerning Ursula's third
point about how it feels to be given a message,
and about the remaining points concerning style of
delivery and clarity.

Julie had been baptized in the Spirit three
years and a few months before our interview.
Early in her new life she had felt as though the
Lord wanted to speak and "I didn't know enough to
be afraid to prophesy." She had started hearing
words in her mind over and over again till she
felt as though she needed to speak them out to her
Life in the Spirit seminar. "I would sit with my
eyes closed. There were no physical feelings
then." The following Fall term found her in a
dormitory household and scared now at the awesomeness of the gift. She didn't want to speak the
Lord's Word "impurely" or at the wrong time. Now
she would feel butterflies in her stomach before a
large group, but she could tell when "I'm just
thinking or it's the Lord's Word." She would prophesy in a household, at subcommunity gatherings,
or over people for the Baptism in the Spirit or
who asked for prayer. (The prophecy quoted above
for Isidore was delivered by someone in just such
a prayer context of a small group of students
praying for one another.) Somewhat

counterphobically she exclaimed, "The more nervous
I was, the more sure I was I should give the word.
I was young in the Lord, but there was only two of
us doing it." She felt responsible. She would be
getting a sense of the message and knowing the
words as she went along. When I inquired what
themes predominated in those early days, Julie
replied:

> It was different depending on who we
> were praying over. For unsure people, the
> Lord spoke words of reassurance. I didn't
> get any "Repent, sinner" prophecies! There
> were directive prophecies like "Pray more for
> X-virtue" or "Pay more attention to the
> Lord's Cross and Resurrection."

Early in the Spring of 1972, one of the leaders in the Community met with the prophets to discuss problems in prophecy and attitudes toward the
gift. (This is the first attempt, which this researcher was able to discover, to move toward institutionalization of this gift. The Community
would not be five years old until the following
October. Out of this and subsequent meetings
would grow the "prophecy group" and the circle of
recognized prophets for public gatherings.) Problems such as not giving the Word because one was
afraid, not giving it clearly, not knowing when to
give it, were aired and discussed. The group was
instructed to exercise the gift freely and listen
to the older prophets. I asked whether the Community elder was concerned about content. Her
reply:

> No. The leader of a prayer meeting
> should later discern a prophecy. You don't
> have to discern it, just give it. He didn't
> ever contradict me, but he did others. It
> would be clear that the stuff they prophesied
> wasn't from the Lord, but a non-prophecy. It
> didn't fit in with what the Lord was saying.

The leader would be fairly certain that it
wasn't right. I would pray and ask the Lord
to quiet people so I could prophesy. It was
like sitting and listening. There would be
certain specific words and phrases the Lord
wanted to use.

We shall return later to Julie's story because she
provides a clear discussion of the history of the
prophecy group, but here the focus is on the experience of giving a prophecy. The principle is
clearly enunciated here: the prophet is to speak
out; it is the function of the leader to discern
the prophecy's applicability, not the prophet's
role. We note another conflict in this calling:
besides the tension between inner urgency and timidity, there is an expectation latent in all prophets that they could be told by a leader that
their prophecy is impure, not the Lord's wish for
this particular time, etc.
     Quentin's comments reinforce Julie's but de-
rive from someone not appointed to the official
prophecy team. By reading between the lines, we
can tease out the influence of Community socialization from the spontaneous experience.

          In a spoken prophecy, I experience pray-
     ing and receiving a clear idea of what needs
     to happen, or what the group needs to under-
     stand. For a long time, I just experienced
     frustration at not knowing what to do with
     this. I was built-up when others would share
     what I was thinking about. I can't work up
     the right set of vibrations. At alot of
     meetings I don't get anything no matter how
     much I seek what the Lord wants to do. When
     I do prophesy, I might get the first few
     words, then a sentence at a time, a thought
     at a time. I'm in the middle and don't have
     a clear sense of where I'm going or where
     I've been, just a sense that I'm being led
     logically with lines coming spontaneously. I
     prophesy at district gatherings, and

households, but never at General Community gatherings. (Why not?) Partially because I'm chicken, not old enough, mature enough in the gift. (Your understanding of maturity?) Not being centered on yourself with the temptation to think, What if God stops? Maturing means becoming able to listen to the Lord and having some self-confidence that you <u>can</u> hear the Lord even if the idea comes from out of the blue!

From listening to both Julie and Quentin, we gather that a prophet moving with the flow of a meeting, or in tune with the life and needs of an individual for whom s/he is praying, suddenly intuits a "sense from the Lord" about a message for the individual or the group. This sense takes concrete shape in the form of a few words or sentences, but no more. The prophet must embark courageously on the proclamation with trust in the Lord that He will see him through to the end of the speech; that it will be preserved and protected from any influence of the prophet's own desires, ideas, or any other contaminating influence; that even if the content makes little sense to the immediate recipient (as in Ursula's frightening revelation), the prophecy must be told forth. Then it is up to the leaders to "discern" how the Community is to respond to the Word. We recall from Julie's biography that a leader had once admonished her for a "too Catholic" prophecy, and for changing the direction of a meeting without consulting him first. (But we are getting ahead of ourselves here: it is only later in the history of the group that a prophet must <u>antecedently</u> consult the leader of the prayer meeting before proclaiming the prophecy. Earlier on, the prophets were simply to speak "boldly" and discernment would <u>follow</u> rather than precede delivery.) Yet already in the first gathering of the prophets with an elder, there is contained an instruction to listen to the more experienced prophets to see how they speak and so to learn from them, apprentice-fashion. In Quentin's statement,

150

we see reflected the Community's practice of encouraging novice prophets to try their wings in small groups where, presumably, they would have fewer distractions from nervousness, and a wrong direction would not influence the larger body; but only "mature" prophets may speak at the large gatherings. Among his characteristics for maturity, Quentin fails to mention explicit approval by the central board of coordinators, but lists only the subjective criteria from the side of the prophet!

Ned, because he had joined the Community so early in its history, provides a nice summary statement of the prophetic experience prior to its greater institutionalization:

> When I prophesy to others, I feel minor physical manifestations, but mainly a psychological sensation of "God wants me to say something," I have conscious knowledge of the first word or two; after that, it's open. I have to surrender to trusting that the Lord will say what He wants. The validation is my internal sense that it's correct. I have no responsibility to see that what I say becomes law for the hearers: this makes me comfortable. The message content is not my own, but it is phrased in my own language, experience, my understanding. The Lord uses me and my experience as a vehicle of His message. There are visceral sensations of tension -- in your gut, you know: like wanting to implement a new program, or having an interview before your boss.

Earlier we had pointed to the inner conflicts in the prophetic vocation. Here at least is a note of consolation: the prophet is not charged with enforcing His word, only with delivering it.

Thus far we have been moving through a consideration of the characteristics of personal prophecy and prophetic delivery to a small group. Logically, we should move now to an understanding

151

of proclaiming a prophecy before the whole WoG Community, and we shall combine this study with an analysis of the evolution of the "prophecy team" or "prophecy group" since the four main informants about both topics are the same; namely, Julie, Daphne, Geraldine and Sheila. We shall continue Julie's narrative interrupted a few moments ago concerning the history of prophets' meetings.

In November of 1973 (Sheila remembers the date as 1972, a date confirmed by others) Bruce Yocum, the author of the handbook on prophecy cited above in chapter one, called together a group of persons who prophesied frequently so as to give them a chance to share together and grow in the gift of prophecy. These friends gathered every other week for an hour and a half of prayer. About twenty prophecies, on the average, would be spoken at such a gathering. At the end of each meeting, Julie recalls, there would be time set aside to discuss "what the Lord had said." At other meetings of the group, topics would be assigned for discussion such as overcoming one's fears, the direction in which the Lord was leading the Community, the role of prophets, a prepared list of biblical citations on the Word of the Lord in Scripture. Because her regular prophecies in the subcommunity had been heard, Julie was invited to the group by a coordinator. I asked her what changes she had noted in herself, and she first stated that she had gotten more sure of herself, and her prophecies had gotten better; she sensed that she was able to hear the Lord more clearly. Again at this part of the interview, she repeated what she had stated previously: her prophecies to groups (as to individuals) contained assurances from God that He was pleased with the behavior of a group, and directives to the group on how best to function. "For example, I got prophecies about service for the service-team; for the child-care group, I received things the Lord wanted for the kids, for us (the child-care workers), for the parents."

On the prophecy team, the members would discuss what was going on in each others' personal lives and pray over each other. Replying to my query about how she felt she had benefited from the meetings. Julie responded enthusiastically that these were "my favorite meetings ever!" (In a community with meetings of one form or another almost every evening and on weekends, this is quite some praise!) She claimed to have felt the Spirit present. "I talked about my problems, fears, questions. Others did too." Members would practice "stirring" of the gift, that is, would ask the Lord to speak through them. "I'm here, Lord, eager to speak your word. It was deep, rich prayer, and the meetings were fun too: we all got along." The meetings seemed to follow the school calendar and stopped for the summer, but would resume for the Fall.

The next change documented by Julie (without being asked) was the appointment of official prophets for the public Thursday night prayer meetings. Her explanation of this decision by the leaders was that "it's easy for the body to receive the Word of the Lord if it comes from a familiar voice, from someone older in the gift." Only five people in the Yocum group were not appointed to become Thursday-prophets. The latter would meet before a prayer meeting and pray as a group. (For terminological clarity, we shall refer to the Yocum group as the "prophecy team," and the special Thursday appointees as "official prophets.")

Daphne repeated many of Julie's observations, but her story adds further interesting nuances.

After Daphne's conversion (reviewed above in the biographical section) when she had first come to the Community, she had known about the spiritual gifts. At the meeting when somebody had prophesied, she had been impressed. "It could be from God," she mused. "If God was gonna speak, that might be the way He talks." She had prayed at a meeting that God give her a sign that the next prophecy really was from Him. This was a crucial experience for Daphne: "It was four years ago last October. I had a sense that a person was gonna prophesy. He did, and it was 'I want you to come to me right now. If you wait, it'll be too late.'"

Originally, despite her own conversion experience, Daphne had been skeptical of the prophets' claims. A woman friend of hers in the dorm claimed she could hear God talking to her mind. "I felt, 'Oh dear, you poor thing. She's kinda emotional.'" In her own life, nevertheless, she did experience "God's really being present in the room (where she was praying). I have an underlying sense of God's presence all the time. God's around. It's a stronger sense in prayer." The phrase, "My yoke is easy and my burden light," came to her mind. That this was really God's special Word to her was confirmed soon afterwards when she attended the annual Charismatics' Conference at Notre Dame and this scriptural text was the theme of the Conference. (Again, as with Ned previously, no sense was conveyed that there was any stretching of logic or time between event and interpretation.)

Three days after first hearing the phrase, she sat down at a prayer meeting, closed her eyes, was struck by the presence of God and wanted to respond. She felt that the Lord was giving a message to the group through her. "I didn't prophesy because everyone else was. The content was that the Lord wanted to give us all His gifts, and He didn't want us to limit His gifts." After the meeting she had felt badly that she had not gotten the Word out, but still her sense of God's presence was great: "I didn't have an 'or else' sense about it." Her first actual delivery of a prophecy was to a single individual with whom she was praying. Three components of the experience are still with her; first, a sense of God's presense; second, that some response was wanted by God; third, a sense of some part of the message, some of the words God said; namely, "I'll give you the desire of your heart because the desire of your heart is me."

Daphne got practice after this in a small group context. As a household head, she often experienced a prophetic message. The themes of her pronouncements tended to be personal because (according to her interpretation) she was a "greeter" (someone assigned to formally welcome new members

154

during their seven week Life in the Spirit Seminar), was assigned to pray over people for the Baptism in the Spirit, and was head of one of the service teams. Most of her prophecies tended to be "about love and trust rather than 'repent.'"

Her first prophecy before a large group occurred two years before our conversation, at a subcommunity gathering. Daphne recalled experiencing turmoil in her life and in her prophetic calling. She recalled needing confidence in hearing God's Word and in her ability to give it. What helped was "having good discernment about my prophecies from my coordinator." For example, a coordinator had told Daphne that she spoke out her own convictions instead of "resting on" God's power, for example, by saying words which conveyed the implication "This is God's Word, and furthermore I think it's true!" (This experience contrasts with Julie's who had happily exclaimed that no coordinator had ever criticized her except when a "too Catholic" prophecy had changed the direction of a meeting.) Daphne had felt fear of giving prophecies at a large gathering. "I could be wrong and lead people astray." After her first public prophecy, a girl had told her, "I didn't have the same sense you did." This made her cautious. Yet her timidity was countered by the internal sense she was give beforehand about whether the Lord was going to speak through tongues, song or prophecy. At one meeting she sensed that the Lord wanted someone to prophesy immediately, so she plunged in and did. The year previous to our conversation marked Daphne's full exercise of the gift. After giving a prophecy whose theme was "I love you alot, but you should trust Me more," a coordinator had encouraged her by suggesting that "The Lord wants to hear more about lack of trust." Daphne's understanding of the permission required to prophesy at a public gathering was advice about whether or not a particular prophecy was appropriate right at that moment. She had been invited on to the prophecy team by its founder, Bruce Yocum, after she had been prophesying more and more regularly. She added the information that the text of his book was used sometimes by the

group for its discussions. An example of a prophecy given just to the prophets was also volunteered by Daphne, "The Lord said a few weeks ago
that we need a deeper sense of awe before the
Lord, respect for His Power." A coordinator discerned that the Lord wanted to teach the whole
Community about this revelation. Daphne is one of
the special appointees to the Thursday group of
official prophets.

In listening to Daphne's testimony, we are
struck by the interplay between the subject's
growing confidence in herself, the gentle leadership of the coordinator, and the inner subjective
"sense from the Lord," or "Lord's leading" her
into fuller use of prophecy. Whereas Julie needed
moderation in her exercise of the gift, Daphne required encouragement which was provided.

Geraldine's story repeats some of the details
and features of both Julie's and Daphne's, but of
course is highly unique. She, like many others
quoted thus far, relates that, at this point in
her development, there is no emotional experience
but rather a "clear sense" of what the Lord might
want to do. "It's not necessarily a direct word
now, but when I first began, it was a direct
word." This sense of what God is going to do
(somewhat parallel to Daphne's sense of the presence of God) is operative for Geraldine not just
at prayer meetings, but "when I'm praying, or even
walking down the street." The sense of what the
Lord will have her to say is related to "how other things are going in my life: reading Scripture; daily prayer; emotional ups and downs." She
claims more confidence now than earlier in using
the gift. She is eager for the direction provided by "headship." She estimates that "maybe
half of what you say could be from the Lord." She
accepts the fact that prophecy can be imperfect,
but knows it can "get purified." When asked to
describe in her own words a particular experience
of prophecy, she remembered giving a prophecy to
the Community in November, 1974 about the "Lord
calling us to ministry to the world, outside the
Community." Simultaneously there had been a
"pull" within her indicating that this couldn't be

156

right. "But it was clear. I had a feeling I wasn't at a gathering, but in a more direct union or communion with the Lord than I've felt otherwise." As she was supposed to do, she asked the coordinator sitting next to her to pray for discernment. But the sense was clear, intense, directive. "I felt like the Lord wanted to say this for sure. But afterwards I was most doubtful." Comfortably self-critical, Geraldine commented that the delivery was overly long, with some repetitions she didn't need to say, but she stuck to her story that she was sure of the direction. (This prophecy was fulfilled among other ways when in the Fall of 1976 the Community did send thirty of its members to Brussels to work with a struggling group there. Geraldine did not know of these plans at the time of the prophecy, nor at the time of the interview.)

Geraldine states that she gets this very clear sense once or twice a month:

> The times I experience this most are when other things are going very peacefully and are not cluttered. I don't look for the clarity, and don't prophesy just when I experience this, but at other times too. Before I go to a gathering, I have a clear sense of the area where the Lord will be speaking or healing. I'll have an idea of the direction the gathering will be going. I'll be praying that the Lord's Word will come through. Lately I've been prophesying without knowing all that the Lord will say. I used to spend alot of time figuring out what to say. I don't think it's a good thing to do: you can discern yourself to death!

As one of the official prophets, she feels responsible for the Thursday gatherings, but notes sensibly that it isn't necessarily right to give a prophecy just because one has a sense of what the Lord is going to say. The point may come out in a talk or a person's sharing his life's experiences

157

just as well.

Like Julie, Geraldine attributed her own growth in the gift and its good functioning in the Community to the prophecy team's meetings every other week. "We share personal experiences while we're praying; we share everything: how we experience the Lord working in us." If one sensed something going on in the Community, he would share it with the others. (Thus the group serves as a monitoring device by means of which the coordinators are advised of even the most subtle ripple of mood change within the prophecy team and WoG at large. This intimate sharing also would provide encouragement for a prophet should s/he decide to offer a pronouncement at the larger group gathering.)

Geraldine also volunteered some information concerning the sort of feedback she was provided by the coordinators. Concerning one of her prophecies she was informed, "The first part was what the Lord wanted; the second part you added from your own mind." She confessed that when she feels awkward about ending, she adds. "since I'm expressive as a person and intense, as things get taken care of in my life, especially emotionally, prophecy will get more pure, clear, settled."

Trying to get her to describe this sense of the Lord's leading, I asked her how she was sure that a Word came from the Lord. Her response:

> The way I'm most sure is that I experience a kind of conviction, knowingness that the Lord wants to say this in this situation. Also in the response people give -- If the Lord wants people to experience something and they do receive His goodness, or if worship is directed by the Word. Sometimes I know it's from the Lord because of faith, but I turn also to my heads and to other people. It's my faith that prophecy is for upbuilding of the body and not for personal gain.

Sheila, finally, presents the case of a

158

person who was given the gift of prophecy without
having ever heard about it previously. At the
time of the interview, she was a member both of
the prophecy team and the official prophets, but
seven years previously she had never heard of prophecy.

> My first experience of prophecy happened
> soon after I first turned my life over to the
> Lord. I was praying after Mass in chapel.
> Besides personal hassles, I was worried over
> my mother's health. I felt very clearly
> something outside myself speaking very clear-
> ly about my mother's health. The Lord told
> me to stop thinking and kneel down and listen
> to Him. I was skeptical of people who
> claimed to hear the Lord. I remember think-
> ing, "I must be thinking this up." My re-
> lationship with God was very distant then:
> I used to ask myself, "Is He real?" A friend
> came in then. It was like a large voice any-
> one could hear. It shook me up alot. I got
> up and left -- it frightened me. The friend
> asked, "Are you O.K.?" The priest asked me
> the same thing. Then I began to "prophesy,"
> in the form, "God said this; I said that."
> Later that evening the priest felt I'd gotten
> the gift of prophecy. I was afraid of the
> gifts and didn't use it for two or three
> years till I came here.

After leaving college where this event had
happened, Sheila had a similar experience as a
young teacher. Again it was in a chapel but this
time there was a physical "anointing," a feeling
of God touching her on the shoulder, like a shock.
Having arrived at Ann Arbor, she was encouraged by
a coordinator to use the gift. She had had many
doubts. She thought it was a "heavy thing," but
now feels it is quite natural, and is as at ease
with it as "in praying in tongues or reading
Scripture." Use of the gift grew in conjunction
with her spiritual life as she grew in her

159

knowledge of the Lord's love for her and the body's love for her. She appreciates the encouragement she got especially in the 1972 meetings with the other prophets. "It was good to hear other people's apprehensions, doubts, victories."

At first, Sheila found it harder to control the physical reactions to feeling the urge to speak: these were not an anointing, but rapid heartbeat, foot-tapping and chest-heaving indicating fear about speaking. Her style of delivery evolved over time. She used to think there was only one right way to speak: solemnly. It was hard for her to understand that on some occasions God speaks in different ways. She had to learn how to "let the Lord use you so the Word comes across in the right way: by singing out softly and sweetly, or loudly and boldly." She was encouraged and found that various modes worked. When she felt very detached personally from the Word, she spoke calmly. When she was personally affected, it came across differently. She wants to make her prophecies shorter. Usually she has only a couple of words, occasionally just the sense. When younger in the gift, she would stumble a lot. Her fluency grew "partially through the response of the body, mostly from a sense from the Lord that 'That's right on to exactly what I wanted to say.'" Sometimes after speaking, she may have a sense that there is more to be proclaimed, and then others at the meeting will say it. During a prophecy, she feels the power of the Lord. Afterwards she might feel weak, or occasionally like wanting to dance. Sometimes she prophesies just to herself. "God's Word, when spoken precisely and simply, puts us in a wavelength of connection with the Lord." If it's a hard saying, she admits difficulty yielding to it as when having to pronounce repentance prophecies. More recently, she has felt a real connection between prophecy and the whole of her life: "I feel a direct sense from the Lord on how to proceed or not to proceed."

Sheila uses her gift in many contexts. The following brief vignette shows Sheila working with an individual.

160

Prophecy works really powerfully for individuals. I get a sense of how God really loves them. I still have trouble with authority figures and older people. At the women's retreat last Spring God spoke through me to a woman about her love, her holiness. She wept. The Lord said to me "You respect that woman just because she's lived that long and is precious to me."

Interested in discovering just how the prophets' sense of "the Lord" differed from their own cognitive processes, I received the following simple reply from Sheila: "It feels better when the Lord does it. I feel more peace, clarity, precision, confidence. When I prophesy over somebody, there's a real confidence that now or twenty years from now there would be fruit."

Addressing the same point, Betty made some comments with her typical humor. She spoke about a definite "spiritual communication" in her spirit an experience which usually happened when she consciously opened herself to it. The previous Fall, her "head" (spiritual counselor in WoG) had admonished her to "quit trying to hear the Lord." Her understanding of the reason behind this unusual directive was as an aid to making her more, not less, like other people. "I was to stop talking to angels!" Because she was actively seeking spiritual revelations, she was getting them: they did not help her relationship with the Community, but were "just a neat thing," and were alienating her from the group, it was felt. Once she was praying in church and

. . . the Lord told me how much He loved me: "Quit praising me for a minute; I want to tell you how much I love you."

"No, Lord," I said. "I'm not allowed to hear you."

"I don't care," He said and went on

talking.

I said "O.K." and a spiritual communication went on. There's a difference when you
remind yourself of stuff and when the Lord
does. It makes more of an impression --
words like "deeper, richer, fuller," deeper
especially.

Before summarizing these varied comments concerning prophecy, we shall provide some information about other different but similar spiritual
gifts; namely, "Word of Wisdom," "Word of Knowledge," "Discernment" and "Interpretation of
Tongues."
It was difficult to formulate a precise difference from subjects' reports between Word of
Wisdom and Word of Knowledge (hereafter abbrevi-
ated WW and WK respectively). The articulation of
the distinction provided above in propositions
nine and ten was not repeated by all since the
terms were somewhat indiscriminately employed.
Nevertheless, the inward experiences just reviewed
for prophecy in its various contexts seem to accompany both WW and WK with the content or the
recipient of the Word determining whether it was
"Wisdom" or "Knowledge." Ned, a man with a sense
for subtle distinctions, volunteered that a "WW is
a prophetic Word or message that tends to be situation-specific as opposed to a more universal
Word." Quentin uses the term WW in the sense of
an "understanding of the causes behind stuff. Our
overall coordinator understands what makes things
work." Daphne phrased the distinction this way:
"A WW is the revelation of a spiritual truth as
related to our personal lives, for example
Christ's Resurrection. A WK is specific, about
an individual."
Examples will concretize this. Both Daphne
and Victor related a dramatic story, perhaps concerning the same gathering. A person at a prayer
meeting was given a WK that "someone here was involved in homosexuality. God wants it to stop because He loves you." The Community prayed for the

162

person and the meeting continued. At the end of the meeting, a young man got up and publicly admitted, "I'm the person. Please pray for me." According to Victor, the young man had his life turned around by this experience. Now married, he "does lots of service for the Community." Victor went on to illustrate other instances. At public gatherings, a person with a WK will announce that "someone here has a certain illness" and describe the ailment. The sufferer will be invited to come forward to be prayed over for healing. Prayers will be offered whether or not someone confirms s/he is the intended beneficiary of the group's concern. Or someone will rise and say, "The Lord gave me <u>this</u> Word. Does it mean anything to anybody?"

Quite often WK is conferred in a counseling relationship as the following reminiscences of Paula and Lois indicate.

Paula, when she had been a high school student, had found herself looked up to as the oldest in a group, and thus was approached by people with problems. "Without knowing what to say or much bible knowledge, I experienced almost supernatural knowledge of what to say!" Girls her age and under would seek her aid to decide what they should do with the rest of their lives. Should they go to college or get married? "I'd say, 'What are your gifts?'" She would ask questions concerning their readiness for the marriage commitment, their sense of direction for themselves in serving the Lord in a career or family situation. She would give advice about problems relating to parents who didn't understand their new Christian lives. She would tell them about "obedience and headship even though I didn't know much about it at all." Her source of Knowledge? "Reading Scripture and the sense I had." (Paula used this word, "sense," with the same connotations implied by the prophets in their employment of the term.) She would suggest that while under their parents' roof, they were obliged to submit to headship and obey, but could make their own decisions if they lived elsewhere. Regarding relationship counseling, she recommended that they be "not too heavy in high

163

school because the students couldn't make a permanent commitment. There were to be no physical relationships -- but that was difficult to keep." Paula would also warn of young people's financial difficulties in supporting themselves.

One could view this testimony from several angles. A minimalist interpretation would see mere common sense in action. Anyone familiar with high school students might be impressed with the extraordinary concern she showed and trust she evoked: while parents might get a deaf ear to such counsel, Paula was sought out and heeded. Paula's viewpoint is supernaturalistic: groping her way along almost like a prophet in the midst of a proclamation, she was given a WK to aid her brothers and sisters in their need.

Somewhat more spectacular are Lois's "interior visions." A young man has shared his concerns with her about where he stood with the Lord; was he "in the Kingdom or wasn't he?"

. . . I prayed for a way to answer him or to put off his questioning in a way that wouldn't hurt him. The Lord gave me a vision of a large banquet hall with people seated passing food to each other. The boy was walking up and down, not taking a seat nor letting himself be served, but picking at the food a little bit here, a little there. This meant a great deal to him.

Another time a person was annoying me, behaving in a childish way. I saw him, almost visually, as a child, eight or nine years old. My irritation vanished with this change of perspective.

Another young man who heard I had some of these abilities came with a problem. As he presented it, it sounded like fornication. Yet I seemed to hear it as a problem of dishonesty. He stated that he was unsure he wanted to marry his fiancee. He worried about how she would take his Christian life

164

and what it meant to him. I felt he was trying to trap himself into a marriage. I
heard a voice within me which was respecting
his privacy and giving me just enough to know
a bit more than he said.

He said, "It's a problem of fornication."

A voice within me said, "That's not
all."

I asked, "Is there any area you're not
being honest? Are you doing anything to prevent a pregnancy?"

"No."

"What should you do?" I asked.

"The only thing to do is get married."

We prayed for his courage to tell her.
Unfortunately, other things happened. She
got pregnant, they married and dropped out of
the Community.

This is a new gift for me: I get a picture. The coordinators asked me not to use
direct prophecy, but I may use the third-
person way, such as "The Lord seems to me to
be saying X." In prophecy there's too much
chance for evil spirits. My own and the other party's ability to be objective is un-
certain.

The reference to "evil spirits" will be dealt
with more fully in the section below concerning
deliverance. Lois described her experience with
these interior visions. Their suddeness and viv-
idness were the crucial differentiating factors.
After realizing that they were fairly reliable,
she would ask for them inwardly, would ask explicitly for a word, a picture, or "an indefinable

sense like, 'Be very gentle.'" This prayer always gets answered, but never in the same way.
"The Lord can't be poured into any specific mold."
When questioned whether she would call this process discernment, or WW, or WK, she confessed that
she didn't know such distinctions, but then said
she never experienced a WK like "That young man,
aged thirty, has a problem with his left foot."
(This statement reveals the common understanding
of WK.) Her final description of her gift noted
"the speed with which it comes and the very distinctive nature of it. When I saw the picture of
the banquet, it's like turning on the T.V.: you
can't change the picture as in ordinary imagining."

Geraldine's statements showed how WK usually
works at a Community gathering. A brother at a
prayer meeting had been given a WK that a married
couple in attendance was experiencing fears about
the Community and was thinking of calling it quits
and leaving. During the gathering, the brother
had gotten up and shared his Word. Afterwards, a
couple approached him and identified themselves as
having been on the point of leaving the group until he had spoken out.

At the meeting just prior to our interview,
she had felt a WK concerning a growth in someone's
throat. She told the leader at the beginning of
the prayer meeting, and ten minutes later he had
asked her to share about this with the group. She
also sensed "a man with stomach problems needing
healing." She delivered this WK in prophecy form,
and that evening two people with stomach problems
came to the "healing prayer room," but during the
prayer "I felt like it wasn't them." The last man
asking for prayers said he'd had an ulcer all his
life, and Geraldine "felt like He was the man."
Yet the individual with the throat problem never
showed up.

Ned too was given the gift of WK and used it
in counseling situations. He defines WK as a
knowledge of a person and his life, an intuitive
knowing of facts about a person's past before
coming to town. For example, he had known about
the pain of a "bad love affair" of one of his

counselees before being told about it. "It's like an intuition except that I really did know." When living in one of the Community's guest houses, he sensed that he had helped about half of "all kinds of strange people who came there." One man had been suicidal, "massively depressed with his life falling apart." The man's spiritual director in another state had heard a speech by a Community coordinator, had sent the man to Ann Arbor, and the man arrived at Ned's guest house. The man had stayed for three months, gotten married, holds a job, and in five years exhibited no depressive tendencies nor rash choices. "Rarely in the mental health field do people go from depressive suicidals to health in three months." During that time, Ned spoke in prophecy to him, told him what to do, constructed a "regime milieu," exhorted him, "You can't be depressed or suicidal here."

A psychologist would describe this as an intensive effort at behavioral modification in a supportive environment whereas Ned, whose psychological sophistication was the highest among the subjects, attributed the success to prophecy and WK.

Moving on from WW and WK to "Discernment," we note that many subjects have already spoken about this gift. By means of discernment, subjects sense when a Word is from the Lord or from themselves. Through discernment, prophets know how a meeting will proceed, and coordinators will intuit whether or not a prophecy should be given, whether it is "pure" and a genuine Word from the Lord. The internal experience of subjects discussing discernment seemed exactly like that of prophecy although it did not issue in a pronouncement, but in the coordinators' case would be expressed in a directive, and in a subordinate's situation, in a judgment about how next to behave.

To cite just a few examples: Chuck spoke of "times when you wonder which way to go; you don't get a real feeling one way or the other. Discernment comes after examining the two: it isn't knowing the consequences, but feeling that something beyond consequences is better."

Some might label Olga's discernment a WK, but

167

the name is not as important as the event. Discernment happens for her "in cases where I'm talking with someone and they're talking with me and I know they're leaving something out. I'll know what they're leaving out. I'll be directed to ask leading questions." For example, a couple was having some problems and the wife was saying "He does this, he does that." She left out the whole area of her input. Olga knew what it was and told her so. This gift is seen as "important for future types of development work the Lord wants to do." Another time she welcomed a troubled person into her home overnight. The Lord gave her directions on what to do. "A friend who worked at a state hospital told me, 'You did everything right.' Yet I'd had no training!" Describing her discernment, Olga comments

. . . In my head there's this knowledge. I feel compelled to share. That married lady was angry at first. Two days later she called me and admitted, "I really needed to hear you say that." To my knowledge this sense has never led me wrong. I focus not on the person but on the Lord. The experience is not always preceded by a prayer, but is not without a prayer. It's more operative when my entire life-space is more conscious of the Lord.

Discernment is also used in exorcism rituals, but will be covered below in the section on deliverance where the deliverer gets a sense concerning just what evil spirits are operating in a person's life.

The last gift similar to prophecy is "Interpretation of Tongues." It is clear to anyone attending even a single prayer meeting that glossolalia is employed in two contexts. Most frequently, an individual or group speaks or sings prayers of praise to God in babbling syllables called "tongues" and thought to be ancient, foreign, or extinct languages inspired by the Holy Spirit.

(See proposition five above.) Secondly and less frequently, someone will speak out a "message" to the Community and use this same garbled speech. After completing the delivery, the same person or someone else, after a silent pause of a few moments, will "interpret the tongue" in the vernacular for all to comprehend and obey. Very rarely is it claimed that the second statement is a "translation" of the first, but rather an interpretation of the Lord's message. Victor recounts his experience with the gift in a prayer group in another city where he first came into the Renewal:

> . . . I remember in _____ that we never had a message in tongues or an interpretation. I had heard of the phenomenon from people outside the Movement. We felt it should happen, but nobody was excited about being the one to do it. One night I knew it had to happen. I spoke out in tongues. I held my breath for what seemed like three minutes. Somebody else gave the interpretation.
>
> That's gone away here, that particular spiritual gift. Now there's not much urgency for it.

Julie, one of the prophets, remembered interpreting tongues for several meetings a year and a half before our discussion. "The Lord gave me the Word as this guy spoke out. I did a sort of teamwork with him." Daphne remembered once getting an interpretation of a message even before the Word was spoken. Then someone gave a speech in tongues she spoke out the interpretation, and the person employing glossolalia "confirmed" that her interpretation was accurate and in accord with his own sense of the message.

This concludes our presentation of personalized reports concerning prophecy and related spiritual gifts. Before moving on to the area of healing, we might offer a few organizing comments (but save the main interpretative summary for the chapter which follows). First, let it be noted that every subject except Frank, Max and Roberta contributed some materials from his/her experience of these gifts.

Secondly, not all the materials from each were quoted, but only a representative sample of comments. Many more anecdotes could have been included, but all were included which diverged in any way from the main thread of the story (for example, the different ways of labeling what has variously been called WK, discernment and interior vision). Hence, the quotations and stories included represent the unanimous experience of these subjects -- with the exceptions noted -- and, therefore, are typical of WoG members.

Next, we refer the reader back to the propositions at the beginning of this section so that s/he may see whether the data presented support the suggested generalizations. (See especially propositions one through seven, nine and ten.)

Fourthly, we may comment that the five gifts above (prophecy, WW, WK, discernment and interpretation of tongues) differ in the ways they are exercised, used and understood, but are similar in that their "essence" (in Husserl's and all the phenomenologists' sense) lies in an experience of interpersonal communication with the Divine. However, a theist/atheist explains or explains away this reported experience, the subjects themselves are firmly convinced of its validity with a knowledge that is rooted in a whole set of personal and communally shared "marvels and wonders." For these people, proposition one, for example, concerning God's existence, has an existential validity: for them, a "proof" for the existence of God by means of reasoned argument would be a hollow shadow of their deeply felt interpersonal relationship with Him whom they name, with fond familiarity yet reverential awe, "the Lord." Their experience of all of the "gifts" come in response to His promptings (proposition two) rather than being something they initiate. The prophet, therefore, is most crucial for the community because through him comes direction for individuals and for the

170

group about how the Lord wants concrete behavior, and even thoughts and feelings, guided and directed. WoG participants, then, are not persons whose religious experience focuses on a creed, a code, or the cult: while they have their dogmas, their rather strict ethic, and their public religious ceremonial, all this remains commentary to the essential and crucial relationship of each and of the whole body with the Lord. Granted the shaping effects of socialization and institutionalization, there still remains room for the individual and the group to hear a new Word and change direction radically. In prophecy, and its related gifts, there occurs a dynamic interplay between the inner and outer words: between the body and spirit of the prophet; between his physical anointing/urging and his natural timidity to speak out; between the word spoken and the discernment of the leader in a group prophecy; between the encouraging and exhortatory contents and themes; between the prophet whose only duty is to proclaim and the community whose primary duty is to obey; between the clarity and "boldness" required in articulated proclamation and the usually vague and hazy "sense" of the message. Our task in the final chapter will be to reflect upon the implications of this data psychologically; here, we wish only to order and arrange it somewhat.

Healing

Members of WoG use this term for two different but related spiritual gifts:

(1) Healing of memories, by which is meant the removal of subjective pain surrounding memories of past events, plus the termination of reactive effects on others like bitterness to family members, inability to relate lovingly with one's parents, etc.

(2) Physical healings of all sorts of body ailments, major and minor. In discussing their

171

healings, subjects often spoke about both types occurring together. To parallel the presentation of the materials contained in the previous section on prophecy, we shall speak first of the experience of being healed; then about praying for another's healing; then about the healing team; finally, we shall handle some related topics such as how these persons deal with healings which have been prayed for and perhaps prophesied but not accomplished.

The following table presents a partial summary of the physical healings claimed by the subjects of this research. The list is partial because subjects were requested to concentrate especially on one instance of healing, but would frequently spontaneously relate others. (See Table I.)

TABLE I

LIST OF PHYSICAL HEALINGS

Abigail:	myopia; gastro-enteritis; bronchitis; emphysema; high blood pressure
Betty:	stomach aches; dislocated kneecap; sore throat; nerve spasms
Chuck:	headaches; pulled tendon
Daphne:	asthma; swollen tonsils
Elaine:	pain in back and legs from strain in furniture-moving; ingrown toenail healed without surgery
Geraldine:	strep throat
Karen:	severely cut foot; chipped bone in ankle; dislocated kneecap
Lois:	cancer

Max:	wife and children healed of severe ear infection; allergies; visual perception problems; tumor
Ned:	leg lengthened
Olga:	leg lengthened
Paula:	hereditary degenerative bone-disease
Quentin:	food allergies
Roberta:	myopia
Sheila:	pregnancy-related pain; child's ear infection
Thomas:	kidney infections; asthma; arthritis
Ursula:	leg lengthened; lower back pain

All of these healings will not be narrated because, while the particular maladies and symptoms vary widely, the procedures employed in the healings and the internal states of the healees are quite similar and so concentration can be directed to technique and psychological mind-set.

At the outset, we can recall the distinction (noted in the literature review) by Oursler and Nolen between "functional" and "organic" cures. Physicians at Lourdes call "miraculous" only the healing of an organic disease which must continue for at least a year without regression (Oursler, 1957, p. 52). Nolen declared that all the healings he had investigated were for functional ailments. Most probably, Nolen would classify most of the healings in the list above as functional. Therefore, when subjects speak of "miraculous" healings, they do so not in the narrowly medical sense, but in the theological context outlined by Macquarrie (1966, pp. 225-232) wherein miracle is an event where they believe that God is present in some special way, that He authorizes it, that He intends to achieve some special end by it. Still,

we shall begin by narrating two healings which
would perhaps come closest to being termed "organic," those of Paula and Thomas.

In December of her junior year in high school
Paula had had pain and swelling of her right kneecap. She recalls that on a Tuesday, she had gone
to her family doctor who, after X-rays, had diagnosed her problem as the same hereditary affliction which had troubled her older sister and younger brother. At this point, much of the knee-cap
and the bone beneath it had already degenerated.
The usual treatment indicated was the wearing of a
cast or brace for six months, and the administra-
tion of a medication which would arrest the de-
terioration, but not restore the bone tissue already affected. She was to return the following
Friday for the cast. Thursday of that week, she
and some other high school students had been
scheduled to speak before a group of other black
Pentecostal students to share about how they had
given their life to the Lord. In Paula's words:

. . . My sister felt like the Lord wanted to
heal me as a sign to people that God was
working. I was popular, and she felt that
this would be a good sign. My sister had
kept encouraging me to ask to pray to be
healed. I wasn't sure that this was what God
wanted so I made a deal with the Lord and
prayed, "If you want me to be healed, have
somebody else ask." At the end of the meeting, this man said, "I feel like there's a
girl here with a problem with her knees. If
she has the faith and comes forward to be
prayed with, she'll be healed." So I re-
joiced and said, "O.K., Lord, this is your
answer, I believe that you want me to be
healed." So I limped up to the front of the
auditorium and the group of elders prayed
over me, laid hands on me, prayed over me. I
didn't experience anything in my knee. It
was still very swollen and still hurt very,
very much, and I limped back to my seat. But
when they prayed with me, I really

174

experienced the presence of the Lord in a very, very direct way. I really experienced believing that God would heal me. I felt like a little baby believing something very strongly, even though there was no evidence, that God had healed me.

So I limped back to my seat, and limped to the car and went home. Our parents had been worried about us Catholic kids hanging out with Protestants! But they saw the fruits in our lives: how we were more helpful at home and were joyful. That Thursday night we came home and woke our parents to tell them, "I'm healed." My father, half-awake, said, "Paula, I love you. I don't want you to be hurt. Go to the doctor tomorrow: if he says you don't need the cast, O.K. But if he says you need the cast, I want you to have it on." I felt fine about that.

The next day, my mom drove me to the doctor's. The knee was still swollen, still really hurt, but inside me I really believed that God had really healed me. I didn't feel like I was being crazy about it, or just excited, but I really felt very definitely that something had been done.

There are eight steps going up to the doctor's office and I felt in a lot of pain going up, but I remember praying, "Lord, I really believe that you love me and care for me, but how are other people going to give glory to you because of this, because look at this -- it still looks very bad." So I sat up on the table and he was preparing the plaster for the cast. I asked him to stop doing it because I knew I had to tell him something, about what the Lord had done the night before. Then I looked down, and the swelling was gone! I hadn't noticed it going away: I wished I'd been looking at it, but at the time I was looking at him. I exclaimed, "Look!" and I bent it up straight. I jumped from the table and started jumping around on it -- I was very excited at that point. He was very clam about it and said, "O.K. let me check it out." So he re-examined it, went through the whole examination again. It looked fine, and the bone that had been deteriorated was there: the bone that had been gone was there. He said that he believed that God could do things like that; that if I had any trouble with it, I should come back and he would put a cast on it.

My mother didn't want to come in and be embarrassed. I came out running and said, "Oh mother, look. He said it's O.K." She started crying and said, "God is doing something. I've been praying for you. God is about something new."

Paula did not broadcast this incident, but told some friends she trusted. Reflecting afterwards about the delay between the prayer for healing and the cessation of symptoms the next day, Paula recalls feeling not doubt in her cure, but somewhat perplexed: how could she "witness" so that others would glorify God if she still had the pain, cast, etc.? Her own explanation for the delay lies in the conclusion that, had she been physically changed immediately, she might not have returned to the doctor's. To "share," she needed the doctor's testimony: for example, the nuns at a Catholic High School where she had been invited to tell her story requested a note from a physician. Her doctor wrote a brief letter with no attempt at explanation, but simply a record of the before/after contrast in the condition of her knee. Again afterward, she reasoned that the need to tell the doctor herself about the healing and before the symptoms disappeared might have been a test for her faith. The Lord required her to "step out in faith" before the evidence was all in.

The actual moment of prayer for healing will be described in others' stories, but we might note here that different views are stated by various subjects concerning the need for active faith in the healee. In Paula's faith, her belief overwhelmed even the continuing pain. In others, the subject is totally unaware that healing had happened (e.g., Abigail) or asleep (Betty). In many, there is faith in the mind of the healer, but doubt in the (potential) healee. Cases will be reviewed below.

Ned provided the best explanation of the unusual linguistic usage of the phrase "I have been healed" while symptoms still persist. Subjectively, this act is called "claiming a healing." Referring to the fact that his wife's spinal curvature had been "healed" even though the curvature remained, he explained that "her back was healed, but the physical expression hasn't happened yet." To my startled inquiry about just what this could mean, he noted that there is a "change in faith state. It's sort of Gnostic really, a pointing to a higher reality: I have been healed or am about to be by assurance even though symptoms may be there." Ned's wife does use a water-bed, however, and the pain has been eliminated as they confidently await the straightening of her spine.

Now to Thomas's story. Two year prior to our interview, Thomas had had a bad kidney infection, and was taken to the hospital with bleeding. After an examination, he was put on medication.

. . . When the doctor would leave town, he would give me a hundred pills. I took four a day. A year later, halfway through a prayer meeting, a brother got up and said, "I feel the Lord wants to heal those with kidney problems." I stood up -- was one of the first; closed my eyes, folded my hands. People around me put their hands on my shoulders, head, waist. People around me were praying and praying. I expected to receive something. I took deep breaths. I'd seen so many cases of people with cancer cases,

177

kidney cases, kidney machines. Somebody
said, "You can sit down now." It took about
two minutes. The brothers and sisters around
hugged me. From my neck down, I was sweating
inside my clothes, I was soaking from sweat.
I felt uplifted, felt I was healed.

Two weeks later I went for an examination because I had received a letter of acceptance and a scholarship for a three-week
course at a New England University. The doctor wanted an intravenous pyelogram. I told
the doctor "I've been healed." The doctor
didn't make fun of it but wanted the exam
anyway. "Let's get it on record," he said.
All was normal.

He wanted another exam, an expensive
one, before leaving (for New England). When
the doctor was examining the films, I asked,
"What do you see?"

He said, "Two healthy kidneys"

"Would you give them away?"

The doctor said yes.

I took no medication on the trip. When
I got back, the doctor wanted to go into the
bladder to see if it was O.K. After surgery,
the doctor said, "I didn't see a thing:
everything is normal."

We interrupt Thomas's account to make several
comments. The man at Paula's and at Thomas's
prayer meeting who had announced the "feeling"
that the Lord wanted to heal was exercising the
gift of "Word of Knowledge" treated previously in
the section on prophecy. The "laying on of hands"
by the elders at Paula's meeting and at Thomas's
is often used during prayers for healing with application to the sufferer's head, hands, shoulders, waist and frequently also to the afflicted

178

body part. Two minutes is an average length of time for the actual prayer. Thomas's expectation that he would "receive something" is called "expectant faith." (See proposition eleven.) During prayers for healing, "evil spirits" are routinely cast out as the sequel demonstrates.

. . . The doctor wanted one more examination; "If everything is normal, I won't bother you again." They found an irregular heartbeat. I never had that before. In church I got chest pains and pains down my left arm. I went out and told the Lord, "Lord, you healed me. I believe I've been healed. In the name of Jesus, would you ask Satan to leave my arm alone, leave my body alone?"

In the test, they injected a tube in my leg artery with dye to illustrate my kidneys. Everything was normal. I started to laugh and giggle as when I was baptized in the Spirit. I was to lie flat. They took my pulse every fifteen minutes. The nurse said, "You're going into shock." My wife and my daughter prayed over me. It was due to Satan. The urologist said, "I've been defeated." I said, "You're not the only one," (referring to Satan).

A month before the exam there had been odor in my urine, a dark color to my skin, a lump in my back. I had been tired. The doctor had feared cancer and didn't tell me till after all the tests were over. That was two years ago, and I've taken no medication since. I bawled all the way home, "Lord you're so good to me." The Lord really worked. Satan tried to give me a hard time. After the renal arteriogram there have been no more pain, infections or chest pain. After the last exam, the symptoms all went away.

Unlike Paula's, Thomas's healings (of the kidney infection, asthma and arthritis) were all instantaneous. We notice just above that Thomas and many members of WoG attribute physical difficulties to "Satan," "the Evil one," and "demons." Hence, prayers of exorcism are routinely employed during the healing ritual. The forms are two: either God is asked "in the name of Jesus" to "bind up and cast forth" the power of the devil, or the demons themselves are directly addressed and commanded to depart.

In Paula's account, we heard the idea that God was testing her in the process. Though Charismatic Movement theology frowns on it, the opposite sometimes happens, i.e., people will also test the Lord as the account of Thomas's second healing indicates:

> . . . I had had asthma for twenty-five years. I told the Lord, "I'm tired of it." My healings are instant. I wasn't in a charismatic group then. I was testing the Lord. He gave me more peace, relaxation the whole year round. I could run and play.

Thomas's third healing was the most dramatic for him "because I was alone with the Lord." He had suffered from crippling arthritis until "late April three years ago." He had driven his wife and some friends to Toledo and back to hear Pat Boone speak at a Full Gospel Businessmen's Fellowship. They had sat up talking that Saturday night "until 2 a.m., talking about the Lord and how much he had given us." At his wife's bidding, he had prayed, "Everything you've given is really yours. If I've not done it before, I give you everything. Everything is yours." This had been an intensely emotional experience for Thomas because the next morning "I cried and cried after church. My father used to say, 'Men don't cry.' I took one step forward, went down on my knees, and said, 'Lord, if this is of you, heal my hands.'" Again the healing was instantaneous:

. . . I hadn't worn my wedding band for
three months. I slipped it on, shook hands
with myself, banged it on the table. I felt
like my chest was gonna burst. Everything
became joyful. I met a man with the same
problem. I shook hands, but he just touched
my hand. I said, "No, shake it!" That was
three years since April. I've taken no as-
pirin since.

While most of the healing accounts make for
extraordinarily fascinating listening, for our
purposes we shall more briefly narrate the remaining stories which add to an understanding of the
methods employed and the interior experience of
healees/healers.

It might seem that healings always take place
in an emotionally charged atmosphere. Quentin's
story, already partially related in the biographies above, indicates the contrary. His allergies to certain ordinary foods had even gotten him
excused from the draft. "My first summer in the
Community, the guys in my house made a sacrifice
for me not to eat those foods." His analytical
approach is revealed by his reaction to the girl's
prophecy that "The Lord will heal you soon. I
thought, 'Great. Soon means tomorrow, next week:
not a year, that's too long.'" The following Fall
it was announced at the gathering that a "healing
prayer room" would be opened after the meeting.
Quentin

. . . turned to the Lord and prayed, "Do you
want me to go to that?" I was surprised; the
Lord said, "Yes." (What was that experience
like?) An inner conviction. Words were
formed in my mind -- a very affirmative, positive feeling, "The answer to your question
is yes."

Not satisfied, Quentin went and prayed with
somebody. He had said, "I'm wondering if I should

do something. Please pray with me. I won't tell you what it is." The person replied after prayer, "I think you already know the answer."

> . . . In the prayer room, the leaders said, "We want you to believe that the Lord is here and He wants to heal people. We'll come around and pray over each person." I felt it was good prayer, but not a very emotional experience.

> They came and asked, "What do you want?"

> I told them of my allergies. I felt the presence of God close to me, not awesome or fearful. I knew that He was awesome and powerful and coming close, but simultaneously was very aware of the love between us. I didn't have to be terrified, just "struck" that the almighty Being would come so close. I knew I had been healed. The next day I started eating all those foods with no recurrence of difficulties. That was two years ago this Fall.

> There was no arm-tingling or sensation, just a conscious perception of being touched. They laid hands on my knee, maybe my throat. I can't remember. It was easy and natural to be focused on God. I knew that His promise of four or five months ago had been fulfilled. The most emotional part was testifying several months later at a Thursday gathering. I was scared!

Quentin's description of his being told that he should enter the healing prayer room parallels the "sense from the Lord" spoken of above by the prophets. The centrality of one's relationship with God is what is emphasized in Quentin's account rather than any accompanying emotional fireworks. Finally, his explicit rejection of "arm-tingling" was made most probably because such sensations are sometimes reported during healings. These sensations also have their counterpart in the physical reactions to a prophetic "anointing."

Abigail and Lois described what happens when being prayed over by a group. (Later we shall recount the usual procedures of the specially appointed healers.) Lois, it will be recalled, had been healed of cancer, a condition from which she had suffered since 1946 until her cure in 1972. Prior to her medical examination, she had to cease taking medications for six weeks and was suffering intense pain. In the healing prayer room she had doubled up in pain. A brother sitting beside her knew that something was wrong and prayed a little with her. He opened his Bible and came upon the verse, "They that are bowed down shall be lifted up." She then opened hers and read "One generation shall declare the truth to another."

> . . . He was one generation younger than I. He prayed for me. The pain stopped so suddenly I felt almost silly. I didn't expect this from someone who wasn't a coordinator or clergyman!

A few days later, she was lying in bed at home and had the experience narrated in the biographical section above with the feeling of hands healing the afflicted areas. Three weeks later, she went to the isotopist and the scan was totally negative. The examiner said three times, "I wouldn't expect it; I can't explain this." She testified to her "miracle" at the next prayer meeting. (We note here the absence of the intense sense of expectancy which characterized Paula's and Thomas's healings immediately above.) As for the non-cancerous fibroid tumor, it was still there on the scan, but there was no more pain. "It used to produce intense pain, but all that's gone. You might say that's harder to explain <u>with</u> the fibroid than without it!"

At the prayer meeting, the leaders had prayed for her also, but the pain had stopped immediately

when the brother had prayed. The latter had put
his hands on her shoulder and asked the Lord to
take the pain away: he had prayed that if no other way were possible, then let the pain be transferred to him! It hadn't been so transferred, but
he had been frightened that it just might have
been. Lois then described the usual procedure:

. . . The coordinators pray directly to the
Lord. Then they rebuke the disability with
or without a direct exorcism. Then they
thank the Lord for what He's already doing.
(In my case, the pain had already gone, of
course.) Sometimes someone gets a relevant
Scripture passage. There is praying in
tongues or in silence, usually accompanied by
laying of hands on the shoulders, hands or
head. I've had exorcism done in the healing
room, but I don't remember if there was one
at that time. (Did it seem appropriate to
you?) I think that the direct action of the
devil takes place more in my spirit than in
my body during illnesses, tempting me to discouragement or despair. But I never object
because I want to cover the waterfront, touch
all bases!

Abigail's statement reinforces Lois's and
indeed that of all the subjects who might not mention all the steps as Lois just did. Abigail had
asked for prayers for healing at a different community's meeting two months before joining WoG,
but the approach was the same.

. . . I asked prayers for my arthritis, diabetes and alcoholism. The minister in charge
prayed for a "general overhaul." He laid
hands on my shoulder. All the people praying
put hands on each other's shoulders. A nun
held my hands. I shed tears, but wasn't
crying intentionally. The Lord said to me,
"Tears are healing." The minister prayed in

184

tongues, rebuked the sickness, used "Jesus, Jesus" over and over. I was thinking of my arthritis, diabetes and alcoholism. I felt lifted from the chair. I opened my eyes to make sure I was still grounded. We then prayed for the others. On my way home I sang songs which had been unknown to me before. This was an emotional rather than a physical healing because there were no changes.

The one additional detail mentioned by Abigail is the mutual imposition of hands by the healers. Abigail did describe the other successful cures noted on Table I, but her remarks concerning alcoholism are worth quoting:

. . . I had been drinking a fifth a day. Now I can drink but not to excess. I tried A.A. but didn't like it. I didn't hear God mentioned and was upset by the people's tales. I told the Lord I couldn't go back, and would give over the problem to Him. There's been a gradual change; no more hiding the stuff. God wants control, not quitting, for social reasons or to relax.

Some disagreement among the subjects was manifested concerning the place of an need for faith or expectancy on the part of a healee. Lois's long bout with cancer had brought her to the following conclusions:

. . . I've had a subtle change in attitude: whatever happens, the Lord has it in His hands, and will use it. Does the New Testament mean that faith is an inflexible conviction that this particular healing would occur? No. We're supposed to "give thanks in all circumstances." A burden is put on a sick person when you say, "The Lord wants all persons healed here and now." I had a time

185

of discouragement in '62 when I felt like
that. In '61 I had been convinced there
would never be a problem again. Then I was
blown to pieces and decided never to have
that kind of faith again. I'm convinced I'm
free of cancer now. Next year and five years
from now are no concern of mine. The Lord
will take care of me then. Probabilities are
strong I'm over it, but I don't speculate.
The blessing received is enough for right
now.

Hilary, a member of the healing team, implies
that "faith healing" is a misnomer if by that one
means faith must be found mostly in the healee.
He provided the following subtle and succinct account of an interplay between healer and healee:

. . . We mainly try to build up people's
faith. My theory is that expectant faith
plays a real part. When there is a real gift
of charismatic faith in a healer, it doesn't
really matter what the other person is thinking as when Jesus healed. Yet I do experience it making a difference. Generally we
just pray for healing among us. Even with
Jesus it worked both ways. Often in the Community it's not just when someone with the
gift is praying over someone that something
happens. It's when we pray together and turn
to the Lord in faith that God hears our
prayer. The person himself does have something to do with it. Generally if a person
doesn't expect, I'd have a hard time expect-
ing God to do something. Faith means a basic
expectancy for God to work. There might be
doubt some place that's not completely dealt
with. I can still pray.

Ursula's theology is perhaps more standard
among persons who look for healings through prayer:

I think it's your faith and the faith of others. "Your faith that heals you," the Lord said. When you pray for a person, their faith is limited. God wants to heal. Unless a person believes, expects to receive, there won't be a healing. I don't know why they won't believe. (Have you ever had a problem believing yourself?) Yes. I've prayed with reservations, "I guess God might want me to suffer." There's a little doubt in my mind sometimes. The source of healing is there: just sit down and ask the Lord.

Occasionally, people's expectant faith leads them to take steps which, from a medical or just a common sense viewpoint, seem imprudent. Hilary relates one such tale:

. . . I prayed with a sister who had polio as a child. She tripped and sprained her ankle often. She came into the prayer room and we prayed. I don't often get this sense, but I felt that the Lord wanted her to take off the bandage and walk with it. I sensed God had healed it. I had to step out of my own fear to get her to do it. First I asked her to move it around. She said it felt great. She walked on it: it felt great. The doctor had said two days before that she'd be on crutches for a couple of weeks. I was surprised and delighted as she was. This was an intuition, but an inner sense that's not the result of something I'd reasoned out: some kind of assurance. I had lifted up her foot when praying. I had not warmth in my hand. (I don't experience all kinds of "charismatic" signs and feelings.) It was an intuition but something that needed to be responded to in faith. A couple days later she tripped and sprained it again. She remembered what had happened the other night, prayed and was healed again. It was unusual for her: before it had taken a real long time to heal.

187

It is clear that Hilary is talking about the same experience as the prophets' "Lord's leading/sense from the Lord." In the latter case, this "sense" goads people into making public exhortations; in the former, it overcomes a societally-induced norm that "doctor knows best." What was stated by Hilary is true for most of the healers in WoG; they work in tandem with the medical profession rather than at cross-purposes. Yet such incidents as this account of Hilary's demonstrate dramatically where their ultimate allegiance lies: in their sense from the Lord, subject indeed to discernment, rather than in, say, a physician's prescriptions.

Two more incidents of "stepping out in faith" will be related. Even though both involve leg injuries, the metaphor applies more broadly, of course!

After relating how her father had prayed over her and her sisters while asleep, and how her stomach problem had been healed while she was unconscious, the first healing mentioned by Betty concerned her kneecap which had slipped out of place as she practiced "splits" for cheerleading. She got it bandaged up and the girls in her household prayed over it. The difference between her own idea and the "sense from the Lord" came home painfully to Betty when she thought about taking off the bandages, did so, and her leg continued to hurt. Later that very day, however, "the Lord said, 'It's O.K. to take your bandages off now.'" She did so and felt no pain. "I have no idea why He wanted it later and not immediately. You can't pin the Lord cown, but He does talk to you."

Betty senses the difference among people praying for healing between those with expectancy and those without expectant faith:

> . . . I once prayed and the pain didn't go away. I asked others to pray. I got the impression that they weren't expecting anything just saying words, you know. I asked others and sensed their expectancy. I was anointed with oil and I was healed.

188

This is only one of two references in all the testimonies to the use of oil in a healing ritual. The infrequency of its being mentioned reflects the researcher's understanding of the Community's practice: it is used occasionally, but seemingly without any pattern.

Betty continues her reflections about expectancy:

> . . . There were no deep spiritual repercussions: the Lord just healed my knee. You can't put it into a magic formula, into terms like "faith" because as a child I hadn't even known what had happened when I was four. . . People go to Kathryn Kuhlman not even believing in God, just expecting to be healed and they are. I sensed that one group praying over me expected and the other didn't. They ought to be expecting and they weren't.

In Karen's account of the chipped bone in her ankle, the student health service physician thought that she should be on crutches for three weeks. Just three days later

> . . . some brothers laid hands on me: there were four guys. They put their hands on my ankle, another on my shoulder, another on my head. We made known to the Lord that brothers and sisters are concerned. The Lord said I wasn't open to His healing in other areas. I repented of those other areas. The swelling went down. After unwrapping it I jumped up and down, put my crutches on my shoulder, got onto my bike and went home.

By the "other areas," Karen meant her emotional and moral life. In Abigail's and Betty's remarks, we have heard mention of the belief that these latter healings often precede or accompany the physical healings. The subject's proper response

189

is to "repent" of the sin involved in one's life, and to expect healing there first.

We have seen that the belief in healing may cause a subject to violate "doctor's orders." It may even lead one to ignore pain signals as Karen's further account of her dislocated kneecap makes clear:

> . . . During prayer time I was dancing in the spirit and dislocated my knee. The doctor said I'd have to be on crutches for awhile. I prayed and it didn't get better. I and others felt the Lord wanted to heal me.
>
> I was supposed to go away. I prayed and decided I'd have a walk in faith. I wanted to go home with a sister who said, "I guess we'll have to take the crutches." I cried. She said, "You gotta believe." I took the crutches and put them in my closet. She said, "Go climb the staircase, you're healed." I did it. It was hard; it hurt. I felt sick to my stomach, faint and the whole bit. But it was O.K. Now I occasionally have twinges of pain depending on the weather. The Lord dealt with my expectant faith.

Taking faith to this extent is not officially encouraged by the leadership, but can be seen to flow logically from the common understanding of faith-in-practice.

Shifting now to emotional healings, "healing of memories," we notice that the same techniques, even to the laying on of hands and rebuking of evil spirits, are employed by healers. The perspective, however, is still that of the healee.

Along with her several healings, Abigail reported being healed from violent temper-tantrums and resentment at some of the persons entering her office.

Betty's words are graphic:

190

. . . I learned last Fall that I don't need
to be so emotional. I'd have atomic bombs
going off inside, and every so often I'd
throw hand-grenades outside. Now, I just
have fire-crackers inside! I feel less self-
ish. I got healed of a lot of things. (Such
as?) A bad sore throat, being sick to my
stomach; I was generally sick once. (A non-
believer would say, "It just went away."
You, a believer say, "The Lord healed me."
Why?) The same things used not to go away so
quickly. It happens a lot. I'm generally in
better health. Something I learned from a
Christian Scientist friend was: the less you
think about yourself, the better you do. As
a nurse's daughter, I'm more aware of the
physical. I'm sick less often, I'd bet.

In this brief statement, we see woven together a
natural transition between emotional and physical
ills. Betty struggles too to explain her faith
somewhat empirically: illness didn't used to be
cured so quickly. Other subjects will refer especially to the "support and concern of brothers
and sisters" in explaining emotional healings, but
all will attribute progress ultimately to the
Lord.
    Sheila, who works in the prophetic ministry,
as well as in deliverance (see below) made this
comment:

. . . Evil isn't just war, but a personal
attack on us. As Christians, we can expect
to be protected. Lots of times, the stuff
people share isn't evil spirits, but is the
need for a healing of rotten images of themselves. Lots of people have had images of
themselves. At our last deliverance session,
a woman had a real spirit of fear through her
life, a pattern. She feared dying and her
kids' not being taken care of. I pointed out
all the connections. I prayed that she be
delivered from fear and anxiety. Deliverance

191

is an ongoing process. Prophecy really works powerfully for individuals. They get a sense of how God really loves them.

This statement shows how one practitioner uses all her gifts when confronting a suffering sister. Prophecy and deliverance are put to the task of accomplishing an inner healing. While many simply blame any unpleasant, immoral, or emotionally trying situation on "evil spirits," the majority of the subjects interviewed made some distinction like Sheila's between psychological and spiritual causes; appropriate remedies, however, rarely included therapy because of the difficulty some had experienced (and shared with their heads) in finding a counselor/therapist who took religious experience seriously. Hence, inner healings were prayed for, and common sense remedies like Betty's maxim ("the less you think about yourself, the better you do") were invoked to aid the unfortunate.

It will be recalled from all the biographies that Ursula was the most practiced among the subjects in inner healing. We can notice in her testimony the interweaving of psychological and demonic factors:

> . . . I met with X and Y weekly for a year. They did all the talking. I prayed at the beginning and at the end. Both were suicidal. I sensed a spirit of self-destruction. I felt the Lord wanted me to pray for deliverance. X broke down and cried a lot. He said he felt relieved. He hasn't talked about it with me since. Also Y: for awhile he came everyday since he worked nights. He was so upset, so distressed, so disturbed. Before seeing him, I spent two hours in prayer. I had no training. We were members of the same household though. I didn't know what to do. I thought, "Take a long walk." We walked around campus. He was sent to another city. After ministering to him

there, they said they couldn't minister to
him any more. Then he came back here to live
after trying yet another city. He came to me
on _____ Street where I live and said,
"You're the most mature Christian around, an
older person." I asked my head who said,
"There's no one else." Y said, "I need the
support of the Community."

I remembered in prayer time the verse,
"Christ stood before Pilate and didn't answer." He was very disturbed this one day.
I didn't know if he would attack me. So I
was quiet -- thought that's what the Lord
wanted.   >

The Lord said, "There's a spirit in him
trying to destroy him. It's named self-
destruction."

He asked, "What's the matter with you?"

"I'm fighting a battle with the Lord."

"You better do what the Lord says."

"I don't want to."

"You better."

I addressed the Lord and then said, "In
the name of Jesus I cast out the spirit of
self-destruction."

After I prayed some time, he just
changed, relaxed and was peaceful. As he was
going out he was joyful. He said, "You
really love me, don't you?" He couldn't believe it.

The Lord brought me to this situation.
I thought, "I really ought to go and study
counseling." But it's the Lord who's doing
it for them. I see a great change in them.
They're not strong and well yet. People were

scared of Y; I never was. He was angry.
Once he kicked a barrel and it went rolling
down the street. I'm not called to pray for
just anybody: a specific prayer for healing
must come from God if He moves you. If a
person asks, that's kind of a sign. With
Jesus, people would ask, make the first
approach.

There will be a section concerning deliverance below; here we can see how it blends into the
ministry of inner healing as it does for regular
physical healing to which we now return. We shall
find, however, the same reliance upon the inner
sense among the healers as we found among the prophets, the same interweaving of explanations and
procedures drawn from the human, divine and demonic realms.
This next section will treat the experience
of healing others. We shall begin with individual
healers and conclude with the combined testimony
of the four healing team members interviewed.
Sheila, quite experienced in prophecy, is
just beginning to exercise the gift of healing.
"I'm at the point with healing where I once was
with prophecy and deliverance: it's hard to grasp
it." She had prayed over her children when they
were ill, but they were not cured. Then a guest
came and prayed over her child, and he stopped
suffering from his ear infections. Her approach:

. . . I need to let the Lord clear up my
thinking on it. I need more understanding
and faith. When I see people who have faith,
my faith is built up. If I were God, I
wouldn't want anybody to be sick. Part is
accepting your humanness, and part is knowing
God wants to intervene in the course of
nature.

Once at a meeting I felt that the Lord
wanted healing, and the coordinators said,
"Not now." Once I was asked to walk around

and sense what the Lord was doing. I prayed
and prophesied over a sister that she was
healed of a breast infection. The doctor
confirmed that she was healed.

In her statement, Sheila relies on the gift with
which she is familiar, namely, prophecy to be employed at the discretion of the coordinators for
healing.

Quentin's testimony is the briefest:

A guy playing paddleball twisted his
ankle. He was lying on the ground writhing
one minute, and then after prayer over him,
he was up and finishing the game.

A brother on a dorm picnic twisted his
ankle playing soccer. People spontaneously
gathered and prayed. We knew that our Father
in heaven can fix it. He calmed down, then
got up and played.

My roommate had a cold. I pray over
people against sleepiness. They may need to
repent for running their body ragged and getting sleepy or a cold. I feel perfectly
natural about doing this. I really believe
it's God's will to heal people. It's a natural part of Christian life to be experiencing
miracles, and experiencing God's power. He
really wants us to have that power in a daily
way.

Many of the subjects made Quentin's last point
over and over again: that healing did not have to
wait for the experts in the healing prayer room,
but was meant to be an ordinary, daily occurrence.
Indeed, by the time of the last interview with
Victor, the use of the healing prayer room was declining because "people were coming in for every
hang-nail!" A deeper theological reason stressed
by the coordinators was that the power to invoke

healing resides in the whole body, and so spontaneous healing services would occur during the large prayer meetings. Hilary, a member of the team admitted frankly, "I don't feel I've got any particular gift. The Lord's used me this way. It's the way the Lord wants people in general to pray with people for healing." He does believe that several people in WoG do have a special charismatic gift for this ministry. "I have a spiritual sense that the Lord's given them a gift. A fair amount of revelation has been given to them." Ursula agrees with Quentin and Victor: "Everyone has the gift to pray in the body. Power seems to be in the body as a body rather than with individuals. I see the body as Jesus present today with the same power, the same desires, the same spirit."

Chuck, Paula and Thomas work in hospitals, and they exercise their ministry there unobtrusively. Praying silently at work, Chuck has noted drastic and dramatic changes for the better:

> . . . There was a non-cooperative lady who wouldn't take her pills. I prayed for her cooperation and the lady took 'em all. The nurse said, "I can't believe this. She never took 'em before. Something's going on."

Paula works on a medical unit with terminal cases:

> . . . I love serving people in this way. I can support them. They want to hear that there is a Jesus who loves them. There was a lady with lung cancer. I prayed with her that she have an easier time breathing. She was expected to die, but a week later she was discharged. I don't know if the cancer was cured, but she walked out breathing fine.
>
> I don't feel free in my work situation to evangelize. My main witness is to be a

good nurse. It's very demanding: patients want, then don't want a drink of water, a blanket. They are incontinent. Nurses get into complaining. I got a gift not to be afraid of people dying. People have asked me where I get the strength to do what I'm doing. I tell them about WoG. I pray for situations where I can talk about God. Other nurses will ask me to go see a patient. I talked to the head nurse. She said she trusted me not to become a hospital preacher.

Paula explained that there are three bases of her decisions: the written word of Scripture; the circumstances of her life; prophecy, wisdom and knowledge. "When these three things line up, I'm sure God is speaking. I don't wait for these all, but if I experience a situation, I do what the Lord directs."

After he had recounted the story of his own healings, I had asked Thomas if he had ever been involved in healing others:

. . . Yes, it scares me so much. A man would come in yearly for kidney stones. He had a stone that wouldn't go through his ureter. My wife had told me, "The Lord will use you in the healing ministry. Use it." I went up to the guy and asked where it hurts. He said on his right side. I held my hand over the guy and prayed. Next morning I asked what had happened. He said the stone had passed, but the pain had stopped "after I left you guys by the elevator."

Another woman had cancer of the bone in her skull. I prayed to myself for her healing. She hasn't been back. The Lord might have cured her.

There was a black minister with blood clots in his bladder. He asked me to pray over him "right now." I put my hand on his shoulder and one on his abdomen. "Lord you are so powerful, release your power through me." After I opened my eyes, his arms were up and he was praising the Lord. The next morning he was discharged.

Parenthetically, we might note that in these hospital cases just reviewed, with the exception of the minister, the "expectant faith" was found only in the healer rather than in the healee. We come now to the statements of the four members of the healing team who were interviewed. Lois already described in a schematic and detailed way the methods of the healers so we shall here add only what is particular to each. We have previously gotten acquainted with Hilary from many comments already recorded so we shall continue with an examination of his approach. First, a brief healing success:

. . . I prayed with a brother who had a problem with tiredness. He would be sleepy all day, couldn't get into his work. I sensed an evil spirit bothering him. I had an understanding, insight, intuition that the cause was an evil spirit, a spirit of fatigue. I commanded it to leave. The brother shared about it at a gathering: it had happened for a long time. He wasn't bothered subsequent to prayer. The thing indeed was changed.

Hilary's interaction with the spirit is dubbed "taking authority over" the evil spirit. Hilary, university educated, struggles to put into words his experiences with "spirits" while preserving his modern viewpoint and identity:

. . . We prayed twice with someone who had begun losing his sight. The first time I sensed something would really happen when we prayed. God was working in our prayer. We

198

prayed a second time. It wasn't a case you could see something resulting immediately. My partner took authority over an evil spirit. I was thinking about it, but he did it. That was a factor. It's real vague, hard to sense what connection that might have with physical reality. I often sense that evil spirits are involved as a real factor. Sometimes I can name the spirit, often I can't. It might be a mean or angry spirit, a harrassment weighing someone down. I internally get angry at it.

In this case, the eye ailment was cured as mysteriously as it had come on. The physicians had prescribed mega-vitamins; the healers had used prayer and exorcism. The person got well and thanked both sets of professionals!

Hilary's comments about his attitude during work on the team are contained above in the quotation concerning expectant faith. Picking up on his comment that the presence of spirits made him angry, I remarked that I had seen him in action, and that he behaved "vigorously" during prayer and exorcism. I wondered if he had been instructed in his procedures. He responded that there were no specific guidelines, that his approach varied:

. . . Sometimes I'm vocal, sometimes not especially when I don't know what's going on. I'd do more than the sister I pray with (his partner on the team). Implicitly, I take the initiative leading the prayer; she would make suggestions. Afterwards we share, ask questions. There's nothing real formal right now.

Here we have Community order preserved with the male taking the leadership position on the two-person team. Even though Hilary denies that there's anything "formal," the stylized pattern described by Lois has become quite standard among

both the appointed healers and anyone else attempting to offer such a prayer.

Geraldine, a member of both the healing and
prophecy groups, has also been quoted at length
above. After she herself had been healed of strep
throat, she was attending a heads-of-household
meeting when she had been asked to join the team
by a coordinator. The commitment involved praying
an hour and a half weekly, as well as time in the
healing prayer room after a Thursday evening gath-
ing until all who presented themselves for prayers
were attended. Team members worked in male-female
pairs. She more than others devoted a large por-
tion of her remarks to the need for faith in the
healee:

> . . . Whenever I'm sick, I do experience
> faith to turn to the Lord and confidence that
> the Lord wants me to get well. . . . I be-
> lieve it because I've seen it. Two weeks
> ago, the healing team fasted for the Thursday
> gathering. We each had a listening session
> for twenty minutes alone before the Lord. My
> general sense was that the area of faith
> needs building. God wants to begin healing
> people more miraculously. He wants us to
> heal because of who He is, not just to get
> people's faith. Healing will be more a thing
> people can look at and believe. Strong
> Christians have doubts like "He doesn't want
> to do that stuff regularly. Prophecy and
> teaching are O.K. in a Christian community,
> but not healing." It's an obstacle when
> there's not enough faith. Often I pray not
> for a specific healing but for people's be-
> lief.

"Fasting for" means, in practice for WoG members,
going from sundown to sundown with no food except
liquids and juices. Fasting for something means
adding this discipline to the prayers that some
gift be given by the Lord, in this case, some revelation from Him as to which direction the

Community was to go with respect to healing. Geraldine gives vent here to the frustration felt over the constant uphill battle against the mind-set of even "strong Christians" that the age of miracles has passed, that such things don't happen nowadays. She, Hilary and Quentin have already been cited as expressing the Community's teaching that "miraculous" healings are meant to be an "ordinary, day to day" part of a Christian Community's experience.

Although physical concomitants seem to occur regularly with prophecy, and the literature quoted above in chapter one indicates that healers too experience sensations, among the healers interviewed only Geraldine said she has felt such; in fact, Hilary has already mentioned not having these "charismatic signs and feelings." In Geraldine's own words:

> . . . A month ago, a sister came to be prayed with for her knee: she had had an accident. I didn't feel we even needed to pray: she seemed to have faith from her expression. I felt like the Lord was there and wanted to do something immediately. It was the only time I experienced something happen in my hands. They were hot as I put them on her leg. I was telling the Lord of His goodness. Then she stood up, started shaking her leg. Something was cracking. The pain was gone. She limped for a few days but the pain was gone. I don't feel that God doesn't heal because a person doesn't have enough faith, but the way a person looks at the Lord has a lot to do with when and how the Lord will heal.

Healers in other traditions regularly report heat or tingling in their hands, but this feature seems notably lacking among these subjects and others questioned informally.

While Lois's outline gave the main steps in the process, we now hear Elaine discussing what happens as she and her teammate, Frank, go from person to person:

. . . We meet after the Thursday gathering.
We try to make them feel relaxed. From two
to twelve people might come. (There were
usually more than twelve on the several occasions I had visited the healing prayer
room. Perhaps Elaine means that she and
Frank would see this many.) There's a spirit
of praise in the room. (After prayer together) we go around and ask what each wants
healed. Sometimes we just ask the Lord for
healing. Our approach is not to figure out a
person's whole life and get everything worked
out, but if we sense more is going on, for
example anxiety, we suggest they talk to
their head if they're in the Community.
Sometimes we take authority over evil spirits. If they're not in the Community and we
sense lots is going on, the best thing is to
cast out evil spirits, ask the Lord what's
best and give them words of encouragement.

After praying with each awhile, we ask
why they came and what they want praying over
for, for example, eczema. Sometimes we feel,
"That's it," and pray for it. Other times we
ask more questions like "How long have you
had it?" (When do you ask more questions?)
It's a combination of our own sense that we
need to know more, and how much time we have.

So much is out of our hands. There's no
formula. The Lord gave us power to heal; He
gave us instructions to lay hands on the
sick. It's different for each person. We
don't consciously seek the next step, but
just trust the Holy Spirit to lead us. We
ask them and they pray too. We ask how they
experienced our prayer sometimes. Sometimes
we give advice: "See your head."

If, say, there's a pain in their arm or
they're not able to move it, we sometimes

202

advise them to use it. We tell them to act
in faith and do things never done with their
arm before.

We end all together. The leader concludes with words about faith, about healing,
etc.

Again in this narration, we hear about reliance
upon the internal "sense from the Lord" about how
best to proceed. There is also a balanced awareness that not all problems can be solved at once
or even prayed for on a particular occasion. A
distinction is made in the "prescription" given to
Community and non-Community members. While
Christians generally pray for the absent sick, the
leader of the large prayer meeting always an-
nounces that only people with personal ailments
should go to the healing room. Earlier in the
Community's history, people could go for prayer by
proxy, as it were, but this practice had been
abandoned in favor of the presently described procedure.

Elaine's partner, Frank, adds his commentary.
He, like Hilary, behaves forcefully and vigorously
during healing prayer services though his soft-
spoken conversational tone would not lead one to
anticipate such intensity. He repeats a theme emphasized by Elaine: praise of God is an important
element in a healing ritual. Notice too in his
speech the frequent use of the words, "real" and
"really." (Perhaps the attentive reader has
caught on already to the somewhat idiosyncrati-
cally frequent usage of these words by WoG
members.)

. . . I've been on the healing team since
January. I missed about a month and a half
because of a hundred and one special reasons.
People have been coming with real serious
kinds of illness to more minor things. When
we pray with people in the healing prayer
room, we experience really having a lot of

203

faith and really believing that the Lord is really doing something to them and promised something or working some sort of healing. We encourage people not to get real worried and uptight and put pressure on themselves, but to look to the Lord. They should expect a healing from the Lord -- maybe not this particular night, but maybe later on. Spiritually I felt real good about this.

We have saved Frank's testimony to the end of this secton because he recapitulates so concisely a number of major themes running through both the healing and prophecy sections. In this brief statement, he has already suggested a way to balance the need to help a healee relax while appealing for his faith-response. He puts the emphasis on the healer's expectancy while also working to draw it from the healee. Frank continues:

. . . I didn't see a lot of miraculous healings. I prayed over a guy who was bubbling over with praise of the Lord. I felt that at that time he really was healed. There was an improvement, greater freedom, lack of pain.

About a year and a half ago, Hilary prayed with a crippled brother whose foot straightened up and he could walk with a degree of freedom not experienced before. I prayed with him two or three times in the Fall and Winter. Each time he's made some improvement.

Both Frank and Elaine feel that healings should take place in an atmosphere characterized by praise as much as by expectancy. Yet Frank does not expect instantaneous healings the way Thomas does. We may wonder whether the delay in experience shapes the reduced expectation or vice-versa. Frank then spontaneously brought up the day of fasting already alluded to by Geraldine:

. . . Three weeks ago we fasted and had a day
for the healing team, the first such. I felt
the Lord encouraged us to take more authority.
Since then there's been greater faith and
more people are getting healed. I prayed
over a brother with running ears. They
stopped running while we were praying. While
he was telling a friend later about the healing, he was feeling skeptical about the cure
of the ear and it started to run again! He
rebuked the Evil One, told him to stop, and
it stopped running! From this he learned a
spiritual lesson: we're to take authority
over our own body in the name of the Lord.

By hearing many such vignettes as these repeated
many times in public sharings and in private conversations, the WoG members' sense of the immanence of both divine and demonic activity is
shored up, and finds echoes in the experience of
each.

Whereas the prophecy team meets biweekly for
an hour and a half, the healing team members meet
for only five or ten minutes after each Thursday's
session and review what went on, such as

. . . the general tone, whether it was wor-
shipful. We comment on each other like,
"You should look more to the Lord, be less
concerned about yourself."

I don't know why I got on the team --
they asked a number of people from the dorms.
They thought I could pray in faith and that
it would build my faith: it has. I like it:
it's a situation where you need to turn to
the Lord to do something specific now. I
feel the Spirit speaks to me about a person's
life. (Describe the sense.) I'll turn to
the Lord, worship Him, come into His presence. The spiritual sense is different from
a mental image or emotional feeling. I try
to be receptive rather than giving Him praise,

205

thinking of His deeds. I believe the Lord is hearing my word; I don't rely on my feelings. Sometimes I will hear a voice; I get a sense of where they're at with the Lord. I'm with the Lord loving them. We're seated with Christ at the right hand of God, seeing things from His point of view. I get a mental image of a healing taking place, for example, of a nasal passage clogged or a limb not working. The Lord impresses me with a picture of what's going on: in the picture, the Lord is setting it right. I pray that the life of the Lord may run through our crippled brother's body like water.

This is an expectionally candid and full report of a healer's inner thought process while working, so to speak. Frank's inner "pictures" are often accompanied by forceful activity. He goes on:

. . . I take authority in different situations. As sons of God in the name of Jesus, the Lord has given us the name, Jesus. Not just healing, but our whole lives are supernatural, not just one department. I'll speak to an ailment, "Go away; be destroyed; die; wither" to a cancer or tumor. When you treat it that way, something happens. I'm more personally getting into the battle.

Frank now goes on to describe his team-work with Elaine:

We greet people and start with a song. The leader gives an introduction about the Lord's love and desire to heal. "It's not us, not our prayers; you're to have faith in the Lord." He explains how the hour is to be spent. The whole time is in an atmosphere of worship and praise. There may be twelve, fifteen, twenty people sitting in a circle.

Elaine and I will start anywhere. We'll tap
someone on the shoulder, ask "What do you
want to pray for?" The team approach is
helpful. Often just one person isn't open to
all the Lord wants to do.

It's mostly people from the Community or
their guests. Directions are given at the
large meeting to pray only for physical healings: there's not enough time for more.
People are to take up inner healings with
their heads, or we take their names for later
contact.

We may pause to note the specialization developing. Earlier in the Community's history, all
types of healings were prayed for in the prayer
room, for those present as well as far away. Yet
with increasing structure, heads provide counsel,
advice and prayer for inner healings, and healings
at a distance are simply not done in the healing
prayer room. To return to Frank:

After I turn to the Lord in prayer, my
sense grows. We ask the person what the disease is; we ask if they believe. Even if
they don't believe, we pray anyway: "Let's
turn to the Lord now and worship him." We
kneel before the people sitting in a circle.
Elaine prays immediately for healing. I worship and am receptive. A mental picture may
come. I listen to Elaine's prayer, pray
along the same line especially if I'm not
feeling real inspired. I'll verbalize the
prayer, "O Lord, may your life fill our
brother." I'll take authority over the illness; "I come against you, you tumor; we want
no part of you; the Lord doesn't either." I
can be real stern too in coming against this
evil. I'll get an inspiration about how the
Lord wants to finish. We'll close and ask
the person how he feels. Elaine and I share
our reflections; we'll encourage them to have

faith, try, for instance, to control their hands, make a fist; exercise faith right there in the room; walk.

The importance of this is that God be glorified, that there be a God-centered atmosphere. If we think of His love, people's faith is kindled. Last time, we agreed that we would pray only sixty seconds with each 'cause there were twenty-five people there. It was one of the best times we had.

(Do you do anything during the rest of the week involving your healing ministry?) We agreed to spend one hour a week praying, being before the Lord. I may fast once a week. My approach would be to read lots of stuff. Our coordinator said, "We know enough. Let's just come before the Lord." We don't need to increase our knowledge, but be before the Lord about it. It's a matter of growing in spiritual maturity.

With Frank's testimony, we conclude the accounts of healing experiences except for one special category, that of leg-lengthening. This is treated separately because all other ailments are subjected to the procedures described above, but this difficulty has a slightly different tradition of treatment. None of the members of the healing room mentioned it, but Chuck, Ned, Olga and Ursula reported its occurrence, and to them we now turn for an understanding of the phenomenon.

In a household where Chuck had lived, one of the men complained of back problems. Ursula, who lived there at the time also and who had similar pains, had inquired, "Could it be due to your legs' being unequal in length?" Chuck goes on:

. . . The technique is to have the person sit in a chair or against a wall so that the back is flat. We pulled on his feet by the ankles, and pushed the legs so the hips are

square. There was a half-inch difference.
Someone said, "Let's just pray but mostly
praise the Lord." He was holding, but mostly
pushing the legs. We prayed for maybe, five
minutes. I saw the shorter one come up to
the longer one. From then on, he had no back
problems. At the start, the brother had been
skeptical.

It was done to my brother too by some
radical Christians. He felt this guy pushing
on his legs as hard as he could, but at the
same time could feel the leg stretching out,
building cells, growing out to the point. He
had a hard time walking for two weeks since
it causes a sore neck.

I've seen arm-lengthening too: the person will be backed up against a wall with his
arms out, his hands to the side against the
wall. You bring the hands forward till the
fingertips touch. You hold the hands and
push.

Ned and Olga, husband and wife, corroborate the
procedures, but do not mention the pushing. They
do speak about their inner reactions of simultaneous humor and faith. First Ned:

I was always extremely skeptical about
physical healing. It strikes me as Holy
Roller-ish. This guy visiting our house
talked about leg-lengthening: it had happened to him. My wife had curvature of the
spine and one leg shorter. If she'd wear
flat shoes, her dress would hang. Well, we
had her and my short leg lengthened. The
technique is to sit in a straight-backed,
hard chair, put your legs out and see where
the heels fall. He supported my ankle, but
didn't pull on my leg. The four of us
prayed. There was no stretching sensation in
the hip, but in the calf there was sensation;

209

I felt like the calf stretched. In fact, I've had less problems with my feet than before.

My wife sat in the chair next. There was three-quarters to an inch of difference. He didn't pull, she didn't push, and the legs wound up even. Her back is still curved though. She has less pain in her back now, but we have a water-bed too . . . We had prayed in tongues and in English too in an emotional tone. "We don't believe, but want to." I watched her leg get longer. I was joyful, awestruck; it was a boost to our faith. She said, "It felt like somebody pulling my leg." But it wasn't Sam (the fellow who had suggested doing this) because he was supporting the leg. There is a point to the prayer of lengthening and not "making the legs even" because Sam had heard a story where a short guy got upset because when they prayed to make his legs even, one shrank!

I can't not believe because I saw it happen. I felt a sense of tension in the large part of the calf. I didn't feel pulling. There was a momentary sharp pain like a cramp. The pain went away, and the observers were giggling. This became a high point in our house's relationship, a joyful, exciting experience. I was "up" for a few days, but decided not to share it at work. There's a pervasive, anti-religious sentiment at work.

Then we asked the Lord to straighten her back. We put our hands on her head and shoulders and prayed ten minutes. There was no sense of anything happening as we did have a sense of God present in a special way at the time of the leg-lengthening. Sam said, "God has healed her back." Olga wanted to believe, but the curve in the back didn't change: I felt the vertebrae. She said it had changed somewhat. There's no pain now

210

either because God healed her, because of the water-bed, or both.

Olga's memory of the incident was the same as her husband's but she emphasized different details:

 . . . There was graphic proof; my skirt no longer hung right. It was a very strange experience. It felt like someone grabbing my ankle and pulling as hard as he could, but Sam was only holding my heels up. We all had a giggling fit over my slanted skirt. It took about five minutes. Ned had been in a frame of mind to test the Lord. Sam had said, "O.K. let's do it." I had a feeling of peace, of being refreshed and rested. This is a different kind of contact with Him; His doing a thing for me. I thought He was going to heal my curved spine; I probably always will. My hips were out of line too: with the leg being lengthened, the hips got back into line too.

Finally, Ursula who has both worked in this specialized form of ministry and had her own leg lengthened, describes very precisely the feeling of having it done:

 . . . They measured my leg: one was a half-inch shorter than the other. I felt it; you feel bones shifting and things straightening out. It's like when you're tense and can't relax: not psychological tension, but because things in your body aren't right. It felt relaxing, warm and straightening. I relate it very much to the praising of God.

Then, when she was prayed for lengthening others' limbs, the following happens:

. . . I can sense it, but it's hard to describe; like a shifting into place of something that's out of place. Bones, muscles,
sinews, whatever -- they make the adjustment.
You know how when you're all tensed up and
tight and then in prayer, all relaxes and
gets adjusted. You can almost hear it. It's
more gentle than when you crack your knuckles.
There's a gentle shifting of bones and
muscles.

When I put my hands on a person, I can
sense two things: I can sense that the person is experiencing healing from the relaxing
of the body. I can feel the Lord's power
going into the body, can feel the warmth.
Some people can't feel anything. The person
feels a release, warmth. I feel warmth in my
hands. People say, "I felt warmth, power in
your hands."

Thus far in this section we have tried to
capture the two experiences of being a healee, and
of acting as a healer. The emphasis has focused
on procedures employed, and especially on internal
emotional states. We conclude this part of the
chapter by trying briefly to articulate the theology of healing which emerged from the subjects
when explicitly asked. This is important, of
course, because what people think about something
is as relevant as what they directly feel and experience. We shall divide the treatment into two
sections: a more positive overview of the phenomena of gifts; then, answers to the question posed
about dashed expectations, i.e., a prophet or
healer had a "sense from the Lord" that a healing
would occur, and it didn't. The perspective here
in this chapter will continue to be that of the
subjects interviewed, of course.
Cognitive explanations have already been
hinted at along the way. We recall the struggles
of various subjects to articulate for themselves
and the researcher the place of faith and expectancy; the need for praise of the Lord during a

healing; the difference between a "sense from the Lord" and one's own thoughts; the ordinariness of the miraculous in the life of the Community. Two subjects, Elaine and Karen, provided some useful summary comments which we can insert at this point; first, then, Elaine:

> . . . Soon the Lord will work more miraculously, more often. It's not the result of wisdom gained, but of His power. I don't feel we have to "get better" at it. I feel rather a security about my physical health; there are doctors, medicines and the Lord's hands. As for prophecy, I have questions when to speak the Word of the Lord and when to pray for others to speak it. I must exercise it regularly. It's a part of me I can give to others.

Here succinctly stated is a dynamic view of the gifts: Elaine sees them originating with the Lord and being basically His work. As a result of receiving those gifts, she grows in security and has a gift which she, in turn, can share with others. There is movement and flow, therefore, of "power" from the Lord to the Community and herself, and out through herself to others. Though she has questions, she believes that repeated exercise of the gift brings greater wisdom, but ultimately it is the Lord who is producing the effects.
Karen's summary is longer but equally instructive:

> Healing is not super-important, but normal in your own and in the Community's life. It's a promise of Scripture. I'm on the Evangelism team, and I don't want people to come to the Lord for side effects or fringe benefits. It's not the most important thing.

Here Karen emphasizes Community teaching that

213

faith in and love of God are what counts, and that the gifts are by-products. She goes on: "I don't want to make it a sensational thing because that's based on feeling. The Lord is fact." Again, WoG members are instructed to be suspicious of their feelings which fluctuate according to the mood of the moment. Instead, they are called on to "stand firm on the Lord."

> . . . Jesus is constantly healing, for example, the ten lepers. Yet only one came back. I want the Lord to deal with stuff as he sees fit. It should go on all the time as in the days of the early Apostles. When he doesn't heal, it's for a purpose.

In another section of her testimony, Karen linked physical healing with emotional, inner healing, and implied that when healing was absent it was because the Lord showed her she was not open to healing in "other areas of sin."

> . . . Playing it up wouldn't help other people's faith. They might think healing happened because I was special. God gave healings out of His love: I want to emphasize God's love and not the healing.

As with Elaine, there is a subordination here of the individual and her worth to the power and love of God. Yet she gains in self-worth too, paradoxically, for she goes on to say:

> Sometimes I thought God was punishing me. Until the time the ankle healed, I didn't really communicate with the Lord the way I could. There was sin in my life. I told the Lord to "shut up," especially in the area of my boyfriend. I came from a background where the Lord is punishing. He

214

healed me because He loved me: it was a clear case where I had nothing to do with it.

The statements from both Karen and earlier from Betty contain a view of a Lord who has, as it were, a priority of concerns, the highest of which is a moral life for His people, as an expression of a relationship of communication with Him, but who does not hold back His gifts, in the manner of an angry parent, until His children reform.

Quite often, people's understanding of healing would be further revealed when asked how they handled healings which didn't "materialize." Ned's answer, already quoted, is not all that uncommon a reaction: one is to "claim the healing," i.e., say publicly that one has been healed even though the "symptoms" of the ailment remain. The basis for this reaction can be found in giving literal obedience to the command found in Romans 9:9-10,

> For if you confess with your lips that Jesus is Lord, and believe in your heart that God raised him from the dead, you will be saved. Faith in the heart leads to justification, confession on the lips to salvation.

A friend, not one of those interviewed, referred to this text when I shared with him my confusion over the Community's bizarre (to me) usage of the phrase, "I have been healed," by someone quite ill. In this mind-set, "confession on the lips" means "I have prayed in faith and been assured in faith that I am healed: therefore, I am, despite pain, etc." As Ned suggested earlier, the change refers more than anything else to a change in faith state.

Those subjects of less fundamentalistic persuation find other explanations. We continue Karen's testimony:

215

. . . Basically, I don't understand. A sister in South Quad hurt herself. We prayed for healing and she didn't get better. She got better gradually, the usual way. I went to the Lord and said, "I don't know why you won't do this. I accept the situation, but still want the healing." I can trust him. I don't like to analyze so I won't get too introspective. Too, I don't want to pressure her so she feels she <u>has to</u> be healed. The Lord will do it, but <u>people</u> feel it has to be themselves. Healing is an area where we're young: we think it has to be ourselves. Being healed slowly, naturally is the Lord's doing too. It's just a question of how miraculous it looks to others. A miraculous healing is one that's not explainable. A healing from the doctor is from the Lord.

In this brief statement, there are contained five themes which have occurred in others' responses:

(1) Taking the Lord to task for not healing. Such a prayer is typically -- as here -- accompanied by a reaffirmation of basic trust in His Providence.

(2) Don't delve too deeply. Difficulties not understood are best left unexamined. Because most of the subjects are University trained, this alternative gets lip service at best.

(3) Don't pressure the healee into guilt. Even more than a desire for understanding, a deep intention not to add further to the suffering of the sick permeates the teachings and practices of WoG. The basis for this stance? The teaching that God is the one healing, not the person him/herself.

(4) The Community is "young in the gift;" whereas many felt that WoG was growing in "maturity" with prophecy, in healing there was still a

lot to learn.

(5) Redefine the miraculous so that "all is gift." Even an ordinary slow healing is God's work, therefore miraculous.

Max, who came to our interview to speak about his wife's and children's many healings, had a swollen ankle from ruptured blood vessels. His family had prayed over it daily but no healing had occurred. In Max's words:

> . . . It's truly a mystery. God wants to heal. God sometimes works in spite of blocks, for instance, with the demoniacs in Scripture. I feel awe at the mystery. You should expect the best and don't despair if it doesn't happen at first.

Here are two more reactions: awe at the mystery of healing, and a dogged perserverance in prayer.

Sheila recalled that her household had prayed for a young father with leukemia. At first people had no sense that he would live; then later their sense was that he would be healed. "Then he died; it was hard."

Chuck recalls this same case:

> . . . The Lord has answers and He's not giving 'em yet. I prayed during my lunch-break for these girls' father's healing from deathly illness; also for the man with leukemia. People felt the Lord wanted these guys healed. These are questions the Lord hasn't answered for me yet.

What is not found in these testimonies is as significant as what is declared. What is not found is any doubt that the Lord does speak His mind and will to His people. At most, there is expressed a wish to get better at hearing Him, to

"grow in maturity and wisdom in the gifts."
People are firm (without becoming adamant) that
they can and do discern between their own imagin-
ings and the Lord's Word to them and to the group.
A prophet who predicts that someone would get well
would be categorized as having given an impure
prophecy should the person die. I say "would be"
because in the grief of the moment, few bothered
about explanations. Yet the fact that several
brought up the case of the man with the leukemia
in response to a very broad question about unrealized healings shows that the problem was on their
minds still.

Hilary, who had faced the death of his father
from cancer and an unhealed malady of his own of-
fers these reflections:

> . . . I was praying for my father, for his
> cancer, but he had died. I wasn't open at
> first. But I'm just a man, and God is God.
> Often He can use our prayer, but we don't
> have a handle on God. I don't understand why
> people don't get healed. As for my case --
> well, most people don't get healed right
> away. Ideally more people would be experi-
> encing it. I used to wonder what I should do
> to get it to happen. I would fast, meditate
> on God's love. All we can do is simply ask
> Him. I don't feel anything we're doing is
> wrong. God would tell us if we needed to
> change. We can't ever guarantee results. It
> doesn't shake my faith in God's love: it's
> just He's holy and I don't understand Him.

Hilary here renounces his early efforts to manipulate God into dispensing His gifts through fasting, meditation, etc. Yet his acceptance of
things could hardly be characterized as stoical
because it is fundamentally grounded in his ongoing relationship with God. In fact, he relies
on prophecy or the Lord's Leading to redirect the
Community should they be doing things wrong.

We shall offer just a few summary remarks

here, as was done at the conclusion of the section
on prophecy, while saving the bulk of our comments
for the fourth chapter. An attempt has been made
to present the experiences of healees, healers,
leg-lengtheners, and the cognitive theological
orientations of the interviewees. Insofar as possible this was done in their own words with explanatory notations added, but with as little
biasing interpretation of the researcher as possible -- though, of course, an essential element
of the phenomenological method employed calls for
active interaction with the subject. The methodological reminders at the conclusion of the prophecy section hold for this part too: i.e., not
all incidents of healing were reported so as to
avoid repetition, but any significant divergences
from the usual methodology or usually reported
inner experiences were noted. (Hence, a special
section on leg-lengthening had to be included.)
Propositions eight and eleven best summarize this
material. Proposition six points to the essential
similarity between the gifts of healing and prophecy: both are exercised in response to the inner sense from the Lord. At the time of the research, it was the consensus of those interviewed
that WoG members were "mature" in the gift of prophecy, but "young," i.e., quite inexperienced,
still needing more "Wisdom" in the gift of healing.

Deliverance

A personal pre-note is in order. From my
psychological and theological training, both liberal and modern (adjectives applied analogously to
both traditions), I was conditioned against taking
seriously the following materials. General Psychology courses begin with an historical overview
of early attempts to explain human behavior, and
pooh-pooh all references to the demonic as at best
superstitious, at worst leading to such horrors as
witch-burning. Similarly, from my theological upbringing, I was taught that the biblical writers
employed literary borrowing from the Persians:
since the Jews originally had no place for demons

in their cosmology, they imported them freely from surrounding cultures, and simply employed projection to impart to devils an existential reality. Yet members of WoG take the "Evil One" with utmost seriousness, and convincingly impart their conviction that yet another gift from "the Lord" is their ability to "bind up and cast forth" the "powers of Hell." References have been made in the previous section to the use of deliverance during healing rituals, but we now take up this curious practice for separate study and reflection.

Members of the Community shared the conditioning of the author regarding demonic forces. Since most were members of Catholic and mainline Protestant denominations, they simply had never been schooled to pay much attention to demons. Hence, it is important here to trace historically the rise of belief in occult powers and the Community's reaction to their felt presence.

Victor provided the most systematic account concerning the various stages and phases of the deliverance ministry. His account will predominate here with some references to others' memories and experiences.

Victor's first words were that deliverance "came out of nowhere," but that since then there has been growth and development. This statement is, of course, not quite accurate because the Pentecostal churches are the source of most of the practices and techniques chronicled here, and deliverance is no exception. It all started on a Monday in March, 1970, known ever after as "Deliverance Monday." Two preachers from Florida had come to town and were "amazed that Catholics were getting baptized in the Spirit." At supper with the leaders, they shared about deliverance and prayed for the gift. In those days, prayer meetings were held on Mondays, and the ministers came to explain about deliverance of people "from the work of Satan in their lives."

After the prayer meeting, they held a deliverance session in an apartment across the street from St. Mary's Student Chapel. Victor goes on:

. . . People were told to denounce the spirits that might be operative in their lives. The ministers were into certain kinds of cultural, Protestant fundamental things.
They're into jumping up and down, screaming when you pray. They feel there should be a dramatic physical manifestation of spirits' leaving like rolling on the floor, drooling, vomiting. It caused quite a stir.

The ministers wandered around the room. People were in various states of disrepair on the floor screaming. They were acting out the departure. People were coughing, hacking, wheezing.

The police came. Someone explained and the police went away: they were used to weird things in those days!

People thought this was a real breakthrough. Everybody had stuff in their lives they couldn't come up against. The ministers prayed for people, laid hands on them violently, moved people about. Our coordinator was watching it all from a corner.

For six or eight months thereafter there were two big opinions: first, it's the greatest thing that ever happened; secondly, it's crazy -- let me out!

Victor himself believed it was a good thing, but wasn't sure the approach was best. People got "too hung up on blaming evil spirits instead of working things out in other ways." One couple wound up with opposite opinions. At the house where Victor resided, there began to occur basement deliverances day and night. "People foamed, shrieked in the cellar all hours of the day and night."
When Victor himself got delivered,

221

. . . I felt absolutely obliged to do something. The best I could work up was coughing. For certain Fundamental groups, you can't be baptized in the Spirit without praying in tongues; can't be delivered without physical manifestations. There was an unconscious social pressure. Yet I saw people I respected flying out of their chairs: they were literally thrown from their chairs. It struck me as odd but real. Their experience was that they were being acted on. Things happened I couldn't explain.

I prayed gently one time, and the guy was thrown to the floor, was drooling. We were in shock: nobody knew what to do next. I thought it was something genuine, but was work of evil spirits. I knew from the Gospel it could happen. The fine distinction between possession and oppression was not yet worked out. Because we did not know much about it, possession was the most common thing from the New Testament.

Victor here spontaneously explains many of these early phenomena as being due to social pressure. The distinction referred to comes from the Catholic Exorcism ritual where "possession" means the taking over by demon(s) of someone's personality whereas "oppression" or "obsession" means forms of violent physical harassment of people and places by the evil spirits (Weller, 1964, pp. 636-644).

After half a year, the next major phase occurred, namely, talking to the spirits, sometimes for hours on end. People kept in touch with the ministers and began reading "old Catholic works." People were told to say aloud what the evil spirit had in mind to say. The deliverers were getting beaten up. "Unuseful," foul talk was heard like that in The Exorcist. People's characters were assaulted; sin in their lives was revealed. Though they were told that they didn't need to give vent to violence, blasphemy, indecency, some people had been "pretty messed up and into the occult."

> . . . I remember being called to a cellar. A brother and I got our heads bashed. A woman had said, "We need strong men around." This yound guy had been around but not in the Community. He had been into drugs and the occult. He asked for deliverance one Thursday night. When we got there, the guy couldn't sit still anymore. He was on the floor screaming with people holding him down. The heads wanted it to be gotten over with. All of us were praying; the main person would address spirits, command them to leave. There would be conversation with the spirits as needed. It was supposed to be useful to find out how spirits got in and how they worked in people's lives. We got back-talk. I really experienced something more than normal going on. He's not a particularly strong guy. We got smashed together, my friend and I.

> It went on for a long time, a long night of needless talking. People from all over would come in in the evening and pray till "dawn's early light." It had good effects because the guy seems to be doing much better.

As with healings, not all deliverances "work." Victor narrates such a case:

> . . . This guy was into drugs and having flashbacks from hallucinogens. When we prayed with him he got physically violent: one guy took on the dozen of us! We prayed and he did too. The leaders would address him, "Spirit of such and such, I cast you out in the name of the Lord Jesus." When they started this, he became extremely violent; he became so powerful. We couldn't hold onto

him, the dozen of us. The leader said it
would be better to take care of the doors
and windows and let Willy do his thing. Some
people got pounded. He made his escape out a
door, went to a dorm, smashed Michael in the
mouth and went on his way. People have kept
up with him. He's into Hare Krishna, has
been back a few times. He's such a hurt person; he needed lots of repair work to get his
act together.

Deliverance is not without its occasional humorous
moments too: "One nice older lady came. We
prayed all night. She was into verbal violence.
A funny thing happened: at 4 A.M. we had a tea
and chocolate chip cookie break!"
    We interrupt the progression of phases cata-
logued by Victor to narrate a few confirming accounts from others concerning this matter of conversation with evil spirits.
    Frank was praying for deliverance with a
brother once. Frank used to feel he ate too much.
While praying over the brother, the latter said,
"You can'd do that to me, you glutton." Frank
laughed and said, "I'm a son of God. Get away,
evil spirit."
    Frank felt "you can do lots with spirits."
He would take a pad and pencil, write down what
the spirit in the person said, then answer with
the Truth to the stuff on the pad.
    When Frank spontaneously commented that
"there's also the psychological pattern," I requested that he enlighten me on the difference
between a psychological and a demonic problem:

        . . . One is a psychological disorder in
    thinking and emotionally responding. Spirits
    are liars, they want to murder you, Jesus
    says. They tell people things that aren't
    true. But it's not like people have no re-
    sponsibility; they do.

        At a deliverance session, the person

would pick out a spirit and we would too, one by one. Say, fear. I'd ask, "What do you do?" The spirit would reply, "I make Andy afraid of his mother." Then I tell the spirit to leave.

Olga had been present in the early days and recounts her deliverance in a story reminiscent of Victor's:

. . . A couple guys came through town preaching deliverance. Ned did some investigating into Church teachings. The major problem I had was that my life was very bound in fear. I had gone through most of my life terrified of things, people. A brother prayed over me. The person praying would call forth by name the spirits. In the course of praying they would assume that the Lord would show them what they needed to know. They would let the evil spirit respond. I heard my voice say things. Not like what people say happened in The Exorcist. It didn't sound like my voice: it was horrible, raspy. After he left, I was tempted to be afraid. I had to remember that Jesus was my Lord and be reminded that I wasn't alone. Other than that it was just tiring.

Here is an account from someone who actually went through the trauma of having "the evil spirit" speak through her. More emotional still is her narration of helping Xavier, the brother who had "delivered her," with another "client."

. . . We just prayed for him and quiet, gentle Xavier stood up, looked in the doorway, spoke firmly, loudly, authoritatively in tongues. There was a presence there, definitely malignant. We prayed with Xavier and the other guy. When it was over, the guy

fell asleep, utterly exhausted. Clearly he
should have been given over to the authority
of a priest. We were totally drained, totally exhausted; we felt we were holding on by
the skin of our teeth. We had been laying
hands on the guy the whole time. He had
been a heavy user of drugs. Now he's no
longer in the Community, had a couple of
kids, is supporting his family.

Victor had answered my question as to what
was the sign that "now it's time to stop?" "When
those involved felt an end had been reached. When
the discerned spirits had been dealt with. There
was, of course, a continual pastoral care for
these people." Once again we see the interlocking
employment of the gifts: though deliverance is
the gift sought, the leader prays in tongues; lays
on hands; uses discernment to discover what spirits are operative and when to stop. All takes
place within the supportive "pastoral" structure
of the WoG Community. (See proposition four.)
   Ned too provided some reflective input on
this topic of discussing matters with the spirits:

My initial reaction was resistance.
After the first mania, I saw at least some
relief in some people's lives. After six or
eight months (confirms exactly but independently Victor's estimate) Xavier came and
prayed with us for deliverance. In my case
it was a surrender as if in prophecy. It
spoke to Xavier about what it was doing in my
life. We prayed for exorcism; it went away.
There was a major spirit and some little
spirits. The major spirit was greed over my
personal library. The spirit of greed said,
"I make Ned subject to his books, a slave to
them." It was true; I had an inordinate
pride in my library. Another was lust, plus
other garden-variety spirits. Before that
point in time, I had realized my relationship
wasn't healthy with my things. I got freedom.

226

When we moved, I threw half the books away.
The major spirit had a personal name,
"Algernac," a name which seemed to have no
function.

Typically, cerebral Ned first questions a new custom in the group. Then he reads up on it, and
tries it out. He compares the experience of letting the evil spirit speak to letting the Spirit
of God speak in prophecy, a comparison no one else
used, probably because it would have sounded blas-
phemous. Frank had independently confirmed in his
testimony that when he inquired into the names of
spirits, he would most usually be told the name of
a vice, but occasionally a personal name also as
in Ned's case.

Without being prodded, Ned spontaneously went
on to reflect:

... I'm unsure if my unconscious psychological states are involved, but I hold in faith
that there are spirits. Whether they work
this way, I'm not sure. I did research in
Thomas Aquinas.

I had conversations with spirits, an
emotionally trying and somewhat upsetting experience. You feel like you're on the front
line where the metaphysical and tangible
worlds intersect. I feel like here especially we must rely on the Lord. We did it for
people traveling through Ann Arbor, and felt
the power of the Lord.

Sometimes a spirit would name itself,
for instance, lust, and I'd sense it wasn't
true. "That's a lie: tell me who you really
are," I'd say. Through discernment, we would
get to the bottom of it: pride, greed, etc.
It did indeed seem that there was a principal
spirit and subordinate spirits, as in a hierarchy. The mechanism didn't seem to work unless you gave each its name and bound one

from another. The methodology came from
Xavier's behavior with me and my own
experience.

Ned offered further reflections of a more cognitive nature to be discussed later, but meanwhile
we return to Victor's "next phase."

> Xavier developed a new approach. There
> was a change from colorfulness to deal with
> things in one's life more constructively. He
> would explain that things were obstacles in
> your life. Together they would pray: if
> they prayed they were delivered. We moved on
> from there: it's not a cure-all. It became
> much more quiet and peaceful. We don't blame
> the devil. People would discern things.
> It's now routinely done in Week nine of
> Foundations I.

The genius of the WoG coordinators is revealed in
this passage. Xavier is a sensitive, talented,
middle-level coordinator, the father of a family
and head of a household. Seeking to use this new
gift of deliverance, yet make it less spooky and
violent, he took the spectacular element out of it
(talking with evil spirits) while reaffirming the
basic belief in demonic influence. The Foundations courses are several series of twelve-week
lectures required of new members after their Life-
in-the Spirit Seminar, Community weekend, and underway commitment. The courses cover the "foundations" of Christian community living. The main
talks for each session have been taped and are
sold worldwide on cassette tapes through Charismatic Renewal Services.
Victor elaborates further:

> . . . Deliverance was like the Catholic con-
> fessional experience, but now they don't men-
> tion their vices anymore. People don't even

mind having it happen in their basements!
The whole thing was a learning experience:
we went from a cultural thing to a more quiet
way of helping people deal with difficulties
in their lives. It's like a rite of passage
now -- from what people were, into what they
choose now.

In this way, WoG has tamed and institutionalized
another practice inherited from the classical
Fundamentalist tradition of Pentecostalism.
Victor recapitulates the phases by giving a quick
summary of them as they affected his life:

> . . . When I first joined the Renewal in
> in '69, I was demythologizing, wasn't
> believing in a personal Satan. The Lord gave
> me an experience; I met a practicing witch
> who worshipped the old Druid gods. He told
> me things about myself, read Tarot cards. I
> saw personal evil operate in a concrete kind
> of way in someone's life.
>
> In the second phase, I witnessed physi-
> cal violence. They would yell at deliverers,
> reveal sin in people's lives. It was a dis-
> traction while praying. They didn't need to
> say everything, nor do things which weren't
> nice or were blasphemous. I had some people
> say things about me which no one knew.
>
> The signs of a successful deliverance
> are the fruit in people's lives. They are
> able to cope better, make progress in the
> spiritual life. There are a lot of concrete
> changes. Now it's a calm, everyday sort of
> thing.

Frank gives several more practical, less
aesthetic reasons for the move away from talking
with the spirits:

. . . We were paying more attention to spirits than we needed to. We can ask the person
instead about their problems. The less attention given to the devil, the better. It's
more healthy not to dialogue with the devil.

Despite these changes, deliverance, we saw,
is still employed not only formally in the context
of the Foundations course, but also routinely in
healing rituals. The next few selections from the
testimonies show how people discern the presence
of evil spirits as distinguished from ordinary
psychological difficulties.
Elaine begins with a case of anxiety:

. . . I once knew a person was nervous. I
knew anxiety would interfere with trust in
the Lord. At other times there was no out-
ward physical thing I could see. I wouldn't
hear actual words that a person is anxious
-- it's more just a sense. I experience prophecy the same way, just a sense of what the
situation really is. (Does the sense include
what to do as well as the diagnosis?) From
past experience, for example, with anxiety, I
would pray for the person first. I would ask
the Lord to relieve the anxiety. If I felt a
spirit of anxiety, there's a different sense
of what it is. (What's the difference between psychological anxiety and spirit-caused
anxiety?) When I sense an evil spirit, I
feel there's more seriousness, a darkness.
It's not natural, not caused by circumstances
in the world. It's an ugly spiritual force,
against the Lord, evil. Sometimes I feel
fear till I recall the Lord has the victory:
then I feel anger. I come against it, banish
it. I call on the name of the Lord. I pray
that the person is in the Father's hand. In
casting out the spirit, I address the spirit
in the name of the Lord. (Afterwards, do you
feel different?) There's an external difference in sensations, a physical calmness on

them. They'll praise the Lord. I sense that the ugly, dark, evil thing is no longer present.

Several other subjects recounted experiencing a certain extra something present in their inter-actions with people presenting themselves for healing, or deliverance, an "ugly, dark evil thing," an extra "spiritual force."
Frank's account is similar:

We went to the house of a new Christian. We sensed the presence of the Evil One. (What's that like?) There was a darkness over my own spirit, an atmosphere in the room not from the temperature of the room, the ar-rangement of furniture, the color of the walls, an oppressive atmosphere. Sometimes I sense their names. It's like when you used to picture a soul-shaped thing in your body, something S-shaped. I sense them flitting around. I was gonna rebuke it, but suddenly sensed it wasn't there. I talked with my friend later who had gone with me who said that he had rebuked that spirit.

Now that deliverance has become institution-alized in WoG, it occurs frequently in conjunction with the use of other gifts. The following is Sheila's story of the prophecy given to her in a dream which involved deliverance as well. A year prior to our interview, Sheila and her husband were vacationing in a cabin in the woods. During the night as she slept she had a dream:

. . . In the dream, I was at a prayer meeting with lots of free praise. I began speaking a prophecy. I awoke and had a prophecy. I knew I'd give it later. My husband sensed a spiritual interference. Something frighten-ing woke me. I sensed evil flowing up from

231

around the woods, from the floor of the cabin.
I woke my husband. He sensed it too. We
prayed, praised the Lord, rebuked Satan. I
had a physical sense of pushing darkness
back. Later I gave the prophecy. It was
about God's work in the world and His pushing
back the curtains of darkness. He was calling together people to do this.

On one occasion, Daphne was praying for a
girl in her household who was suffering nausea and
cramps in the middle of the night:

. . . She was really white; I was afraid
she'd pass out. I prayed over her; nothing
happened. I woke everybody and we prayed for
five minutes. She went to bed O.K. We all
praised the Lord, asked Him to heal her, cast
out some spirits. (What's the difference in
your sense of praying for healing vs. praying
for deliverance?) If I pray for healing and
feel resistance to faith in them or in me, I
pray against the spirits.

This brief anecdote reminds us of the several
stories in the previous section of the chapter
concerning healing in which deliverance was routinely employed.
Max tells of two deliverance experiences, one
with his wife and one with his child:

. . . My wife discovered a lump in her
breast. Three days later the gynecologist
scheduled surgery, but found nothing. Meanwhile she had been prayed over twice, once by
friends and once in a Pentecostal Church.
She was prayed over for deliverance at the
Church. The minister felt that sin inside
was causing the breast problem. Something
must be wrong in her marriage; she had some
wrong attitudes. It was strange. The

> minister took her aside for work, for firty-
> five minutes. He might have been in the
> Spirit, but it was high-powered and odd.

This reminds us of the early days of deliverance
described by Victor before the procedures had been
normalized.

In the case of his son, the doctor had advised Max that his boy had been physically cured,
but on the day before Thanksgiving severe symptoms
reoccurred which caused the child to be readmitted
to the hospital. The family's interpretation was
that the symptoms "must be a hassle from the Evil
One." His wife and a friend prayed, "cast out the
Evil One," and the symptoms disappeared. He was
released from the hospital in a week. During this
trying time, they stayed at the boy's bedside for
hours, but never simultaneously with the physician.
They also "felt condemnation" because the doctor
got angry with them. Max and his wife got angry
with each other too:

> . . . Even the symptoms were a hassle. They
> were incongruous with the facts. We prayed,
> forgave one another, then forgave the doctor,
> cast out the Evil One. There was a change in
> a few hours. Now the boy is a happy affec-
> tionate child.

In Max's world-view, therefore, and in that of
others who corroborated it, the "Evil One" causes
both physical ailments and misunderstandings between people (himself, his wife, their physician)
who are sincerely trying to achieve a good end together. In other words, the evil spirits work in
both the physical and emotional realms.

Thomas had described earlier how he felt that
his pains were demonic in origin, and related two
brief anecdotes of deliverance in his own case and
in that of others:

233

. . . One time for a whole week I felt someone behind me. I'd turn around and no one
was there. After taking my wife and children
to church, I was taking my t-shirt off. I
could almost see a figure in the doorway,
could feel a presence. I told it, "Demon,
devil, in the name of Jesus, be gone." It
seemed to explode like a balloon. I felt
victorious. (Any experience of deliverance
with others?) Only when I see someone really,
really angry. I ask the Lord to give him
peace and joy. We get things settled and I
thank the Lord.

This testimony combines the notions of a personalized experience of Evil as well as its effects
on interpersonal interactions noted immediately
above in Max's remarks.

Although we gave a long quotation from Ursula
above in the treatment of inner healing, the account would fit just as well here in this section
concerning deliverance.

Ned and Olga both spoke concerning their
prayers for deliverance over their son. First
Ned:

. . . I have an occasional sense that in my
son is an influence in temper-tantrums above
and beyond psychological influences. When
I've prayed, the temper-tantrum subsides to a
usual expectable level. Say, he has a temper-
tantrum before dinner over a lollipop. O.K.,
he's frustrated. If it escalates to something near hysteria, and I can't come up with
a reason why he's particularly frustrated today, I may attribute it to action of spirits.
If I pray, he can't understand polysyllables.
I tend not to hold him, ignore the tantrum,
pray in the hall while he is in his room.

Olga's approach is similar:

234

. . . Our son was once troubled by a spirit
of fear. I bound the spirit of fear, prayed
for his protection. He settled and went to
sleep. He's troubled too by a spirit of rebellion. He's a very independent child.
(What sense do you get between his little
self and an evil spirit?) There's almost a
presence, a sense of someone else here. I
don't give them the time of day. I can tell
the difference between it and normal two-year-
old things.

Elaine answered my query about why there was
no deliverance team to match those for healings
and prophecy. "Deliverance is a one-time thing.
Also, prophecy and healing are special gifts, but
all can pray for deliverance." Yet her skill in
this area was what got her appointed to the healing team in the first place: "I'd prayed with
people a lot and had been able to discern during
exorcism what spirits were at work. I don't have
the gift of healing, but as a daughter of God, I
can pray for their healing." We recall that
Hilary had made a similar disclaimer, and provided
a distinction between those with the (charismatic)
gift of healing and himself who simply prayed and
occasionally was heard. Part of such a statement
by Hilary and Elaine may be attributed to humility
perhaps, but their remarks indicate a different
understanding of the gifts (which they employ) and
the gifted (among whose special ranks they do not
count themselves).
We conclude this section of the chapter with
a somewhat hair-raising tale of Sheila's own
deliverance.

. . . My first experience of deliverance was
of being delivered five years ago in _____.
I'd had a lot of trouble with it beforehand,
had heard about this new thing in Ann Arbor,
but didn't believe in those spooks. There
was trouble in my own life. I was into the
Peace Movement, but not healed from family

experiences. I was becoming more and more bitter and knew that something had to snap. The priest I was going to for spiritual direction was messed up too.

I felt I should go home for a weekend. Friday before leaving, I was in the chapel and a nun was talking to me. All of a sudden, I felt, "Shut up!" I walked around the room restless. I began to think, "Don't go home." Yet I knew the Lord wanted me to. I left the chapel and was walking across campus. I felt like three trucks were attacking me at once. Stuff I'd worked through all came back, like hating my parents, wishing they'd die. I remembered a priest-friend saying that he had seen people attacked by evil spirits. I felt something push me to the ground. I was crying. I got home, trembling and frightened. I read Scripture. In Luke (11:24-26) it says that if an evil spirit is cast out, then it gets seven more -- well, I felt like it was seventy! I tried calling the priest. He was scheduled to start Mass just then, but he came right over anyway and prayed over me.

I threw up! Rolled around! I hadn't heard about that stuff here. Yet it was tremendously freeing the next year. I talked about my life in general with a coordinator, and he suggested we pray for deliverance. Stuff came out that I remembered at four or five years old. It was the beginning of a real personal healing, clearly different from psychological hassles. It was the first time in my life I'd experienced blatant evil outside myself.

Sheila's story thus ended happily with the process of healing of memories and deliverance, but in the telling of it, she went right on from this point to tell of other harassment by this same unknown force:

. . . This thing drove me to the chapel earlier. I'd had dreams about death, dying, violence. While driving a relative to the hospital as she was having a heart attack, I'd found myself praying, "I hope she dies!" I dreamed I was gonna kill this person. And me in the Peace Movement! This was really out of character. When I awoke from the dream I had been trying to crawl out of the second story window. I felt this thing telling me, "You're gonna visit and kill her." I was driven by it into church. God touched me on the shoulder, moved His hand across the evil. Evil isn't just war, but a personal attack. My priest-friend had said, "As a Chrisian, you can expect to be protected."

This statement concludes the section on deliverance. Though shorter than the two previous sections on prophecy and healing, our treatment of the subjects made references to this gift along the way. As in those cases, all the thematic lines of development have been presented, historical and experiential, for the group and for the individuals interviewed. We proceed now to more extended commentary and analysis.

CHAPTER IV

PHENOMENOLOGICAL ANALYSIS AND DISCUSSION

Data on the experience of the spiritual gifts, most especially prophecy, healing and deliverance, have been set out at some length in the previous chapter. The task remains to subject these data to a phenomenological analysis according to the method outlined in the second chapter. The task might be formulated as a question: just as we have been exposed to the myth of the charismatics, how do we incorporate these experiences into psychological mythology? The goal is to demonstrate from this case of WoG how the method could be applied to other human experiences, religious or otherwise. A practical grasp of the method leads to an understanding of how other Pentecostal groups, for example, and other forms of religious or psychological experience can be studied in the tradition of the "human sciences." The summary of findings and the penetration into the eidetic essence of this Community's experiences could possibly be generalized to other similar times and settings but not a priori, that is, not automatically without undertaking similar research with the comparison group. (At this point, the reader may wish to refamiliarize himself with the section headed, "A Generalized Description of the Method" in Chapter II so as to become aware again of just how the development will unfold.)

Investigation of Particular Phenomena

The first step in the process of phenomenological methodology has been undertaken in Chapter III, as we investigated particular experiences of the various spiritual gifts. The first subphase of step one, the pointing to experiences, was accomplished in the biographical accounts and recorded statements of the interviewed subjects. The analyst's efforts consisted at that point almost entirely of arranging the utterances by topic since they were originally offered in a stream of consciousness flow, and of providing an explanation of word usage idiosyncratic to WoG, e.g., "headship," "asking for a Scripture," etc.

The second subphase of the first step, the analytic examination of the phenomena through an isolation of certain linguistic expression, was performed by the author subsequently to the data-gathering, but has already been partially offered to the reader in the form of the twelve propositions in Chapter III. Furthermore, Table II below contains a collected list of specialized vocabulary employed by the subjects in describing the gifts. The more unusual terms were defined in the reporting of the testimonies, but they are gathered here for convenience in one place. Many have biblical connotations; most have been imported from the terminology of Pentecostal Churches. Further explanations are added in parentheses after some of the terms.

TABLE II

Special Vocabulary

act in faith
anger with spirits
anointing
area (of one's life; of sin)
ask/pray for a Scripture
authority (speak with; pray with)

baptism in the Holy Spirit the body (the whole WoG Community)
bondage
build up (encourage)
bulwark (of faith, against evil)

cast out (evil spirits)
charism/Charismat-. ic Renewal
Christian Living Situation
claim a healing
clear sense (from the Lord)
come before the Lord (in prayer)
come soon (the Lord's second coming)
come to the Lord (a conversion experience)

TABLE II (continued)

commitment (to WoG)
common finance household
community
confirmation (of a pro-
    phecy)
coordinator
covenant

darkness
deal with
deliverance
demon
devil
discernment

edify/edification
Evangelization team
Evil One
expectant faith

fasting (for some gift)
fellowship (noun or
    verb)
freedom
fruit (effects of gifts
or action in one's
    life)

gift
greeter
growing/growth in the
    Lord

handmaid
hard times
headship
healing
    healing of memories
    healing prayer room
    healing team
household

impure prophecy
inner healing
interpretation of
    tongues
in the Lord (e.g.,
    living)

joy

Kingdom (of God)

life in the Spirit
lift someone up to
the Lord (e.g., in
    prayer
limb lengthening
listening to the
    Lord
Lord
Lord's leading
Lordship

mantles and veils
maturity in the
    gifts
ministry (use of
    the gifts)
miracle

normal

obedience
order (Community
order; have one's
    life in order)
ordinary

peace
a People (called by
    God)
perfect plan, Lord's

TABLE II (continued)

personal transformation
power
praise
pray
    pray for a passage
        (of Scripture)
    pray over someone
prayer room
presence (Divine; de-
    monic)
prophecy
    prophecy group
    prophecy team
pure prophecy

real, really
rebuke (an evil spirit,
    sickness)
redeemed dating (under
    headship)
repentance
revelation
the right way (accord-
ing to Community or-
    der)
roles, men's and women's

Satan
sense from the Lord
sharing
slain in the Spirit
something new (done by
    the Lord)
speak in tongues

stand firm on the
    Lord
step out in faith
stir up the gift
    e.g., prophecy
submission/sub-
    ordination

teaching (noun, in-
struction given at
    prayer meeting)
tongues
turn to the Lord
    (in prayer)

underway (going/
    being)
unpeaceful
uplifted/upbuilt
urgency (to pro-
    phesy)

victory (over Satan,
    sin vision)

witness
Word
    Word of Know-
        ledge
    Word of Wis-
        dom
world

yield (to prophecy)

The twelve propositions had provided an overall thematic structure for the terms used by the
Community members to designate the spiritual
gifts. It is the researcher's claim that the verbal reports of the subjects quoted lend sufficient
support to his generalizations with the exception

of proposition twelve. That statement contains the view of history taught at WoG prayer meetings, but never explicitly alluded to in the testimonies quoted here. It was included for the sake of placing the other terms, propositions, and overall meaning structure within an historical context, the context implicitly assumed by the membership but not explicitly in evidence above. With this exception noted, however, the other eleven propositions, or theses, can be said to have been demonstrated as an explicit articulation of the individuals' subjective experience of the gifts.

The third subphase of the first step, a description of particular phenomena, has been provided by the subjects' words themselves. The negative function of excluding irrelevant data was conservatively employed by the author: he counted as "irrelevant" only those anecdotes or descriptive accounts which repeated materials already provided by at least two witnesses. Wherever a subject spoke "outside the chorus" of voices, his/her opinion or experience was noted and recorded. The effort to be precise "about referents and qualifiers" was noted in the investigator's questions and comments appearing within square brackets in the body of the sujbects' verbatim remarks.

An important purpose of this third part of step one is to differentiate the phenomena from others with which they might be confused. Several such differentiations and distinctions can be mentioned as having been noted in Chapter III. An effort was made then to have subjects describe the felt differences between a spiritual gift or influence from the outside (a prophecy, word of knowledge, discernment, etc.) and their own ideas and emotions. Another difference, one which will be developed in this chapter, was that between the earlier and later practices and understandings of the gifts, i.e., before and after the effects of increasing socialization and institutionalization by the Community. Thirdly, subjects spontaneously set themselves apart from other healing traditions: from Christian Scientists who deny the reality of pain and will not employ physicians' remedies; from healers who experience physical concomitants

243

like warmth and tingling; from all occult practices. Study of the eidetic essence of healing in
the next section will reveal how different the WoG
experience is from LeShan's healings in "secular
clairvoyant reality" (1974) and from Worrall's
technique and theory (1965); typically, most of
the subjects neither experience nor employ the
metaphor of energy transformations, waves, etc.,
but rather act in the context of their personal
relationship with the Transcendent. Regarding
prophecy, it has been noted heretofore that this
gift does not typically manifest itself through
predictions, but instead that the prophet speaks
in behalf of (Latin pro/fari) the Divinity. Finally, we will comment further on the two levels
of discernment: by the individual recipient of a
gift like prophecy, and by the recipient's head at
a prayer meeting or someone further up in the
hierarchy like a coordinator.

Investigating General Essences

The work of step one, the investigation of
particular phenomena, was done mostly in the previous chapter. We can now begin the phenomenological analysis with step two, the investigation of
general essences. (This could have been incorporated in the text of the last chapter at the end
of each of the three major sections, but it was
thought best to put it here so that description
would predominate there, and that the formal work
of analysis might neither seemingly nor in practice subjectively bias the presentation of the
interview data.) We are seeking then an "eidetic
intuition," in Husserl's sense, of prophecy, healing and deliverance, an apprehension of the es-
sentials of the gifts themselves as they impinge
on human consciousness.

Community members experience prophecy as an
ongoing, concrete revelation of "the Lord's" will
for an individual, or for "the body," i.e., the
Community, and even for the world beyond WoG.
Prophecy is felt -- not merely thought, but felt
-- to be the use by God of human speech

244

(vernacular or tongues, spoken, sung or written) to communicate His intentions, plans and desires, and occasionally future events. The core of the experience lies in the prophet's personal relationship with the Lord. When s/he has her/his life "in order" morally and emotionally, and especially when s/he is open to hearing the Word, then "pure" prophecy, with little admixture of one's own ideas and biases, results. The prophet's task consists solely in listening to the interior word and proclaiming it boldly, not in discerning its appropriateness, applicability, feasibility. (This latter mode of "discernment" is reserved for the Community heads. Still, the prophet her/himself must also individually "discern" that a prophecy indeed has been given, and is to be spoken out, and that the ideas and feelings are not merely self-generated.) There may or may not be physical concomitants to prophecies, called "anointings," but prophets tried to describe the internal differences between anointings and natural nervousness or hallucinogenic stimulation. The thematic contents of prophecy range from the encouraging to the exhortatory, but are always situation-specific and more concrete, and focused, and timely than the eternal words of Scripture upon which, however, prophecy is ultimately based and judged. Variations in content and style of delivery increase with practice and are modified by unofficial feedback from hearers, and by official input from coordinators of a prayer meeting, or heads of a subject to whom a prophecy has been rendered.

"Ontogeny recapitulates phylogeny." In the context of prophecy, this dictum from biology has applications in that the group's experience of prophecy is repeated in the life of fledgling prophets. Prophecy was first remembered as being utterly spontaneous and free when it sprang up after early contact with the Pentecostal Churches; after five years, a prophecy team is appointed and only official prophets may speak out at public gatherings. Similarly, each person newly baptized in the Spirit is encouraged to practice the gifts spontaneously in a small-group context; with experience, discernment, modeling, and friendly input, the group recognizes and promotes new prophets and gradually shapes a prophetic style for its open meetings, although theoretically such institutionalization has not crushed out the possibility for new directions to be enunciated.

Prophets gave various personally significant signs of the difference between a "sense from the Lord" and their own ideas. These signs included: most importantly, a confirmation-by-event; confirmation after prophesying by another that he was about to enunciate the same message; interior visions, and thought/speech patterns not recognized as one's own; peace and joy, etc. During delivery, however, prophets have to "step out in faith" because they usually have at most the urgency to speak, a few words to use plus an overall sense of the total message. "Maturity" in the gift includes, among other characteristics, ability to renounce one's timidity and to utter words consistently recognized as "pure" by those whose gift it is to discern the prophets' dicta. Tensions of a trying kind afflict the prophetic soul for s/he must trust the insight without being able to predict reactions of the leadership; must have enough trust in the Lord and in oneself to speak out, with little certainty that one will come to a graceful conclusion and not get caught in the middle; must occasionally be called to deliver harsh messages of repentance. An urgency to speak forth the word is felt not only by those officially in charge of the task but by many others in all sorts of settings, even the privacy of one's room with only oneself as listener or writer. Ursula's five criteria (Chapter III. p. 146) for genuine prophecy provide a useful summary of crucial details: (1) the sense of urgency; (2) the sense that the Word is the Lord's, not one's own; (3) a mental sense of the message; (4) the actual delivery; (5) clarity of presentation. The history of the prophecy team as detailed by four of its members showed the subtle and sensitive interplay between the WoG leadership, the individuals' own subjective sense of their gift and calling, and the natural forces of social shaping and institutionalization.

Next, we shall attempt to formulate an eidetic intuition of healing, again as with prophecy by using the data presented. The term, "healing," is used in the phrase, "healing of memories," to indicate the easing of pain surrounding past experiences, and also in the sense of physical cures.

Healing of memories includes calling to mind events which sometimes have been long forgotten, growing in insight concerning them, but also consciously forgiving oneself and any other participants, living or dead, present or absent, for inflicted pain. This healing is not considered complete until the event ceases to stir resentment, bitterness, anger, etc. Community members are taught the Pauline directive, "Rejoice in all circumstances" (Phil. 4:4-7), and are encouraged patiently to seek and pray for healing until they are actually able to thank God for the misfortune or pain which occurred.

WoG participants believe that in a community relating to the Lord "in the right way," healing of illness, even miraculous healing, should be an ordinary and expected happening. At first the terms, "miraculous" and "ordinary" might seem to contradict each other, but we recall that miraculous means "an event where God is experienced as present in some special way," and "ordinary" implies "daily, routine." "Miraculous" further implies an outcome or rapidity not expected by the consulting physicians, as many of the subjects made clear. While most of the ailments healed were functional, several were possibly organic, particularly those of Paula and Thomas (pp. 174 ff.). Again, as with prophecy, the core of the experience grows out of the individual's and the body's relationship with the Lord. This provides the set and setting for the healing, and an occasion, the Lord may indicate that a particular healing is not to be prayed for at that time.

The wider culture refers to this gift as "faith healing," and we recorded the whole spectrum of complicated and nuanced feelings about the place of faith in this gift. To summarize:

"expectant faith," it seems to be agreed by all, needs to be experienced to some degree by at least one party: the healer or the healee, preferably by both. Somewhat parallel to the faith required in the prophet to "step out on" his incomplete sense of the Word to be delivered is the faith of the healee who occasionally feels the urgency to claim, "I have been healed," even when symptoms persist, or to "step out in faith" and use an afflicted body part despite a physician's warnings. This latter experience is rare, but documented with sufficient frequency to suggest that the true believer trusts his God more than his physician, relies on the methods of the non-medical healers more than the methods of science though, unlike Christian Scientists, members of WoG employ both traditions of healing. "Faith" refers not to belief in a set of doctrines, but rather to the aspect of trust in one's relationship with the Lord such that one expects Him to use His power to heal.

The methodology of the healers is the same for the healing prayer room and for "private practice." Lois (Chapter III, P. 184) described what happens from the viewpoint of a healee most succinctly, and Elaine and Frank, partners on the healing team, present an account from the side of the healers (ibid., pp. 202 ff.). In terms of procedures, healers attempt to persuade the healee to relax either through personal encouragement, or by making the theological point such as "God is doing this, not you or us." A talk concerning expectant faith may be given in the healing prayer room, or at the general meeting of the body. Then an atmosphere of praise and thanksgiving is evoked through communal prayer and song. Next, each sick person is individually questioned about his illness, and hands are laid on the person's head, shoulders, hands, waist, and sometimes the afflicted body part. Petitions for healing are offered by the healers in tongues or in the vernacular. An exorcism may or may not take place, depending on the healer's "sense from the Lord." Frank and others mentioned visualizing the body part as being in the process of healing or completely healed. The illness itself may be personalized and directly commanded to depart. Few of the subjects testifying mentioned the physical accompaniments to healing rituals prominent in other traditions such as heat or tingling in the hands of the healer. The procedures, length of time spent with each person, questions, etc. all vary and depend on the inner "sense" of the healer. The healee may be requested to step out in faith and use his body despite physicians' precautions. The exorcisms, if pronounced, are not done in the reverential style of a prayer, but boldly, vigorously, "with authority." The healers listen to their own interior sense and to each other as they pray silently or aloud. Afterwards, the healers mutually confer to share impressions, criticisms, encouragement, and feedback on the sense each had of how the prayer was being offered, and how the healee was responding.

On the part of the healee, there is, of course, the physical sensation of the hands being imposed frequently accompanied by a feeling of lightness, floating, as in Abigail's case. Other physical signs may occur, like Thomas's heavy sweating, or the actual cessation of pain and the symptoms as the prayer is in progress. The special procedures and feelings occurring in leg-lengthening have been noted in that place (ibid., pp. 208 ff.). In limb-lengthening, subjects feel the limb growing simultaneously with the holding or pushing action (in the direction against the growth) by the healer. Frequently after an instantaneous and obvious healing, there is a reaction of joy, laughter, humor, hilarity. Sometime thereafter, the healee is requested to testify before the Community at a prayer meeting, or in more dramatic cases, before larger gatherings like the International Conference at Notre Dame University each summer. (From these subjects, Thomas reported testifying at Notre Dame; Quentin and Lois spoke of their sharing with the WoG Community.) A number of the Community's healings have been reported in the popular press.

In the case of deliverance, we have an historical account of the development of procedures and reactions to a gift that was extremely

unfamiliar to the membership. Whereas Bible read-
ers know about prophecy from the Old Testament,
and Catholics are familiar with healings from accounts of saints' live and Lourdes pilgrimages,
the area of the demonic has been downplayed by the
mainline churches precisely to avoid the sorts of
hysteria which developed in the early phases of
deliverance. The Catholic Church is extrememly
reluctant to employ the ritual of exorcism: it is
used only after all medical and psychiatric remedies have been tried and found wanting. Each and
every time the ritual is recommended, the permission of the bishop of the diocese must be sought
and granted. In 1975, the Order of Exorcist was
suppressed. Previously all priests ordained would
be received into the Order of Exorcist, one of the
seven "Holy Orders." (Ironically enough, the sup-
pression of the Order occurred just at the time
when interest in and practice of the lay deliverance ministry was spreading!)

Deliverance currently is employed in WoG
routinely during healing rituals, during the Community initiation of the Foundations Course, and
whenever anyone "discerns" the presence of an evil
spirit. Reference has been made to the Community's ability to legitimize and routinize a practice in which the members believe, but which came
to them burdened with cultural baggage. The earliest period, beginning in March, 1970 and lasting
six to eight months, was characterized by physically violent interchanges between the deliverers
and their clients and by acting out the demons'
expulsion. This was followed by a period of conversational exchanges between the deliverers and
the spirits who/which were thought to use voices
of those being delivered. Persons delivered during the second phase reported surprise at the
sound and content of their own speech. As practiced currently, deliverers refuse to condone any
violence or conversation, but pray "with authority
in Jesus' name to bind up and cast forth the power
of the Evil One." Persons need not name the vices
dominating their lives. Such confessing depends
on the deliverer's style. The latter may sense
that a particular spirit is operative, and proceed

to use the binding formula while naming the spirit. What was <u>not</u> expressed by any subject interviewed, or by anyone else, was a sense of shame at being told that one was a bearer of evil spirits. By the time of this research, it was assumed that the human condition involved harassment by evil spirits: the way to "deal with" these was simply to be delivered once and for all of their influence. Places, especially houses where drugs had been used by former tenants, were also considered to be haunts of the spirits and would be prayed over by newly arriving WoG renters. The concluding testimonies in the deliverance section record the efforts of deliverers to put into words the differences they felt between psychological and demonic hassles. Words like "darkness," "evil presence," "oppressive atmosphere," "ugly spiritual force" convey the eidetic intuition. Although spirits are thought to cause both physical and emotional problems, human responsibility for sin is simultaneously admitted. No one ever was heard to claim that "the devil made me do it." Spirits work their way, but in conjunction with human ill will. Remedies include repentance for sin in one's personal life, and taking authority over the spirit by name when its influence is detected. Whereas the scientific community would perhaps scoff at the "superstitious" belief of the membership in spiritual influences, malevolent or benign, WoG participants reply that ignoring or dismissing the reality of spirits is naive and opens oneself up to attack.

This clash of philosophies, of cosmologies, has not been resolved, and the resulting perplexity over spirits forms a legitimate part of the eidetic intuition. We listen once again to Ned as he wrestles with the challenge of integrating and interweaving his scientific and religious beliefs:

> . . . I sensed something other than a person and his psychological self and "id-stuff." My psychological training didn't fit intuitively with what I experienced. Sometimes you can blame a cruel superego, but you can

discern sometimes something more. Exorcism
is the deliverance of the personality from
compulsions and inordinate fears. These fis-
sure the personality. Major psychological
problems become major spiritual problems. In
discerning guilt, for example, you often discern its origin at an early age. It gets en-
capsulated in the personality. The spirit of
greed and guilt builds up "brother spirits."
Greed for my books, for example, was a natural basis for allowing spirits to intervene in
psychological events. But possession is a
different gender (sic; genre?) of experience.
If you throw the spirits out of the fissures,
then you can close the fissures.

I accept the demonic on the experience
of my own life. It's not mere residual
wounding. The demonic explanation inter-
digitates with rational psychological experience.

(Why is Ockham's razor not applicable
to your explanation?) Because of my dualist-
ic system! My knowledge of psychology ex-
cludes knowledge of faith. But my experience
includes a faith-state. I use the two systems. (Have you integrated them?) There's a
better explanation through faith for behaviors of people. Psychological variables
don't explain; spiritual variables do.

Prophecy, for example, doesn't fit with
a rational knowledge of psychology: either
I'm having audio-hallucinations, or something
from the unconscious breaks through. This is
a "nothing-but" explanation by psychology.
Even if you extrapolate to the Jungian unconscious, you still can't explain my knowledge
of individual memories of a guy who showed up
on my doorstep. I can't accept the "good
guess" hypothesis either. Also, you can't
make bones, ligaments and muscles grow in ten
minutes. My observer self says, "I saw it
happen." How I believe it is explained

252

either by faith (God made it happen) or rationalistically (I chose to see it).

(But Olga's dress is still hanging straight.) The tangible evidence continues to be there to support the faithful side. But her back was supposed to be straightened: it's not. The evidence is: something happened to the leg; nothing happened to the back. Here's tension.

But the tension I live is both psychologically and spiritually healthy. It confronts me with something I can't explain despite my knowledge. My scientific viewpoint will carry me just so far. Rationalism, reductionism takes me just so far. Faith is based on experiential reality. I'm a believer who is critical rather than a skeptic who hasn't yet fallen out.

Few were as articulate as Ned in expressing such a sense of conflict in perspectives, much less working the conflict through. Most seemed to divide their consciousness between two realms: their working, social lives -- Ned called this the "rational, psychological" level -- and their religious lives. The traditional "natural, supernatural" split comes to mind. However, the whole thrust of WoG Community life and order aims toward interpenetrating the first by the second such that the supernatural becomes the dominant perspective, motivation, level of discourse and regulator of lifestyle. To this end, many work in Community projects and employment, a luxury not shared by Ned who was thus forced to come to terms with the thinking and values of the secular world around him. Still, even in Ned's case, the religious principles and teachings of faith clearly predominate, but for him and the others who alluded to this problem of conflicting world-views, allegiance to Community teachings was grounded in experience rather than in mere blind loyalty.

Apprehending Relationships Among Essences

The first stage of the analysis consisted in the description of particular phenomena of healing, prophecy, deliverance, Word of Knowledge, etc. in the subject's own words (Chapter III), and a concentration on particular linguistic expression (list of twelve theses; peculiarly idiomatic expressions in Table II, Chapter IV). The negative side of this first stage consisted of making precise certain distinctions between experiences of the gifts and other similar but not identical phenomena. The second stage just completed an attempt to formulate an eidetic intuition for each of three gifts, namely, prophecy, healing and deliverance. This process was grounded in a movement from the linguistic expressions and descriptive modifiers of the first stage into an expressed apprehension of the essential constituents of the gifts as they impinge on the human consciousness of the subjects.

The third step in phenomenological methodology consists in apprehending essential relationships within and among essences. The core, essential experience of the spiritual gifts, as related over and over again by all the subjects, consists in the quasi-interpersonal relationship each has with "the Lord." (The researcher adds the prefix, "quasi," to recognize the analogous character of this relationship to human interchanges.) In the discussion of their biographies and their practice of the gifts, their own conversion experiences or "coming to the Lord" were the central meaning-giving events of their conscious lives.

Four other common factors among the eidetic essences were: (1) the individual instances of communication ("sense from the Lord; Lord's leading"); (2) the need usually to "step out in faith" because never was the Lord's leading overwhelming or absolutely clear-cut; (3) physical and emotional concomitants to living out the relationship and practicing the gifts; (4) the use of discernment in deciding how to respond to the communication.

The experiences of the spiritual gifts can be

considered to be high points, more intense foci of an ongoing quasi-interpersonal relationship. The relationship is felt to be a response to an invitation for such by the Almighty, an invitation that the individual is free to accept by becoming a member of the covenant Community, the Word of God. The relationship is unique to each person, but forwarded by such acts as the communal prayer meetings, household prayer sessions, but especially through each one's daily "prayer time," usually half an hour to an hour of conversational exchange with the deity. The characteristics of the relationship are three: reverance, familiarity and trust. Reverence is shown most frequently by the use of the title "Lord" when WoG members refer to Him. Familiarity is manifested by the members' taking every problem, difficulty or joy to Him for sharing, guidance and comfort. They will take the Lord to task (reverently, of course) for unanswered requests, and be quick to point out humorous and ironic incidents in their ongoing interchanges with Him. Trust is revealed in that they respond to Him as to a friend rather than to a stranger. For example, during "hard times," instead of judging His character by His actions as one would a stranger, they judge His actions, i.e., his causing or permitting events, by His character as revealed to them throughout the course of their friendship. The full gamut of biblical metaphors is employed to characterize their dialogue-partner, but "Father" and "Lord" are the two preferred.

From the discussion in Chapter III and the eidetic intuitions formulated just above for prophecy, healing and deliverance, four other factors have been derived. In speaking out a prophecy, in healing or being healed, in delivering from the Evil One, WoG members feel a sense from the Lord, are led by Him to take the human actions coincident with receiving one of the gifts. Those interviewed have commented at length about what they said, how they felt, actions they took (of laying on hands, speaking out or singing, etc.), but most fundamental and central remains their sense from the Lord. However successful the researcher was in inviting them to describe in words this sense,

and to distinguish it from their own thought-
processes, and whether or not the subjects possessed the requisite eloquence, and powers of description, what remains is their own pointing to
this experience as being real, and special, and
different for them from anything else in their
conscious lives. It might be said to be characterized by an element of surprise: whether or not
a Word or directive from on high agrees with their
own inclinations, some surprising element usually
provides a clue -- never a proof, however -- that
the inspiration is external to themselves.

Next, "stepping out in faith" is seen to be
an aspect of experiencing the gifts which transcends each particular one being practiced. In
prophecy, one gets no more than a sense of the
message and perhaps a few words plus the urgency
to speak. If one "sits on" the prophecy, one is
often chagrinned to hear someone else give the
very same message. In healing, one must pray with
expectancy while knowing that medical science has
often spoken quite precisely about outcomes and
the usual course of recovery. In deliverance, one
comes up against mysterious forces presumed to be
malevolent and much more powerful than one's puny
self. Clarity never seems to get one much beyond
the very next step! Yet motivation is provided by
the never-ending stream of "sharings" about the
benefits of living the life of faith and experiencing the blessings of the gifts. Because the
Lord with whom the members enjoy their quasi-
interpersonal relationship is hidden from their
eyes, their mutual expressions of support and
testimony aid them when the materialistic values
and absence of faith in the dominant culture
threaten to overwhelm their belief.

Thirdly, physical and emotional concomitants
of a similar nature accompany the various gifts.
The "anointing" is a more than ordinarily clear
and strong sense of the Lord's leading to prophesy,
to heal, to "call a person on" in exercising faith
despite "doctor's orders," to move with vigor and
boldness against Satan. Emotions which confirm a
particular direction of action are peace, joy,
clam, tranquility. Subjects sometimes used the

shallow-deep comparison when speaking of a surface confusion or tension in following the Lord's will (e.g., Ursula's fear in pronouncing her prophecy to the couple) accompanied by a deeper peace and contentment underneath.

The fourth factor, discernment, is itself called a separate gift, and through practice, trial and error, Community members learn how to respond to the Lord's leading. Of all the four factors presented here, discernment seems most vulnerable to social shaping and human input. "The right way" to conduct a deliverance prayer service was shown clearly to have evolved through the strong and sensible guidance of Xavier; coordinators regularly discern prophets' utterances; individuals discern their own interior promptings of the Holy Spirit, and the Evil Spirit, and their own spirit. While it is claimed that discernment is ultimately based on the Scriptural Word, in practice Community custom guides many decisions concerning whether a particular behavior is "in the Lord" or "out of the Lord." Of course Scripture and Community custom are not mutually exclusive, and the conscious effort of coordinators serves to mould the latter by the former. But WoG is subject to sociological forces just like any other human organization. Even a theocracy, such as WoG attempts to be, evolves its discoverable roles and rules. This network of interacting expectations and reaction patterns influences the way discernments are made.

Up to this point, our analytical perspective has focused almost entirely upon the phenomena as understood by the participants. Our discussion of discernment, however, will allow us to expand and deepen the inquiry into an understanding of the phenomena as phenomena. We might pose the question, "Is something more going on than the participants are ready to see?" Social scientific observers might have a blind spot if asked to agree that the phenomenal core of the eidetic intuition of the gifts consists in a quasi-interpersonal relationship with the Lord, but do the subjects of the research themselves exhibit any blindness or distorted perceptions? The

257

discernment issue may give a clue.

Discernment is practiced at two levels in dealing with the gifts: at the level of the individual who judges his own interior movements and emotions, but also by WoG heads at every level of authority in the Community's hierarchy. In addition to the experiences reported by subjects, other things also affect what happens: social learning is going on, in that the Community members learn that God works in certain ways not only directly from the Lord, as they claim, but also from each other, especially from their leaders. Furthermore, social control is being exercised in that the coordinators, household heads, etc. define how God works, and when something is or is not of God. Accordingly, the core experience of the gifts is not only shaped "from above" by the Lord (as WoG members would claim), but also "from below" by social learning and social control. With the exceptions of Ned and Victor, no subject referred to the determining effects of the group as group upon their experience. The double level of discernment as described and practiced brings an observer to the awareness of this very crucial aspect of the eidetic essence of the gifts.

Effectively, the board of coordinators serves as the ultimate "discernment team" in parallel with the healing and prophecy teams, except that the discernment team exercises an extraordinary amount of power over people's lives in the Community. These powerful men speak for the Lord even when they are not prophesying. Among a group of people whose central experience is a quasi-interpersonal relationship with the Lord, and for whom the Lord's leading ultimately grounds the metaphysics of their communal life, activity and world-view, the absolute authority of men speaking in His name cannot be underestimated. Nor can it effectively be challenged or criticized. Enjoying the trust and consent of the governed, the coordinators are accountable only to each other, but to no outside criterion or agency. Because the Community has no official ecclesial form, it is not answerable to any ecclesiastical board as, for example, Catholic Religious Orders are subordinate to diocesan bishops and the Sacred Congregation of Religious.

Time and again throughout the biographies and the testimonies about the gifts, we have seen the influence of the coordinators saluted, if only directly. This influence comes through most clearly in the area of discernment wherein a prophet must yield to the Word within, but the coordinators and their surrogates, the prayer meeting leaders, decide upon its validity. This accepted practice constitutes an institutionalized taking-control of the outpouring of the Spirit. According to Max Weber (1952), in classic Judaism an essential feature of prophecy was that no one could rule prophets out-of-order although kings regularly attempted to do so. Historically, the royal establishments of the ancient world tamed prophecy through the institution of the court prophets (Weber, 1952, pp. 103-109), and we would suggest that the formation of the prophecy team represents a modern parallel. Theoretically, of course, it is still possible for a prophet today to function like a prophet of doom, but the social controls are set up such that challenge to the board of co-ordinators through prophecy is extremely unlikely and, to my knowledge, has rarely if ever occurred. Since the leadership decides what is true or false prophecy, a dissenter would need to possess a very clear vision plus great courage to speak out. This combination has been rare in past history, and we would not expect things to be much different today. While the rule of the coordinators strikes most observers as being genuinely benevolent, fundamental disagreement with their principles and procedures brings separation from the Community, an outcome not unexpected in a voluntary organization but still quite traumatic for members who give so much of their lives to the group.

Prophetic discernment provides the clearest instance among the gifts of the place of social learning and social control, but it is operative elsewhere too. Invitation and appointment to the healing and prophecy team was decided by a coordinator. "Maturity in the gifts" could be defined

259

operationally as approval by a coordinator or head that one is practicing them "in the right way." The next section will detail the routinization and institutionalization of the gifts as they were taken over from the Classical Pentecostal Churches, a process under the guidance of the coordinators. Reference could be made to the biographies in Chapter III for more instances of the direction of the coordinators in the personal lives of the subjects, for example, Karen's decision not to date a particular young man in whom she was interested; but multiplication of such comments would take us too far afield from our consideration specifically of the gifts.

A final aspect of this third step consists in free imaginative variation of components to arrive at synthetic a priori knowledge of gifts. Thus we shall see whether the addition or subtraction of these certain factors alters substantially the categorical intuition of the gifts. The specific factors we consider are those detailed in this present section.

Would removal of the central core-experience, the quasi-interpersonal relationship with the Lord, alter the essence of the gifts? Most definitely it would. Prophecy would become clairvoyance or a lucky guess; healing might resemble the cures accomplished by LeShan, or Worrall, or practitioners of Mind Control (to take only those sorts of experiences reported in the literature review of Chapter I).

The three characteristics of reverence, familiarity and trust describing this relationship are also crucial to WoG relationship. Playing down the reverence, as it were, and increasing the familiarity so that one feels comfortable "testing" the Lord, or even scolding and becoming angry with Him is a much more characteristically Hebraic style of relating to the Divine, as the Psalms and other prayers in the Hebrew Scriptures show, than a specifically Christian approach. Emphasizing the reverence and lowering the familiarity and trusting elements would produce an experience found in traditions emphasizing God as Judge, as wrathful. The testimonies of these subjects revealed the nuances of their blending all three of these elements.

Nor could the four additional elements be removed without substantially altering the religious experience. While individual instances of communication, the feeling of the Lord's leading or a sense from the Lord, are not present in each and every experience of the gifts, such a sense was felt on at least one and usually a number of occasions of practicing the gifts. The opposite experience, stepping out in faith and acting when God's presence is not clear and obvious, when His will is not precisely manifest, is also quite common, but not universal. For short periods of time in the lives of many subjects, the Divine seemed startlingly immanent. Yet both feelings seemed present some of the time in all subjects interviewed. The same observation holds for the physical and emotional concomitants to the gifts, the anointings. Seemingly neither as frequent, as intense, nor as desired in WoG as they are in Classical Pentecostalism, they still are a part of the essence of the gifts. The final factor, two-level discernment, was shown immediately above to be the crucial shaping factor in the exercise of the gifts, especially from the human side, and so could not be removed without altering the essence of the gifts.

Could addition of any factors appreciably alter the synthetic a priori knowledge? For example, would subjects still consider leg-lengthening to be miraculous if they knew that it regularly occurs when the muscles holding the sacrum at a tilted angle within the pelvis relax, and various techniques can accomplish this? In other words, would the addition of knowledge about medicine alter a subject's sense of the miraculous? This researcher did not feel that it was ethical directly to challenge subjects' beliefs by asking probing questions like this. Yet because the WoG Community members are generally sophisticated about things medical, they would experience little perplexity, I should presume, with this additional knowledge. We have seen how they deal with the difficulty of a prophesied cure not taking place.

261

Answers are found to keep the cognitive framework consistent. Even with this additional knowledge, subjects would still probably interpret leg-lengthening as Divine intervention because it was healing prayer through which God worked to help along the relaxation process hypothesized.

One factor which did influence the exercise of the gifts among several subjects was the addition of skepticism concerning the wisdom of a head's or a coordinator's discernment. At the time of the interview, all subjects were members of the Community in good standing, but in several who ultimately departed from WoG, and who were having authority problems with the leadership, the frequency of the occurrence of the gifts was already declining. Whether one would call this experience an addition of skepticism or a decline of trust, it did affect the frequency of, say, prophesying, but not the explanations provided since they concurred with reports of other members.

Having attempted this process of variation among the components of the eidetic essence, we can consider that the five factors isolated provide a general and necessary intuition of the gifts.

Watching Modes of Appearance

The fourth step of the phenomenological method consists in an attentiveness to the modes of appearance of the phenomena. One is directed to be sympathetically watchful without being wary. Data for this step was provided in the first chapter: the literature review developed an historical and psychological context in which to place the WoG Community without prejudice to its special uniqueness. In order to perceive anything, one needs a reference point, a figure-ground relationship in which a phenomenon can stand out in all its clarity. The "ground" is provided there when we investigated the questions concerning what was already known about similar movements. The "figure" appeared in Chapter III wherein the uniquely individual internal psychological experiences of the WoG members were analyzed.

It would be useful to review here the way in which gifts appear in WoG. Information on this point was most clearly and fully documented for the gift of deliverance, but there are hints throughout the testimonies that the mode of appearing for all the gifts was guided substantially by the discernment of the board of coordinators. Victor's account of the history of the deliverance ministry illustrates the shifts in the overall Community consciousness regarding a gift. Initially, the leaders are exposed to a custom in the classical Pentecostal Tradition. Then the Community at large is told about it and invited to participate. At the outset, the gift is practiced just the way it is in the source tradition, but gradually modified so that it becomes more acceptable to middle-class practitioners.

While the source of knowledge about the gifts is always Scripture ultimately, and the Pentecostal and Neo-Pentecostal Churches proximately, there exists a delicate balance of infusions from the outside, always reworked to be absorbed more comfortably within the sophisticated, middle-class, hierarchical tradition of the WoG Community. Rather exotic contributions like deliverance were ingeniously reworked by Xavier in consultation with other coordinators, and we may postulate a similar evolution of the other gifts from their free, unfettered earlier manifestations to their present somewhat stereotypical practice.

Thus with prophecy, anyone could speak out at prayer meetings in the early days of WoG. In about five years' time, however, a prophecy "team" and a prophecy "group" are formed and the institutional direction of the gift is solidified. At one time, prophets got feedback after prophesying; now, i.e., at the time of the interviews, a prophet has to ask permission of a prayer meeting head before speaking out and possibly changing the direction of the meeting. Many prophecies heard at meetings urge loyalty and obedience to the leaders, especially in view of an anticipated economic and cosmic cataclysm. Prophets confirmed the imposition of mantles and veils on the membership.

Similarly with healing, there are stated references in the testimonies to a lack of emotional charge in self-conscious contrast to the healing services of Kathryn Kuhlman and more enthusiastic Pentecostal Churches. The formation of the healing team was the culmination of the shaping of procedures by the leadership. The Community's teachings on male and female roles are reflected in the practices of the two person healing teams wherein the male partner leads and directs.

Since this step consists in noticing just how the phenomena impinge on human consciousness, it seems appropriate at this point to reintroduce the topic of suggestibility (See Chapter I, pp. 52-57). The literature reviewed there provides a psychological myth traditionally employed to explain such paranormal experiences as the gifts. It would be easy to end the analysis there where it began: in suggestibility. Having explicated the myth of the charismatics, we might be tempted simply to incorporate it within the more generalized and abstract psychologists' myth of suggestibility and be done! Yet such a solution appears unsatisfactorily reductionistic to the researcher. The suggestibility solution applies most directly to the influence of social control, and explains some but not all of the behaviors and experiences recorded of the subjects. Most especially, it fails to do justice to the core, essential experience related, the quasi-interpersonal relationship with the Lord.

To give suggestibility its due, we can briefly pass in review the nine conclusions of Jerome Frank (1973, pp. 325-329) as applied to the various gifts, most especially healing and deliverance. (Frank's points are underlined; my comments, in regular script.)

(1) A particular type of relationship between the help-giver and the patient, in the context of a group, is initiated. This was seen to be true in the case of the healing-team members, but not entirely applicable to the developing reality in WoG; the use of the sacred space of the healing prayer room was declining as this research was

being concluded, and the whole body at prayer, or any individual in it, was encouraged to pray for healing. A number of healings were recounted here by ordinary people, non-experts, as it were. While a socially sanctioned role was recognized for a few of the coordinators who were thought to be especially gifted with healing powers, many others experienced this gift. In the case of discernment, however, Jerome Frank's point is more obviously supported. Members join WoG seeking to remedy their "Transcendency Deprivation" (Mawn, 1975) and submit their entire lives to the special obedience relationship called headship. Such a personal commitment prepares one for the effects of suggestibility to be exercised through social learning and control by the leaders. Individuals and the body are thus readied for prophecies to be heard and obeyed, and their readiness is augmented by the institutionalization of prophecy and the unlikelihood of anyone's challenging headship through prophecy, much less being taken seriously should he try.

(2) Sacred space for healing was created in the healing prayer room and in the large halls used for WoG prayer meetings. Yet healing is not limited to such equivalents of doctor's offices, hospital wards or healing shrines. Healing prayers are offered any place and at any time with no purification rituals except the subjective action of "turning to the Lord in prayer," a mode of interior recollection.

(3) The "therapies" of healing and deliverance are based on the assumptive system outlined in the twelve propositions of Chapter III. Yet this assumptive system is much broader than a mere explanation of illness and health, and includes a whole philosophy of history. The myth of the charismatics includes the myths of medicine and psychology, but in a role subordinate to the religious elements of their overall myth. (In a way, our effort here is to find some overarching psychological myth large enough to include the charismatics' behaviors and experiences. Thus far, suggestibility seems only partially applicable.)

(4) The function of the procedure

prescribed by the myth aims intermediately at bringing relief to the sufferer, but ultimately to enhance his relationship with the Lord. While the gifts in the Community are treasured, they are looked upon as by-products of something much more meaningful and rich and important.

According to Frank, the four elements of therapeutic relationship, setting, rationale and task together influence patients in five inter-related ways to produce attitude change and therapeutic benefit (1973, p. 325).

(1) They provide clients with new opportunities for learning at both cognitive and experiential levels. This statement is true without qualification in the case of the gifts, except that members of the Community do not "feel like" clients in all cases of employment of the gifts, but rather like God's children, brothers/sisters to each other, etc. Even more significantly, few feel or expressed feeling manipulated by the leadership, but rather in cases of conflict, felt "called on" by their heads to deeper faith.

(2) All therapies enhance the patient's hope of relief. This is true of all the gifts studied here. Prophecy, however, could be called a "therapy" only in the broadest sense of the term. Within the paradigm of suggestibility, however, it would have to be regarded as the ultimate form of suggestion, a divine command! Insofar as the members of the Community are seeking relief from Transcendency Deprivation, and also striving to gain some sense of control and power over their lives in the turmoils of contemporary society (as we suggested above in Chapter I, p. 24), prophecy and discernment provide guaranteed and socially sanctioned interpretations of God's Will, the Lord's leading. What more powerful source of stability in a world changing too fast can be found than a direct link with the divine purpose? (This last question is deliberately posed within the framework of social science, and as such is theologically neutral. Whether one denies the very existence of a Divine Will, or sees God as lovingly responding to current needs by making His plan more available and evident, a social scientist

cannot ignore the employment of suggestibility in a Community which claims to be the official interpreter of that Will.) With regard specifically to healings, the described procedures work both covertly and overtly to enhance the sufferers' hope of relief, as Jerome Frank suggests.

(3) The healing techniques provide success experiences which enhance the sufferer's sense of mastery and competence. This is true both vicariously and directly. Members of the Community feel personally involved in a worldwide force of renewal whose power touches many nations, but also is active in their individual family lives, joys and sorrows. Here we see some inadequacy in the suggestibility paradigm. To take a parallel example: an important ritual moment in American civil religion comes at the playing of the national anthem. During the reverent silence at say, a summer baseball game, a senior citizen may recall his involvement in his nation's wars abroad while simultaneously feeling grateful for his social security check which came that day. These memories and feelings were certainly "suggested" by the playing of the Star-Spangled Banner, but cannot ultimately be reduced to the effect of the music. Similarly, the whole complex of relationships among Community members and their involvement with the divine is highlighted by the gifts, expressed in the gifts, but not to be reduced ultimately to the ritual of the gifts.

(4) The gifts overcome alienation from one's fellows. This binding function of the gifts certainly must be noted. Speaking-in-tongues has been called a "bridge-burning" act (Gerlach and Hine, 1968). The same could be said of uttering a prophecy, being prayed over for healing, serving in a deliverance session. One separates oneself from non-Pentecostal Christians while binding oneself closely to the Community.

(5) Successful therapies arouse the patient emotionally. Emotional arousal can but need not accompany the gifts, may but is not necessarily part of their aftermath.

It was noted above in the third step of our analysis that the gift of "discernment" is most

subject to human "input" which here we might label
more concretely as suggestibility. While it is
the contention of the writer that suggestibility
fails to do justice to the core experience of the
quasi-interpersonal relationship with the Lord
reported by the subjects as involved in but tran-
scending all the gifts, it must also be repeated
that use of divine justification for coordinators'
decisions, for prophecy, for any command rendered
by a head powerfully reinforces social control
over docile members. I fault the leadership of
the Community for failing to be sufficiently
skeptical of its ability accurately to "hear the
Lord" in all circumstances. (A non-believer, of
course, would reject any claim ever to hear from
the divinity: this must, by definition, be hal-
lucinatory behavior, or delusional in mistaking
one's own thoughts for influences from the Divine.)
Yet within the myth of the charismatics as experi-
entially lived, divine communications can and do
occur. Members assert confidently that the Lord
will redirect them should they go astray. Indeed,
prophecies to "repent" have been delivered in
strong terms to individuals and to the whole body,
but never, to my knowledge, to the coordinators.
There are many strong social pressures against
criticizing those in charge for they are "the
Lord's anointed." The alternative to criticism
are submission or departure, but in a Community
which shares many aspects of Goffman's "total
institution" (1961), departure is a painful step.
Historically, such communities have suffered under
leadership which is progressively authoritative,
then authoritarian, then tyrannical, then totali-
terian (Knox, 1950). WoG seems to have few built-
in mechanisms for preventing such an evolution.
    Another way to approach the discernment issue
would be to spell out the Community's implicit
ecclesiology, that is, does the membership feel
itself to be a church, sect, cult, etc.? No explicit ecclesiological statement appeared in the
twelve propositions in Chapter III because the issue is presently confused, and WoG's ecclesiological identity is evolving. The leaders and the
members use phrases like "ecumenical community of

268

renewal" to describe themselves. Unfortunately, for the outsider no theological elaboration of the meaning of this phrase has been very deeply developed yet, so it is difficult to clarify the relationship of the group to existing church bodies. For the group itself, however, such a hazy state of affairs has two consequences: (1) it can go about the business of its own development creatively and experimentally; (2) with such a lack of definition, the coordinators naturally must step in and "discern" what the group stands for. In the Preface above, it was noted that the bulk of the membership are loyal church goers, but for many of the subjects interviewed and many other members of WoG, their affiliative and dogmatic ties are shifting gradually to the Community. During this period of transition, no one ecclesiology has yet been elaborated. For the majority, perhaps, the "ecumenical community of renewal" is a means of personal religious revitalization which, through them, will affect their parishes and churches. For the non-denominationals, the Community is their equivalent of church. For some few, the Community is developing sectarian features in that they accept a vision and a claim that only renewal communities like theirs know where God is really calling His churches. Recently the leaders have applied for official recognition as a "pious union" in the Roman Catholic Church, but such a designation has not yet been granted. Meanwhile, practical and theoretical decisions are in the hands and minds of the coordinators.

In this fourth step of the phenomenological method, we have charted the history of the appearance in the life of the Community of the spiritual gifts. We have seen them being imported from the classical Pentecostal and Neo-Pentecostal Churches, and then shaped and fashioned to fit a middle-class clientele more naturally so that the more bizarre enthusiastic elements are purged, but emotional expressiveness and spontaneous exuberance remain. Social learning and social control by the coordinators direct this process of adaptation, and the psychological "myth" of suggestibility has

269

been employed to describe theoretically some aspects of healing, prophecy and discernment. Yet the myth of suggestibility does not provide a big enough net to circumscribe all elements of the eidetic essences noted in the second and third steps above, especially the quasi-interpersonal relationship with the Lord, and so we continue our quest for a possibly more adequate psychological paradigm.

Constitution of Phenomena in Consciousness

In the fifth step of the phenomenological method, one is to attend to the establishment of phenomena in consciousness. Numerous examples of the growth-process have been provided in Chapter III, most especially those testimonies which reveal change over time and development in facility and "maturity" in the gift. The reader should especially review the parallel accounts of the four official prophets and four members of the healing team for extended examples of people's early groping and subsequent familiarity with the gifts. Those testimonies detail the unfolding of the gifts in the lives and experiences of individual persons designated by the leadership as especially representative of WoG. (In Steps Two and Three of this chapter, we have sought to penetrate to the eidetic essence of these gifts, and the inter-relationship among their essences.)

In the case of an individual's coming into the use of the gifts, we note first the conversion experience or "coming to the Lord," which in William James's words (1958, p. 162) means that "religious ideas, previously peripheral in his consciousness, now take a central place, and that religious aims form the habitual centre of his energy." In other words, a radical shift in the structure of consciousness occurs. This experience may or may not have taken place before joining WoG, but entrance into the Community requires a further commitment of time, energy, shift in friendship patterns, ideological alterations, and most crucially, an effort to cultivate the quasi-interpersonal relationship with the Lord. Sooner or later, the "urgency" to prophesy, heal or deliver overtakes one as a combined interaction of forces: one's inner sense, the needs of the "brothers and sisters," the invitation to participate in household invocations for the gifts, etc. Though suggestibility is present along the way, each individual is personally directed ultimately by his own interior groping after the Lord's leading for him. While Community teaching guides him, and interaction with other members influences his perspective, through the mechanisms of social learning and social control another growth is taking place, the growth in the "Life in the Spirit" which is sought in the Baptism ritual, and is the raison d'etre of all the rest: Community order, mutual support, ethical code, the gifts. While there are individual alterations in the pattern and variations on the theme (noted in the examples in the previous chapter), many if not most subjects reacted initially to the gifts with curiosity, fascination, but also with twentieth-century American skepticism. Some few would "read up on things" (Frank, Quentin, Ned, for example) before taking the plunge, but most would be swayed by the behaviors of their peers. As one gradually began to feel comfortable praying in tongues; as one heard more and more prophecies delivered in small and large group gatherings and perhaps became a subject of a prophecy or word of knowledge oneself; in brief, as the sense of strangeness gave way to a sense of "the ordinary, the normal," one's hesitancies melted and one opened oneself up to further spiritual experiences. Perhaps physical healing is the one gift that seems to good to be true, but because functional ailments and illnesses comprise a large proportion of the most common complaints, it is not surprising that the combination of a supportive community plus the expectant faith required would aid the human body's natural self-curative tendencies. Yet this explanation falls down before the organic healings and does not touch the core experience of the quasi-interpersonal relationship with the Lord.

At this point we want to combine the

materials in the two halves of Chapter III, the
biographical and the testimonial, to further elucidate and discover the significance of these
gifts within the living context of the subjects.
Such a life-historical contextualization will show
how the experience of the gifts takes meaning from
and gives meaning to the rest of the members'
lives.

Thesis four suggests that life in a community
is a necessary condition for establishing a relationship with the Divine, that a community provides the focus and locus for the reception and
practice of the gifts. This statement is not
merely theoretically agreed upon by the subjects,
but is a unifying feature in all their biographies.
Whether their conversion experiences were solitary
or communal, all joined a renewal community rather
than, say, continuing along a path of isolated
religiosity. Even Isidore, the most marginal of
the subjects contacted, faithfully attended prayer
meetings, and received a number of his prophecies
while being prayed over by concerned friends.
Benjamin Weininger (1955) suggests that religious
experience represents a person's attempt to be related to a group. When a person who has hit a low
point in his inner crisis meets a catalytic person
who can communicate through the person's isolation
at a non-verbal level, a religious conversion may
follow. The catalyst person possesses and shares
a feeling of group relatedness. The feeling of
wholeness and freedom from conflict in conversion
probably results from a transient subsidence of
anxiety. Most members of WoG joined in their late
teens and early twenties, a normally stressful
period in identity development exacerbated by the
cultural upheavals of the nineteen-sixties and
seventies. Joining a group brought with it the
solidarity with "brothers and sisters" so lacking
in the dominant culture of privatism and the nu-
clear family. Others, like Sheila who had been
involved in the Peace Movement, had had experience
with communal experiments and alternate lifestyles,
but had found them wanting. Practicing the gifts
provided concrete proofs of one's favor with God,
and of integration into an increasingly powerful

and influential worldwide movement changing the course of religious history (and in the person of born again President Jimmy Carter, of secular history as well).

A first and representative group of subjects, therefore, includes those with genuinely painful pasts who came consciously or unconsciously seeking companionship, comfort, consolation. For Sheila, prophecy opened up new depths of her own self-understanding, brought emotional resolution of past conflicts, and made her a Community validated instrument of others' healing of memories. Not surprisingly, her own prophecy at large gatherings of the Community reflects and reinforces the directions set by coordinators since these have been so positive in her own life. Abigail came to the Community with a whole host of physical and emotional disorders (see Table I, Chapter III), but in the friendly, loving atmosphere of the group has found healing of body and spirit, and is becoming a more happy, hoping person. Through prayers for healing and prophecy, friends are identifying themselves, reaching out to her, communicating their unconditional positive regard, galvanizing the self-curative forces of her own self. Chuck came from a history of heavy drug use, but through Community support has become the first member of his family to graduate from high school, and is now preparing for his immanent graduation from college.

Chuck's case, in addition to illustrating the regenerative effect of the Community and the gifts in his own life, provides an example of a second group: WoG members who show occupational integration. A large number of the subjects have integrated their experiences as healers or healees into their work lives as health care professionals. Among others, this includes Ned, Paula and Thomas in addition to Chuck. In various ways detailed in the third chapter, these persons consciously pray for their patients during their working hours, and are quick to attribute any improvement to the Power of God working through their ministry. Ned and Chuck did not report speaking about healing to their patients; Paula has an understanding with her supervisor that she will be discrete about her remarks to fellow staff and patients; voluble Thomas is most exuberant in his employment of and conversations concerning healing. In the case of these persons, the gift of healing has been a valuable adjunct to their service of the sick. The gift has shaped and been shaped by their calling in life.

A third set of subjects has been employed by the Community in its service to its own members, and in outreach to potential converts. Their gifts have been discerned by the coodinators; their activities have marked them, set them apart for special recognition and duties. Such persons included Elaine, Frank, Geraldine, Hilary (and for a time Max) on the healing team; Daphne, Elaine, Geraldine, Julie and Sheila on the prophecy team or prophecy group. Ursula's gift of leg-lengthening had been so frequently requested that she could not remember all the people she had prayed over. In addition, Ursula's practice of the word of knowledge had brought her several referrals from heads and coordinators of deeply troubled persons whom the mental health profession had not benefited. The activity of these persons functions to keep the group's consciousness raised concerning its special blessings from the Lord. These individuals in turn are rewarded with high status in the Community: in addition to the mark of recognition, prophets are obeyed as spokespersons of the Lord; healers reap the gratitude of their clients.

A fourth group of subjects includes people like Victor, Lois, Olga, Roberta and Quentin, ordinary people with relatively normal backgrounds, for whom the gifts constituted emotional high points in their own developing relationship with the Lord and with the Community, but who did not get chosen for any special tasks by the group. The gifts served as relational mortar, cementing these persons more firmly to WoG. Quentin's relief from his allergies followed periods of personal sacrifice in the eating habits of his housemates. Roberta's temporary relief from failing eyesight made her an object of concern for those who had prayed with her. Olga, housewife and mother, practices her prophetic ministry quietly. Lois's healings from cancer, taking place over a number of years, have taught her immense patience in dealing with the sick and emotionally troubled on whom she refuses to lay the heavy demands of too much expectant faith. Victor's long time in the Community confers an historical perspective to his remarks, and his jovial temperament wins him personal, if not official, recognition. His early work in the deliverance ministry, his employment of prophecy and prayer for healing is integrated into his personal life. He and the others mentioned in this fourth group perhaps represent more than the other subjects the large numbers of WoG members not interviewed who live the gifts in the daily rhythms of their lives, but who have not risen to any official position in the hierarchy of publicly recognized gifted persons.

A fifth group of subjects needs comment: those who have left the Community since the interview (when all were still members). Without wishing to be reductionistic and claim that conflict with their heads in WoG was the only reason or been the main reason for departure, this factor was involved in the withdrawal of Betty, Karen, Julie and Ned. (Ned's wife, Olga, left with him.) All four of these had mentioned some conflict with headship during our interview. Subsequent conversation with Betty indicated that for her, Community restrictions in her common-finance household proved too cramping, and that she simply disagreed with much of the discernment of her head regarding her life. Karen, after breaking up with a young man at the bidding of her superiors, met another man (not in the Community), married him and left the area. Julie's case is that of a young woman whose prophetic outpourings had brought her confirmation from the leadership in the form of membership on the prophecy team. Yet during the months immediately prior to our discussion, she had simultaneously been experiencing clashes with her head, and been prophesying less frequently. Although a very active member of her church community, she chose to leave WoG despite the deep investment of herself and the Community's recognition of her gifts. Just as status through the gifts did not deter departure (Julie's situation), neither did longevity with the Community: Ned, present since the earliest days, disagreed with the overall direction and evolution of the group (as he saw it) away from the church renewal and into an entity unto itself. Despite conversations and letters to the coordinators, he felt that his view was substantially different from the vision of the leaders and so departed with his wife.

In this fifth step of the phenomenological analysis, we have attempted to show how the gifts became incorporated within the biographical gestalt of various groups of subjects. The personal histories of each representative set of people illustrate five ways in which one's past extends into a religious experience as a meaning system which endures and contributes to the constitution of the later experience. Analyzing these person's experiences shows concretely how the WoG Community lives and interprets the gifts.

Questioning the Existence of the Phenomena

As we explained in Chapter II, we shall not attempt the epoche, the suspension of belief in the existence of the phenomena. We skip this step and follow the lead of both Merleau-Ponty and Husserl, the former of whom refused outright to accept the phenomenological reduction, the latter of whom taught that the eidetic reduction of step two provides an adequate foundation for the essential intuition. As specifically applied to this research project, the attempted epoche would lead back once again to philosophical wrangling rather than to a psychological analysis because it devolves into the question of the existence/non-existence of the divine referent in the quasi-interpersonal relationship. For those philosophically and sincerely convinced of an atheistic stance, or even of a deistic position with an uninvolved deity -- members of the first four of Epictetus's five classes of men -- Freud's brilliant characterization (1928) of religion as an illusion provides a satisfactory explanatory myth. Yet for those like the author whom philosophical and theological reflection places with the research subjects in the fifth class, the myths of Freud and of suggestibility, social learning and social control, do not sufficiently contain the data of experience. Something more is required.

Interpreting Concealed Meanings of Phenomena

The seventh and final phenomenological step calls for an attempt at interpreting the concealed meanings of the phenomena. Such an attempt provides the ultimate theoretical reason for seeking an explanatory psychological myth for only in myth do the unspoken implications of human reality get most successfully voiced. The ultimate practical reason, of course, resides in the desire of this author and many "spiritual directors" with whom he has spoken to make available to religious people the methodological concepts and insights psychology of interaction and interpersonal relationships in which not only man but also God and the dialogue between them become objects for anaylsis. In Jung, then, perhaps the most elaborate myth has been woven concerning interpersonal communication with the Divine.

I propose that an even more fruitful approach would be to view the charismatics' and other religious experiences within the mythological framework of Object Relations Theory. Whether a psychologist is a theist, agnostic or atheist, his approach of viewing God as personal and as Father permits him to apply the rich theoretical perspectives and implications drawn by the Object Relations Theorists to the experiences of religious believers who relate to God in that way, i.e., within a quasi-interpersonal relationship. While Freud and much of the psychological and psychiatric establishment could not unfairly be described as negative, reductionistic and even hostile to both institutional religion and the claims of religious believers, such an outlook does not characterize all theorists within the analytic tradition. Even some of those who are antipathetic still struggle to explain the origin and functioning of religious behavior within individuals and cultures.

Helpful insights derive from that branch of Neo-Freudian Ego-psychology known as Object Relations Theory. This tradition views the human not primarily as a biological entity (id-dominated), but as a psychological reality (the ego is the center of personality). Human growth and development then centers not so much on conflicting instinctual forces as in interpersonal relationships which began with the parents, the earliest "objects." Harry Stack Sullivan, for example, centered his theory of the structures of personality on interpersonal relations (Sullivan, 1953; Mullahy, 1952, 1953). Sullivan viewed the person functioning in "situations" rather than in the expression of instinctual impulses. Such "situations," for Sullivan, possessed parameters defined by persons, real or imaginary. Therefore, in every concrete interactional situation, each participant deals with others in terms of his/her own past interpersonal relationships, real or imaginary. Thus using a Sullivanian developmental psychological framework, psychologists need not answer for themselves the existence question with regard to the divine partner in a religious person's "quasi-interpersonal relationship:" even if a theorist or a therapist regards God as an imaginary being, for the subject under study or in therapy a relationship with God has real cognitive and emotional and behavioral effects, and can be analyzed and treated accordingly. Thus, Sullivanian psychotherapy emphasizes the need to clarify negative distortions of the interpersonal field, and relies on the spontaneous, natural, inborn growth tendencies of the client to develop his personality under the influence of currently favorable interpersonal relationships. Psychotherapeutic cure is related to the unfolding of the self, and to the decrease of parataxic distortions and anxiety. Accordingly, spiritual direction or counseling with WoG Community members, or indeed with any religious person claiming to live in a relationship with the Divine, would aim at examining such an interaction according to the developed rules for mature human relationships from within a Sullivanian framework: does the person usually experience reality in the syntaxic mode? How firmly is his vocational identity established? How well has he integrated the restrictions and limitations of his past developments? Does he have adult friendships which are non-manipulative? Is his relationship with the Divine a substitute for human friendships, or of a piece with the latter? Employing such criteria as these, a psychologist can begin to determine whether the relationship with the Transcendent is developing along normal rather than pathological lines. He is not hamstrung by the prior conviction that such an interchange is essentially illusory. Furthermore, Sullivan stressed internalized object relations as basic motivational systems, and his concentration on cultural factors has found later support in Erikson's ego psychological analysis.

Erik Erikson is another theorist in the Object Relations tradition who would make an excellent dialogue partner in opening up further meanings of the phenomena. Erikson (1950, 1956), in his discussions regarding ego identity, provided enlightenment regarding the subjective aspects of the ego as an important psychic structure. He defined ego identity as including a sense of sameness or continuity both in one's self and one's meanings for others. For Erikson, ego identity develops out of, yet transcends the integration of introjections and identifications. He pointed to the importance of social roles as part of ego identity, and the unconscious striving for the continuity of the individual's character and his inner solidarity with group ideals and group identity that ego identity incorporates. Erikson charts the history of the healthy development of ego identity through the life cycle as a configuration evolving together with and under the influence of critical stages of development (1968).

279

In counseling religious persons, therefore, or in
seeking to understand the level of maturity of
their relationship with God, one could employ
Erikson's eight-fold schema of significant life
crises (ibid., p. 94) to determine how well they
are performing the tasks associated with each
critical stage, and whether the religious experience enhances or hinders the resolution of that
crisis. For example, the third crisis of initiative vs. guilt would generate questions like:
does the person enjoy flexibility in role experimentation, or is he stuck in role fixation? Does
his religion contribute to role rigidity or enhance role expansion? (According to this criterion, WoG would be positively analyzed in the case
of males, but somewhat critically evaluated with
regard to females since the latter are taught to
value traditional female roles only.) Does the
person's/group's God image induce guilt or evoke
personality expansion? (WoG gets high marks in
this regard since so many of the members enjoy
self-actualization in a relationship with a caring
Father-God.) Erikson's studies of Luther (1959)
and Gandhi (1969) show just how sympathetically
critical a psychologist can be when analyzing an
individual religious person's identity development
from within this tradition of research.

Another proponent of this school, Paul W.
Pruyser, explicitly applied ego psychology to religion in his A Dynamic Psychology of Religion
(1968) where he studied motivation for religion.
The person's set of beliefs and practices are interpreted "from the point of view of wish fulfillment, drive control, primary-and secondary-process
thinking, object relations, the genesis of conscience and the ego ideal, and the economics of
libidinal and agressive urges" (Pruyser, 1968,
p. 6). It is within this much broader range of
constructs than mere "suggestibility" or "illusion," within a myth like Object Relations Theory,
which can be stretched to respect the claim of the
religious subject to be in a relationship with
"the Lord," that psychologists can frame a non-
reductionistic understanding of the phenomena of
spiritual gifts.

280

Object Relations Theory represents a synthesis of the older more impersonal psychoanalytic meta-psychology with a humanistic view of man's transcendence beyond his biological and psychosocial development. Psychoanalytic Object Relations Theory continues the objective, scientific study of the personality, while trying to retain an awareness of the subjective uniqueness of the individual (Kernberg, 1978). Psychology as such cannot settle the question evoked by the epoche, cannot decide upon the Ontological Reality of God, but it can and does respect the reality (at least within Object Relations Theory) of the intrapsychic effects and manifestations of His presence, of the dynamics of a quasi-interpersonal relationship with Him, and can further serve to illuminate the claims and experiences of charismatics and others who so dramatically witness to His activity.

Conclusion

The task attempted here has not been to generalize from this phenomenon to a whole genus of such phenomena, but to lay bare the structure of the phenomenon itself of the WoG Community's experience of the spiritual gifts. Traditionally, research in the psychology of religion has been entirely correlational in nature, and has not carried understanding much "beyond the classics" (Glock and Hammond, 1973, pp. 409-417). Ethical restrictions prohibit experimentation in such a personal area of life. This research project has sought to illustrate the fruitfulness of an alternative approach, the phenomenological, to deepen understanding of religious experience.

BIBLIOGRAPHY

Alland, Alexander
 1961 "Possession in a Revialist Negro Church." <u>JSSR</u> 1, pp. 204-213.

Allen, R. O. and B. Spilka
 1967 "Committed and Consensual Religion: A Specification of Religious-Prejudice Relationships." <u>JSSR</u> 6, pp. 191-206.

Allport, Gordon W.
 1947 "Scientific Models and Human Morals." <u>Psych</u>. <u>Rev</u>. 54, pp. 182-192.

 1950 <u>The Individual and His Religion</u>. New York: Macmillan.

 1966 "The Religious Context of Prejudice." <u>JSSR</u> 5, pp. 447-457.

Allport, Gordon W. and J. Michael Ross
 1967 "Personal Religious Orientation and Prejudice." <u>J. Personality & Soc. Psych</u>. 5, pp. 432-443

Argyle, Michael
 1958 <u>Religious Behavior</u>. London: Routledge and Kegan Paul.

Argyle, Michael and Benjamin Beit-Hallahmi
 1975 <u>The Social Psychology of Religion</u>. Boston: Routledge & Kegan Paul.

Becker, Howard S.
 1932 <u>Systematic Sociology</u>. New York: Wiley.

Becker, Howard S., B. Geer, E. Hughes and A. Strauss
 1962 <u>Boys in White</u>. Chicago: University of Chicago Press.

Beit-Hallahmi, Benjamin
      1974   "Psychology of Religion 1880-1930:
              The Rise and Fall of a Psychological
              Movement." Journal of the History
              of the Behavioral Sciences. 10, pp.
              84-90.

Berger, Peter L.
      1967   The Sacred Canopy. Garden City, N.Y.:
              Doubleday & Company.

Berger, Peter L. and Thomas Luckmann
      1966   The Social Construction of Reality.
              Garden City, N.Y.: Doubleday &
              Company, Inc.

Blatty, William Peter
      1971   The Exorcist. New York: Harper &
              Row.

Boisen, A. T.
      1955   Religion in Crisis and Custom. New
              York: Harper.

Brody, Nathan and Paul Oppenheim
      1966   "Tensions in Psychology Between the
              Methods of Behaviorism and Phenomen-
              ology." Psych. Rev. 73 (4), pp. 295-
              305.

      1967   "Methodological Differences Between
              Behaviorism and Phenomenology in
              Psychology." Psych. Rev. 74 (4),
              pp. 330-334.

Calestro, Kenneth M.
      1972   "Psychotherapy, Faith Healing, and
              Suggestion." Int. J. of Psychiatry
              10 (2), pp. 83-113.

Casey, Rick
      1975   "Charismatic Communities." National
              Catholic Reporter. XI, 40 (September
              12, 1975), pp. 4-5.

Clark, Walter H.
   1971   "Intense Religious Experience" in
          Merton P. Strommen, Research on
          Religious Development. New York:
          Hawthorn Books, Inc. pp. 521-550.

Coe, G. A.
   1900   The Spiritual Life: Studies in the
          Science of Religion. New York: Eaton
          and Mains.

Cohen, Sheldon
   1962   "The Ontogenesis of Prophetic
          Behavior: A Study of Creative
          Conscience Formation." Psychoanaly-
          sis and the Psychoanalytic Review 49,
          No. 1, pp. 100-122.

Cutten, George B.
   1927   Speaking with Tongues. New Haven,
          Conn.: Yale University Press.

Demerath, N. J. III
   1965   Social Class in American Protes-
          tantism. Chicago: Rand McNally.

Dilthey, Wilhelm
   1944   Selected Passages from Dilthey, in
          Hodges, H. A. (Ed.) Wilhelm Dilthey:
          An Introduction. London: Routledge.

Dittes, James E.
   1968   "Psychology of Religion" in G.
          Lindzey and E. Aronson, Handbook of
          Social Psychology V. Reading, Mass.:
          Addison-Wesley, pp. 602-659.

_____ 1973   "Beyond William James" in Charles Y.
          Glock and Phillip F. Hammond, Beyond
          the Classics: Essays in the Scien-
          tific Study of Religion. New York:
          Harper & Row, pp. 291-354.

Douglas W.
  1963 "Religion," in N. L. Farberow (Ed.),
      Taboo Topics. New York: Atherton
      Press.

Eliade, Mircea
  1960 Myths, Dreams and Mysteries. (Trans-
      lated by Philip Mairet.) London:
      Harvill Press.

Elinson, H.
  1965 "Implications of Pentecostal Religion
      for Intellectualism, Politics, and
      Race Relations." Amer. J. of
      Sociology 70, pp. 403-415.

Erikson, Erik H.
  1950 "Growth and Crises of the Healthy
      Personality" in Erikson, Identity and
      the Life Cycle, Vol. 1. New York:
      International Universities Press,
      1959, pp. 50-100.

  1956 "The Problem of Ego Identity."
      Journal of the American Psychoanaly-
      tic Assn. 4, pp. 56-121.

  1958 Young Man Luther. New York: W. W.
      Norton & Comp., Inc.

  1968 Identity: Youth and Crisis. New
      York: W. W. Norton & Comp., Inc.

  1969 Gandhi's Truth. New York: W. W.
      Norton & Comp., Inc.

Eysenck, Hans J.
  1947 Dimensions of Personality. London:
      Routledge and Kegan Paul.

Festinger, Leon, Henry W. Riecken and Stanley
  Schachter
    1956   When Prophecy Fails. Minneapolis:
            University of Minnesota Press.

Fichter, Joseph H.
    1975   The Catholic Cult of the Paraclete.
            New York: Sheed & Ward, Inc.

Frank, Jerome David
    1973   Persuasion and Healing: A Compara-
            tive Study of Psychotherapy.
            Baltimore, Md.: The Johns Hopkins
            Press.

Freud, Sigmund
    1928   Future of an Illusion. London:
            Hogarth Press, Ltd.

Gerlach, L. P. and Virginia H. Hine
    1968   "Five Factors Crucial to the Growth
            and Spread of a Modern Religious
            Movement." JSSR 7, pp. 23-40.

Gerrard, Nathan L.
    1968   "The Serpent-Handling Religions of
            West Virginia." Transaction 5 (May),
            pp. 22-28.

Gerrard, Nathan L. and Louise B.
    1966   Scrabble Creek Folk: Mental Health,
            Part II. Unpublished report, Dept.
            of Sociology, Morris Harvey College,
            Charleston, W. Va.

Gill, M. M. and M. Brenman
    1959   Hypnosis and Related States. New
            York: International Universities
            Press.

Giorgi, Amedeo
    1965   "Phenomenology and Experimental Psy-
            chology. I." Rev. Exist. Psychol.
            and Psychiat. 5, pp. 228-238.

_____ 1966 "Phenomenology and Experimental Psychology. II." Rev. Exist. Psychol. and Psychiat. 6, pp. 37-50.

_____ 1970 Psychology As a Human Science: A Phenomenologically Based Approach. Evanston, Ill.: Harper & Row.

Glock, Charles Y.
1973 "On the Origin and Evolution of Religious Groups" in Charles Y. Glock (Ed.), Religion in Sociological Perspective: Essays in the Empirical Study of Religion. Belmont, Cal.: Wardsworth Publishing Company, pp. 207-220.

Glock, Charles and Phillip E. Hammond
1973 Beyond the Classics: Essays in the Scientific Study of Religion. New York: Harper & Row.

Goffman, Erving
1959 The Presentation of Self in Everyday Life. Garden City, New York: Doubleday.

_____ 1961 Asylums. Chicago: Aldine Publishing Company.

Goodman, Felicitas D.
1972 Speaking in Tongues: A Cross-Cultural Study of Glossolalia. Chicago: The University of Chicago Press.

Grad, Bernard
1965 "Some Biological Effects of the 'Laying on of Hands': A Review of Experiments with Animals and Plants." J. of American Society for Psychical Research 59 (2), pp. 95-127.

1966   "The 'Laying on of hands': Implications for Psychotherapy and the Placebo Effect." *Corrective Psychiatry and Journal of Social Therapy* 12 (2), pp. 192-202.

Hansford, Jack Tyrus
    1975   "A Synoptic Approach: Resolving Problems in Empirical and Phenomenological Approaches to the Psychology of Religion." *Journal for the Scientific Study of Religion* 14 (September), pp. 219-226.

Harrison, Michael Issac
    1972   *The Organization of Commitment in the Catholic Pentecostal Movement.* Unpublished Doctoral Dissertation: University of Michigan, Ann Arbor.

Heidegger, Martin
    1962   *Being and Time.* (Translated by John Macquarrie and Edward Robinson.) New York: Harper and Row.

Heirich, Max
    1975   "Change of Heart: A Test of Some Widely Held Theories About Religious Conversion." Working Paper, Center for Research on Social Organization, University of Michigan, Ann Arbor.

Henle, Mary and Gertrude Baltimore
    1967   "Portraits in Straw." *Psych. Rev.* 74 (4), pp. 325-329.

Hine, Virginia H.
    1969   "Pentecostal Glossolalia--Toward a Functional Interpretation." *JSSR* 8, pp. 211-226.

Hovland, C. I., I. L. Janis and H. H. Kelley
    1953   Communication and Persuasion:
            Psychological Studies of Opinion
            Change. New Haven: Yale University
            Press.

Husserl, Edmund
    1960   Cartesian Meditations. (Translated
            by D. Cairns.) The Hague: Martinus
            Nijhoff.

Huxley, Aldous
    1952   The Devils of Loudon. New York:
            Harper.

Jahoda, Marie
    1959   Current Concepts of Positive Mental
            Health. New York: Basic Books.

Jahr, Mary Ann
    1975   "An Ecumenical Christian Community:
            The Word of God, Ann Arbor, Michigan."
            New Covenant IV (February 1975), p. 8.

James, William
    1890   The Principles of Psychology, 2 vols.
            New York: Henry Holt.

    1902   The Varieties of Religious Experience.
            New York: Longmans, Green.
            (Quotations in the text derive from
            the 1958 Collier-Macmillan edition.)

Jung, Carl G.
    1933   Modern Man in Search of a Soul.
            London: Kegan Paul.

    1937   Psychology and Religion. New Haven:
            Yale University Press.

    1961   Memories, Dreams and Reflections. New
            York: Vintage Books.

Keane, Roberta
1975   Formal Organization and Charisma in a
        Catholic Pentecostal Community. Un-
        published Doctoral Dissertation.
        University of Michigan, Ann Arbor.

Kelsey, Morton T.
1964   Tongue Speaking: An Experiment in
        Spiritual Experience. New York:
        Doubleday.

Kernberg, Otto
1978   Object Relations Theory and Clinical
        Psychoanalysis. New York: Jason
        Aronson, Inc.

Kiev, Ari (Ed.)
1964   Magic, Faith, and Healing: Studies
        in Primitive Psychiatry Today.
        London: The Free Press of Glencoe.

Kildahl, J. P.
1965   "The Personalities of Sudden Religious
        Converts." Pastoral Psychology 16,
        pp. 37-44.

Kildahl, John P.
1972   The Psychology of Speaking in Tongues.
        New York: Harper & Row.

Knox, Ronald A.
1950   Enthusiasm: A Chapter in the History
        of Religion. Oxford: Clarendon
        Press.

Kuhlman, Kathryn
1969   I Believe in Miracles. Englewood
        Cliffs, N. J.: Prentice-Hall.

Kuhn, Thomas S.
1967   The Structure of Scientific Revolu-
        tions. Chicago: Phoenix Books.

LeShan, Lawrence
    1974   *The Medium, the Mystic, and the Physicist*. New York: The Viking Press.

Leuba, James H.
    1896   "A Study in the Psychology of Religious Phenomena." *American Journal of Psychology* VII, No. 3, pp. 309-385.

Lipset, S. M.
    1964   "Religion and Politics in the American Past and Present," in R. Lee and M. Marty (Eds.) *Religion and Social Conflict*. New York: Oxford University Press.

Luckmann, Thomas
    1967   *The Invisible Religion*. New York: Macmillan.

Lynd, R. and H. Lynd
    1929   *Middletown*. New York: Harcourt, Brace.

MacLeod, R. B.
    1947   "The Phenomenological Approach to Social Psychology." *Psych. Rev.* 54, pp. 193-210.

MacNutt, Francis
    1974   *Healing*. Notre Dame, Ind: Ave Maria Press.

Macquarrie, John
    1966   *Principles of Christian Theology*. New York: Charles Scribner's Sons.

Martin, Malachi
    1976   *Hostage to the Devil*. New York: Reader's Digest Press.

Mawn, C. P., Benedict Joseph
1975   Testing the Spirits: An Empirical
        Search for the Socio-Cultural
        Situational Roots of the Catholic
        Pentecostal Religious Experience.
        Unpublished Doctoral Dissertation:
        Boston University.

May, Herbert G. and Bruce M. Metzger, Eds.
1965   The Oxford Annotated Bible With the
        Apocrypha: Revised Standard Version.
        New York: Oxford University Press.

McDougall, William
1923   Outline of Psychology. New York:
        Scribner.

Merleau-Ponty, Maurice
1964   The Primacy of Perception. (Ed.
        James Edie.) Evanston, Ill.:
        Northwestern University Press.

Mintz, S. W.
1960   Worker in the Cane: A Puerto Rican
        Life History. New Haven: Yale
        University Press.

Mullahy, P.
1952   The Contributions of Harry Stack
        Sullivan. New York: Hermitage House.

_____
1953   "A Theory of Interpersonal Relations
        and the Evolution of Personality," in
        H. S. Sullivan (Ed.), Conceptions of
        Modern Psychiatry. New York: Norton,
        pp. 239-294.

Nisbet, Robert
1953   The Quest for Community. New York:
        Oxford University Press.

Nolen, William A.
1974   Healing: A Doctor in Search of a
        Miracle. New York: Random House.

Otto, Rudolf
    1917   Das Heilige. (First published in
              English as The Idea of the Holy.
              Translated by John Harvey.) London:
              Oxford University Press, 1923.

Oursler, Will
    1957   The Healing Power of Faith. New
              York: Hawthorn Books, Inc.

Pahnke, W. N.
    1966   "Drugs and Mysticism." Int. J. of
              Parapsychology 8 (2), pp. 295-314.

Pattison, E. Mansell, Nikolajs A. Lapins and Hans
  A. Doerr
    1973   "Faith Healing: A Study of Personal-
              ity and Function." J. of Nervous and
              Mental Disease 157 (6), pp. 397-409.

Poblete, Renato and Thomas F. O'Dea
    1960   "The Formation of Sects Among the
              Puerto Ricans of New York," American
              Cath. Sociol. Rev. No. 1, 21 (Spring,
              1960), pp. 25-32.

Prince, R. (Ed.)
    1968   "Trance and Possession States."
              Proceedings of the Second Annual
              Conference, R. M. Bucke Memorial
              Society, Montreal, Canada.

Pruyser, P.
    1968   A Dynamic Psychology of Religion.
              New York: Harper & Row.

Ravenscroft, K.
    1965   "Voodoo Possession: A Natural Experi-
              ment in Hypnosis." Int. J. of Clin.
              and Experimental Hypnosis 13, pp.
              157-182.

Roberts, F. J.
    1965   "Some Psychological Factors in Reli-
             gious Conversion." Brit. J. of Soc.
             & Clin. Psych. 4, pp. 185-187.

Sadler, A. W.
    1964   "Glossolalia and Possession: An
             Appeal to the Episcopal Study Com-
             mission." JSSR 4, pp. 84-90.

Samarin, William
    1972   Tongues of Men and Angels: The Reli-
             gious Language of Pentecostalism.
             New York: The Macmillan Company.

Sanford, Agnes
    1947   The Healing Light. St. Paul, Minn.:
             Macalester Park Publishing Company.

Sargant, William
    1961   Battle for the Mind: A Physiology of
             Conversion and Brainwashing.
             Baltimore: Penquin.

Scroggs, James R. and William G. T. Douglas
    1976   "Issues in the Psychology of Reli-
             gious Conversion." J. of Religion
             and Health 6 (3), pp. 204-216.

Sneck, S. J., William J.
    1973   "Glossolalia: A New Approach."
             Homiletic & Pastoral Review 74 (2)
             (November), pp. 74-79.

Snygg, Donald
    1959   "The Need for a Phenomenological
             System of Psychology" in A. Kuenzli
             (Ed.) The Phenomenological Problem.
             New York: Macmillan.

Spiegelberg, Herbert
    1965   The Phenomenological Movement. 2 Vols.
             The Hague: Nijhoff.

‾‾‾‾‾ 1972   Phenomenology in Psychology and
               Psychiatry. Evanston: Northwestern
               University Press.

Spranger, Edward
       1928   Types of Men, (Translated by P. J. W.
               Pigors.) Halle: Niemeyer Publishing.

Stace, W. T.
       1960   Mysticism and Philosophy.
               Philadelphia: Lippincott.

Stanley, G.
       1964   "Personality and Attitude Correlates
               of Religious Conversion." JSSR 4,
               pp. 60-63.

Starbuck, E. D.
       1899   The Psychology of Religion. New
               York: Scribner.

Stark, W.
       1967   The Sociology of Religion. 2 Vols.
               London: Routledge & Kegan Paul.

Stern, William
       1938   General Psychology, (Translated by
               H. D. Spoerl.) New York: Macmillan.

Strommen, Merton P.
       1971   Research on Religious Development.
               New York: Hawthorn Books, Inc.

Sullivan, Harry Stack
       1953   The Interpersonal Theory of Psychia-
               try. New York: Norton.

Troeltsch, Ernst
       1960   The Social Teachings of the Christian
               Churches. New York: Harper & Row.

Underhill, E.
    1912   <u>Mysticism: A Study in the Nature and Development of Man's Spiritual Consciousness</u>. London: Methuen.

Vawter, Bruce
    1968   "Introduction to Prophetic Literature," in Raymond E. Brown, Joseph A. Fitzmyer and Roland E. Murphy, <u>The Jerome Biblical Commentary</u>. Englewood Cliffs, New Jersey: Prentice Hall, Inc., pp. 223-237.

Vernon, P. E. and G. W. Allport
    1931   "A Test for Personal Values." <u>J. Abnorm, Soc. Psychol</u>. 26, pp. 231-248.

Walters, C. S. J., Annette and Ritamary Bradley, C. H. M.
    1971   "Motivation and Religious Behavior" in Merton P. Strommen, <u>Research on Religious Development</u>. New York: Hawthorn Books, Inc., pp. 599-654.

Weatherhead, Leslie D.
    1955   <u>Psychology, Religion and Healing</u>. Bungay, Suffolk, England: Hodder and Stroughton, Limited.

Weber, Max
    1952   <u>Ancient Judaism</u>. (Translated and edited by Hans H. Gerth and Don Martindale.) New York: The Free Press.

    1963   <u>Sociology of Religion</u>. (Translated by E. Fischoff.) Boston: Beacon Press.

Weininger, Benjamin
    1955   "The Interpersonal Factor in the Religious Experience." <u>Psychoanalysis</u> 3 (4), pp. 27-44.

Weller, Philip T.
    1964   The Roman Ritual.   Milwaukee: Bruce
            Publishing Comp.

Wilkerson, David et al.
    1970   The Cross and The Switchblade.   New
            York: BJ Publishing Group.

Wilson, B. R.
    1966   Religion in Secular Society.   London;
            Watts & Company.

Winter, G.
    1962   The Suburban Captivity of the Chur-
            ches.   New York: Macmillan.

Worrall, Ambrose A. and Olga
    1965   The Gift of Healing.   New York:
            Harper & Row.

Yinger, J. Milton
    1957   Religion, Society and the Individual.
            New York: Macmillian.

Yocum, Bruce
    1976   Prophecy--Exercising the Prophetic
            Gifts of the Spirit in the Church
            Today.   Ann Arbor, Michigan:
            Servant Books.

Zaehner, R. C.
    1967   Mysticism Sacred and Profane.
            London: Oxford University Press.

Zaner, Richard M.
    1967   "Criticism of 'Tensions in Psychology
            Between the Methods of Behaviorism
            and Phenomenology.'"   Psych. Rev. 74
            (4), pp. 318-324.